POETRY, MEDIA, AND THE MATERIAL BODY

Autopoetics in Nineteenth-Century Britain

From the Romantic fascination with hallucinatory poetics to the turn-of-the-century mania for automatic writing, poetry in nineteenth-century Britain appears at crucial times to be oddly involuntary, out of control of its producers and receivers alike. This elegant study addresses the question of how people understood those forms of written creativity that seem to occur independently of the writer's will. Through the study of the century's media revolutions, evolving theories of physiology and close readings of the works of nineteenth-century poets including Wordsworth, Coleridge, and Tennyson, Ashley Miller articulates how poetry was imagined to promote involuntary bodily responses in both authors and readers, and how these responses enlist the body as a medium that does not produce poetry, but rather reproduces it. This is a poetics that draws attention to, rather than effaces, the mediacy of the body in the processes of composition and reception.

ASHLEY MILLER is Assistant Professor of English at Albion College. Her work on a wide variety of topics in Romantic and Victorian literary studies has appeared in *Victorian Literature and Culture, Studies in Romanticism, Nineteenth-Century Contexts, Literature Compass,* and *Nineteenth-Century Gender Studies.*

T0371070

CAMBRIDGE STUDIES IN NINETEENTH-CENTURY
LITERATURE AND CULTURE

General Editor
Gillian Beer, *University of Cambridge*

Editorial Board
Isobel Armstrong, *Birkbeck, University of London*
Kate Flint, *University of Southern California*
Catherine Gallagher, *University of California, Berkeley*
D. A. Miller, *University of California, Berkeley*
J. Hillis Miller, *University of California, Irvine*
Daniel Pick, *Birkbeck, University of London*
Mary Poovey, *New York University*
Sally Shuttleworth, *University of Oxford*
Herbert Tucker, *University of Virginia*

Nineteenth-century British literature and culture have been rich fields for interdisciplinary studies. Since the turn of the twentieth century, scholars and critics have tracked the intersections and tensions between Victorian literature and the visual arts, politics, social organization, economic life, technical innovations, scientific thought – in short, culture in its broadest sense. In recent years, theoretical challenges and historiographical shifts have unsettled the assumptions of previous scholarly synthesis and called into question the terms of older debates. Whereas the tendency in much past literary critical interpretation was to use the metaphor of culture as "background," feminist, Foucauldian, and other analyses have employed more dynamic models that raise questions of power and of circulation. Such developments have reanimated the field. This series aims to accommodate and promote the most interesting work being undertaken on the frontiers of the field of nineteenth-century literary studies: work which intersects fruitfully with other fields of study such as history, or literary theory, or the history of science. Comparative as well as interdisciplinary approaches are welcomed.

A complete list of titles published will be found at the end of the book.

POETRY, MEDIA, AND THE MATERIAL BODY

Autopoetics in Nineteenth-Century Britain

ASHLEY MILLER
Albion College

CAMBRIDGE
UNIVERSITY PRESS

University Printing House, Cambridge CB2 8BS, United Kingdom

One Liberty Plaza, 20th Floor, New York, NY 10006, USA

477 Williamstown Road, Port Melbourne, VIC 3207, Australia

314-321, 3rd Floor, Plot 3, Splendor Forum, Jasola District Centre, New Delhi - 110025, India

79 Anson Road, #06-04/06, Singapore 079906

Cambridge University Press is part of the University of Cambridge.

It furthers the University's mission by disseminating knowledge in the pursuit of education, learning and research at the highest international levels of excellence.

www.cambridge.org
Information on this title: www.cambridge.org/9781108408585
DOI: 10.1017/9781108292474

First published 2018
First paperback edition 2020

A catalogue record for this publication is available from the British Library

ISBN 978-1-108-41896-6 Hardback
ISBN 978-1-108-40858-5 Paperback

Contents

Acknowledgments

This book would not have been possible without the boundless intellectual generosity and support of Andrew H. Miller, Mary Favret, Ivan Kreilkamp, and Nick Williams. The striking passages that were the seeds of this project were first discussed with them; I am indebted to each of these remarkable mentors for years of encouragement, critique, and conversation as I've worked to develop those early thoughts into this manuscript. Dahlia Porter, Anne Frey, Rajani Sudan, Beth Newman, and Linda K. Hughes offered invaluable feedback on drafts along the way. Other colleagues, instructors, and friends have generously read and undoubtedly improved various pieces of this manuscript in various stages: Rae Greiner, Patrick Brantlinger, Lee Sterrenburg, Madeleine Thompson, Melanie Brezniak, Deborah Strickland, Ursula McTaggart, Meg Foster, and Robin Vogelzang. This book has also benefitted from more public conversations: I'm lucky to have had the opportunity to present and discuss my work on this project at many NAVSA and INCS meetings, as well as at the extraordinary Meter Matters conference at Exeter. At the Dickens Universe, too, I had conversations that contributed to and improved my thinking about automatism, materiality, and media. I am grateful to all of these audiences and especially to the Transatlantic Nineteenth-Century Group at SMU for inviting me to share my work there.

This work was supported by a grant from the Hewlett-Mellon Fund for Faculty Development at Albion College, Albion, MI, which enabled me to complete the project; its earliest stages were funded by the Patrick Brantlinger Dissertation-Year Fellowship at Indiana University. I'm also grateful for permission to reprint material that appeared previously in the following journals: parts of Chapter 1 were published in "Striking Passages: Memory and the Romantic Imprint," *Studies in Romanticism* 50.1 (Spring 2011), and "Involuntary Metrics and the Physiology of Memory," *Literature Compass* 6 (February 2009); a small section of Chapter 3 appeared in "Speech Paralysis: Ingestion, Suffocation, and the Torture of

Listening," *Nineteenth-Century Contexts* 36.5 (December 2014), republished in a volume titled *Nineteenth-Century Energies: Literature, Technology, Culture*, edited by Lynn Voskuil (Routledge 2016: 85–99). My thanks go to the editors at these journals and presses, as well as to the Trustees of Boston University, for allowing me to reprint my research here. I also thank the editors and copyeditors at Cambridge University Press, especially Linda Bree and the two anonymous readers whose careful attention and generous feedback helped make each draft of the manuscript better than the last.

Over the years, this project has moved with me from Indiana to Texas and finally back home to Michigan; in each place I'm grateful to those who gave me the support, guidance, and friendship that sustained me in my research and writing. At Albion College I'm indebted to my colleagues in the English Department and beyond, especially Danit Brown, Nels Christensen, Mary Collar, Scott Hendrix, Judy Lockyer, Ian MacInnes, Helena Mesa, Jess Roberts, and Deborah Kanter. At the University of Texas at Arlington, special thanks go to the Sixth-Floor Lunch Club and to Jacqueline Stodnick, Tim Morris, Penny Ingram, Jim Warren, Kathryn Warren, and Stacy Alaimo for their intellectual camaraderie. At Indiana University I was lucky to have a fabulous cohort as well as an extraordinary group of colleagues at the *Victorian Studies* journal. Bike Gang Swim Club and the illustrious Prospect Hill Basketball League kept me from ossifying at my desk. And I survived the last year of grad school and the first year of motherhood only because of the incredible support and friendship of the Bloomington Moms.

Of course, my deepest debts are those closest to home. My sister, Meredith Miller, has been my partner in everything since forever: she is my lifeline. There's no way to adequately thank her here, but I hope she knows how heartfelt this is. The same is true for my parents, Lora Vatalaro and Gerald Miller, whose unconditional support I am grateful for every day. I'm grateful as well to Nan and Richard Zaitlen, along with the rest of the Zaitlen family, for their warm welcome and inexhaustible generosity of spirit. Finally: this book is for Ben, Leopold, and Solomon, who give me joy beyond words.

Introduction
The Material Muse in Nineteenth-Century Poetry

What does it mean to be an agent of poetry? This is a question that was asked with increasing urgency throughout the nineteenth century, and for good reason. With literacy on the rise, more people were reading and writing than ever before; changes in media technology meant that these readers and writers were encountering poetry in newly material ways; and in the midst of it all, the status of poetry as a genre was shifting in relation to the rise of the novel. Querying the role of poetry in the modern age, nineteenth-century writers repeatedly attempt to determine its contours, to dictate what it means to write poetry and even what it means to read it. Yet from the Romantic fascination with hallucinatory poetics to the turn-of-the-century mania for automatic writing, poetry in nineteenth-century Britain appears at crucial times to be oddly involuntary, out of control of its producers and receivers alike. *Poetry, Media, and the Material Body* investigates precisely this phenomenon: the ways in which nineteenth-century readers and writers are not, in fact, agents of poetry. Instead, poetry is imagined to promote in them involuntary bodily responses, and these responses enlist the body as a medium that does not produce poetry but rather *re*produces it. Alongside a well-established poetic tradition that insists on poetry's immediacy, in other words, runs an alternate tradition of theorizing poetic agency (in both literary and nonliterary texts) that demonstrates a deep engagement with theories of material embodiment and mediation. Uncovering and articulating this alternate tradition is my project here. As I aim to show, the relationship between poetry and material mediation – mediation that is often involuntary, physical, and reproductive – plays an integral role in the production of modern poetics.

   In considering the ways in which poetry comes to be mediated throughout the century, I argue, it is necessary to consider the ways in which nineteenth-century thinkers conceived of the human body as one of the material media of poetry. In order to do so I investigate the often surprising intersections and overlaps between three infrequently related fields: studies

of poetry, studies of media, and studies of the body. It is at these intersections that we can see the development of a nineteenth-century theory of
poetry – what I call "autopoetics" – deeply invested in automatic reproduction. I use the prefix "auto-" here to invoke a variety of meanings: "by
hand" (i.e., by the body), automatically (i.e., mechanically), autonomously
(by itself, independently). This is a poetics that depends upon evolving
theories of physiology that establish the embodied mind as a material
medium. At the same time, this poetics develops alongside the media
revolutions of the century – from the rise of mass print culture and its
attendant silent reading practices to the development of telegraphy and
phonography – which make poetry's mediatedness, materiality, and reproducibility increasingly obvious. My argument, then, expounds upon two
parallel premises: that nineteenth-century theories of poetic agency are
deeply engaged with questions of the materiality of the body; and that these
same theories of poetic agency are equally engaged with questions of the
materiality of poetic media. Part of my goal here is to make clear the extent
to which these premises are indeed parallel – the extent to which an
increasing awareness of materiality, on multiple levels, comes to impact
theories of poetic agency. Most important, however, is the end result: that
these materialist theories of poetic agency drive toward a way of being with
poetry that in fact has very little to do with agency. Instead, in the theory of
poetry I outline here the material body is at the mercy, as it were, of poetry.
Throughout the nineteenth century, poems are imprinted on retinas and
on nerves; they dictate directly to hands and to hearts; they make readers
listen and listeners speak. This is a poetics that draws attention to, rather
than effaces, the mediacy of the body – its instrumentality, its complex and
intermediate agency in the processes of poetic composition and reception
alike. Privileging automatic responsiveness over imaginative agency, the
autopoetic tradition rewrites the muse as material language. When
Coleridge dreams of Kubla Khan, it is no coincidence that he dreams of
it as an already-written poem.

   In its investigation of the role of material mediation in theories of poetic
agency, this book traces two central and interrelated narratives. The first
narrative focuses on the mediacy of the body in nineteenth-century poetics – a body that is seen as increasingly material, as a means of retaining
and reproducing information. The second narrative concerns itself with
the material mediacy of nineteenth-century poetry itself: its investment in
a logic of quotation, fragmentation, and allusion. As increasing attention is
paid to the mediating body, material poetry appears to attain a surprising
degree of autonomy. Indeed, if poetic automatism displaces writers and

readers as agents of poetry, it seems to install in their place the material poem itself as independent, autonomous, and self-replicating. Throughout the long nineteenth century, in other words, these two forms of material media – poetry and the body – are imagined to be deeply interactive. When and why they become so intertwined – and when and why they cease to be – is this book's governing line of inquiry. Why are questions of poetic agency so embroiled in discussions of and debates about materiality – the materiality of poetry, of media, of the body? Why did it become productive for nineteenth-century writers to imagine (in contravention of a longstanding poetic tradition that exalts the spiritual and immaterial) the human body as one of the material media of poetry? And what are the limits and rewards of a model of poetic agency that conceives the bodies of readers and writers as automatically responsive to – even physically at the mercy of – the material poem?

The Automatic Body in Nineteenth-Century Science

Physical responsiveness to language and literary form has proven to be a productive topic in nineteenth-century literary scholarship ever since the "neurological turn" challenged critics to historicize models of textual affect and its relationship to the body. By now we are especially familiar with the anxieties surrounding the problem of involuntary responsiveness in the reading experience, by nature compulsory and even addictive. This is particularly true in novel theory: from Nicholas Dames's *The Physiology of the Novel* (2007) to Elisha Cohn's *Still Life: Suspended Development in the Victorian Novel* (2016), studies of the physiological experience of reading have proven to yield rich and rewarding interpretations of Victorian fiction.[1] Building on this rich tradition, this book aims at the same time to expand and at times trouble our picture of the bodily medium that literature acts upon. I want to do this in part by shifting our orientation – taking a broad step sideways, as it were, to consider poetry in general, but also refocusing our attention on the particular formal qualities of poetry that constitute its materiality. I am not the first to consider the somatics of poetry, of course. Compared to the wealth of material on the physiology of the novel, far fewer critics have examined the problem of bodily responsiveness in encounters with poetry; but the field is a rich and growing one. Within it scholars have been particularly attuned to the role of meter in the physiology of poetic affect. Jason Rudy's *Electric Meters* (2009), for example, identifies in Victorian physiological poetics a focus on "rhythms that pulse in the body, a rhetoric of sensation that readers might feel compelled to experience" (2); Kirstie Blair's *Victorian Poetry and the Culture of the Heart* (2006) traces the history of a poetics in which "the rhythm of a poem draws the reader into participation in a bodily sense, affecting blood and health" (17). Rudy, Blair, and other critics working on poetry in material culture have helped us to reconsider the place of poetry in studies of nineteenth-century reading.[2] What many of these studies share is an emphasis on the way meter, with its rhythms and pulses, can act on those physical systems of the body that best exemplify what makes us human: our hearts, our brains, our nerves. This book, instead, asks us to consider aspects of bodily mediation that often seem to work against or athwart humanist models of the body. Looking beyond the pulses of the heart and the nervous system, I work here to uncover elements of poetic materiality beyond rhythm and meter. As a result, the mediacy of the body comes to look quite unfamiliar in these pages: nineteenth-century auto-poetics often bypasses the heart and the brain – both traditional seats of embodied consciousness – and registers instead in seemingly disparate and disjoint bodily phenomena. Randomized fragments of print poetry operate like visual hallucinations, appearing unbidden in front of people's eyes; vocalized poetry attains a strange autonomy in the ears and mouths of its speakers and listeners; hands of automatic writers are used to substantiate a global network of excerpted and plagiarized poetry. In short, I focus on instances of bodily mediation that function in unnervingly fragmented and autonomous ways, ways that unsettle models of the body as an organic or coherent system.

It's necessary at the very outset to consider what I mean by media and mediation. Clifford Siskin and William Warner's provocative study of Enlightenment media defines mediation very broadly, as "work done by tools" (5). My own use of the word here draws from a somewhat more focused, yet still capacious, definition of mediation as a kind of physical process of communication or transmission, one that includes the mediation between mind and world. In one sense, then, I use the word "medium" to mean an instrument or channel of communication. In nineteenth-century physiology, the body was increasingly understood to be such a medium, as scientists began to investigate the way the body literally mediated sensation, expression, and even seemingly mental phenomena. Physicist David Brewster's 1832 treatise on the retina's role in mediating impressions, which I discuss at length in Chapter One, makes this evident: "This wonderful organ may be considered as the sentinel which guards the pass between the worlds of matter and of spirit, and through which all their communications are interchanged. The optic nerve is the channel by which the mind peruses the hand-writing of Nature on the retina, and through which it transfers to that material tablet its decisions and its creations" (10–11). The retina here functions as a material channel of communication between the mind and the external world. Yet the body-as-medium depicted by nineteenth-century physiology (and, as we shall see, theories of poetry and media technology as well) also invokes another sense of the word "medium" as any kind of physical material used for recording or reproducing data. And we need look no further than the same text – Brewster's study of the retina – to see this model of the body's mediacy at work as well: "we find the retina so powerfully influenced by external impressions as to retain the view of visible objects long after they are withdrawn," even reproducing them at random (which, according to Brewster, accounts for the phenomenon of spectral illusions) (37). In addition to acting as a channel, the retina is also an inscribed medium that retains and reproduces impressions. When I refer to the mediacy of the body, then, I mean to implicate both senses of the word "medium" – an intermediate means of communication but also a means of material reproduction.

This complex sense of bodily mediation lies at the heart of nineteenth-century physiology's investigations into automatism – that is, the ability of the body to perform without voluntary or conscious control. For nineteenth-century philosophers and scientists, the emerging problem of bodily automatism became crucial to understanding the mind-body relationship. A body that was capable of operating automatically challenged humanist and antimaterialist claims about intellectual agency. In this way, the burgeoning science of physiology drew upon (and yet significantly departed from) eighteenth-century associationism, which attempted to explain mental phenomena via the habitual "association of ideas." David Hartley – philosopher, physician, and onetime hero to Coleridge – was the first to propose a physiological theory of association in his 1749 *Observations on Man*. Hartley linked the association of ideas to the vibrations of the nervous system: "Any Sensations A, B, C, etc., by being associated with one another a sufficient Number of Times, get such a Power over the corresponding Ideas a, b, c, etc. that any one of the Sensations A, when impressed alone, shall be able to excite in the Mind b, c, etc., the Ideas of the rest" (41). Hartley's associationism accounts for automatism, which he describes as motions "of which the mind is scarce conscious, and which follow mechanically, as it were, some precedent diminutive sensation, idea, or motion, and without any effort of the mind"; these automatic motions, he writes, are "to be ascribed to the body [rather] than the mind" (104). For Hartley and the associationist school, the habitual association of ideas allowed the body to operate automatically; and yet the automatism modeled by associationism remains subservient to the mind's ability to train its own habits. While the theory seeks to explain seemingly random associations, it is at bottom a theory of reliable habit, of governance and predictability. This sense of the importance of habit and predictability is precisely what nineteenth-century theorists of automatism abandon as they explore the involuntary workings of the body.

Romantic physiologists were among the first to model a post-association automatism, a body whose involuntary impulses were not in fact predictable or habitual, and whose workings were beyond the management or direction of the mind. Romantic studies of hallucination, which I discuss at length in this book's first chapter, depicted the retina as a literal retainer of images, which could be "renovated" in front of the eye at random. Scientific studies of vision, as we shall see, began to depict the body as an unruly collection of material imprints unconnected by any links of habit or association. Take, for example, the testimony of a celebrated "ghost-seer" whose materialist analysis of his hallucinations prompted scientists to study the phenomenon more closely: after being haunted by phantasms for months, and "having fairly proved and maturely considered it," he concludes that "these visions in my case were not the consequence of any known law of reason, of the imagination, or of the otherwise usual association of ideas" but were simply the involuntary productions of his body (Nicolai 167). Over the course of the century the issues at stake here – the body as capable of operating automatically, of reproducing impressions spontaneously – became part of the scientific lexicon as writers debated the role of physical automatism in mental or cerebral processes.[3] By the late Victorian period, it was well understood that bodily automatism was an established phenomenon, one that needed consideration in any attempt to explain the relationship of the body to the mind. Noted physiologist William Benjamin Carpenter's 1874 *Principles of Mental Physiology*, for example, is careful to distinguish the ways in which doctrines of automatism have diverged from eighteenth-century theories of association:

> By far the larger part of our Psychical operations depend on the mechanism by which past states of consciousness *spontaneously* reproduce themselves: and while the Metaphysician accounts for this reproduction on the principle of "association of ideas," the Physiologist holds that in the formation of such associations, certain modifications took place in the organization of the Brain, which determine its mode of responding to subsequent suggestions;

so that, under the stimulus of new impressions either from without or from within, the long-dormant "traces" of former mental states arc caused to reproduce themselves as Ideas and Feelings. (465–466)

For Carpenter and other nineteenth-century scientists, physiology provided a new way of conceiving of the body's role in mediating our experiences: not only does it act as a medium of transmission, turning sense impressions into mental phenomena, but it also stores these "past states of consciousness" in order to "*spontaneously* reproduce" them as ideas and feelings. The body is both signal and archive, transmitter and instigator.

Nowhere is this complex bodily mediation more evident than in discussions of linguistic automatism. Physiologists often turned to the problem of language because of the way language seemed to operate at both a mental and a physical level: words may be formed in the brain and expressed by the body, and yet both processes may be automatic. Carpenter writes in *Principles of Mental Physiology* that

> the act of expressing the thoughts in Language, whether by speech or by writing, may be considered as a good example [of automatism]: for the attention may be so completely given-up to the choice of words and to the composition of the sentences, that the movements by which the words and sentences already conceived are uttered by the voice or traced on paper, no more partake of the truly Volitional character, than do those of our limbs when we walk through the streets in a state of abstraction. (280)

In this example it is merely the physical expression of language that is automatic. However, Carpenter goes on to implicate the mental production of language in a similar kind of automatism: "great talkers, like Coleridge, sometimes run on automatically, when they have got patient listeners; one subject suggesting another, with no more exertion or direction of the will than we use in walking along a course that has become habitual" (393). Poor Coleridge: he appears frequently in these studies as an example of impotent agency and mental automatism, in keeping with William Hazlitt's more widely known depiction of him in *The Spirit of the Age*.[4] Carpenter, in a footnote, elaborates: "We have seen that the whole mental life of Coleridge was one of singular automatic activity, whilst there was a no less marked deficiency in the power of volitional self-direction" (*Mental* 393n).[5] However, the opium-addled poet also contributed an important study of linguistic automatism to the canon of Romantic and Victorian psychophysiology, one to which scientists returned throughout the century. In his *Biographia Literaria* Coleridge relates an anecdote about a young German woman who becomes multilingual while suffering from a nervous fever: "She continued incessantly talking Latin, Greek, and Hebrew, in very pompous tones and with most distinct enunciation. . . . Sheets full of her ravings were taken down from her own mouth, and were found to consist of sentences, coherent and intelligible each for itself, but with little or no connection with each other" (I: 112–113). According to Coleridge, this "feverish glossolalia" (as Jerome Christensen calls it [111]) can be traced back to the young woman's childhood, when her learned guardian used to "walk up and down a passage of his house into which the kitchen door opened, and to read to himself with a loud voice, out of his favorite books" (I: 113).

In Coleridge's anecdote, the woman's involuntary and meaningless quotation – her automatic reproduction of phrases impressed upon her memory long ago – proved to be a fascinating object of analysis for physiologists, partly because it revealed memory to be an automatic and at times ungovernable faculty. Moreover, it linked mental automatism together with a model of the physical body as a reproductive medium: Carpenter writes that the phenomenon displayed "the automatic action of the 'Mechanism of Thought'" and claimed it was the result of the "recording process" of the cerebrum (*Mental* 439). Along with the body's bizarre ability to record and repeat past impressions, however, Coleridge's anecdote exemplifies another important trend in studies of automatism: a focus on the phenomenon of being *out of control* of language. For physiologists of automatism, even more intriguing than the idea that the physical body could function automatically was the idea that our relationship to language could also be automatic and involuntarily reproductive. Coleridge's garrulous German girl resurfaces in a wide variety of texts, deployed throughout the century as writers grapple with the relationship between mental and physical processes. Her recurring presence is testament to the fact that language – reproducible language, in particular – plays a key role in defining and delineating theories of bodily automatism. Physiologists of vision, for example, draw upon stories of sleepwriting and involuntary recitation in order to make their claims about the material functions of visual memory; later in the century, developing discourses of phonography engage with contemporary theories of the body's ability to reproduce spoken language, and the advent of spiritualism gives researchers a new venue for experimenting with automatic writing and speech. In the chapters that follow, I trace the role of automatic language in Romantic and Victorian theories of physiology – theories that, I argue, fix upon language as evidence of our own lack of control over our bodies and minds.

Involuntary language, in other words, comes to be the most productive confirmation of psychophysical automatism.

Poetry – deployed so often to exemplify a certain kind of intellectual creativity, a certain kind of relationship with an immaterial muse – offers a particularly potent site for considering linguistic automaticity. We tend to think negatively of automatized, mechanical interactions with language; interacting mechanically with poetry is perhaps an even worse offense. The nineteenth-century archive is rich with evidence of this same distrust. Alexander Melville Bell (celebrated elocutionist and father of Alexander Graham) voices a familiar complaint in his 1887 *Elocutionary Manual*:

> There can be no doubt that the school methods of *scanning,* and of reading poetry by the line, are directly productive of this worst and most prevailing oratorical taint. It is but rarely that a reader can be found whose voice is entirely free from this blemish; and the habit is speedily extended from poetry to prose, so that the expressive irregularity of prosaic rhythm is entirely lost in the uniformity of time to which the reader's voice is set. Pinned, as it were, on the barrel of an organ, his accents come precisely in the same place at every sentential revolution, striking their emphasis, at one turn, upon a pronoun or a conjunction, and, at another, impinging sonorously on an article or an expletive. (10)

Bell objects to this mechanical form of reading, one that seems to begin in poetry's regularity and spread even to metrically irregular prose in a kind of reverse Wordsworthian contagion of metrics.[6] In reading mechanically, the body imposes an unnatural rhythm that overlooks the nuance and even meaning of language. However, if poetry's rhythmic regularity was apt to set the body's automatism in motion, it could also be used to advantage. Even Bell goes on to offer a corrective to mechanical poetic reading – in the form of a poem:

> Some writer has happily expressed the principle of pausing in a metrical form, which is worth committing to memory:
>
> > "In pausing, ever let this rule take place,
> > Never to separate words, in any case,
> > That are less separable than those you join;
> > And, which imports the same, not to combine
> > Such words together as do not relate
> > So closely as the words you separate."   (12)

Here the poem's metrics are expressly what recommends it to Bell, who advises his reader to commit it to memory.[7] He relies on its rhythms and rhymes to imprint it in his reader's mind – the same rhythms and rhymes that tend so dangerously toward mechanical reading. Poetry's unusual relationship to memory, in other words, complicates Bell's attempt to do away with mechanical reading entirely. This is an important relationship, one that I will return to throughout the book. However much we might idealize language – and particularly poetry – as antithetical to automatism, poetry's history as a mnemonic device in oral cultures grants it special powers to bypass mental agency and operate at the level of automatic memory.[8] If the automatic body is a language-producing machine, it's a machine that is particularly susceptible to being played upon by poetry.

Yet what is perhaps most striking about the role of language in studies of automatism is that both poets and their audiences come to be figured as involuntarily susceptible to the machinations of poetic language. If this book aims to provide a more complete picture of the role of involuntary responsiveness in nineteenth-century literature and science, another way it does so is by considering the writing body alongside the reading body. As I hope to show, concerns about automaticity are not limited to acts of creation or acts of reception alone: nineteenth-century depictions of poetic automatism suggest that being out of control of language is equally relevant to writers and to readers, to speakers and to listeners. As a result, the automatic body affords a new perspective on the relationship of bodies to language more broadly. In this schema of seemingly random or isolated acts of mediation, production and reproduction appear as strikingly similar processes. Writerly intuition and readerly absorption alike are revealed to be embodied and automatic: they both demonstrate the body's automatic mediation of language. In short, the automatic body underwrites authorship and readership simultaneously, further complicating our picture of the responsive body as a medium for poetry. Attending to the automatic body enables us to see something we've overlooked even in our recent attention to poetry's somatics: the degree to which other people's language can act on the body as a powerful material muse. In so doing, it suggests one possible avenue for reconsidering the complex relationship between creativity and receptivity in the history of poetic theory and – most broadly – in the history of our discipline.

Agency and Automatism in Poetic Theory

According to longstanding critical tradition, automatism became central to poetics in the twentieth century, with André Breton's Surrealist manifesto of "pure psychic automatism." One of the aims of this book is to radically expand and revise our understanding of the significance of bodily

automatism in poetic theory. Such a poetics of automatism has its roots,
I argue, in the media ecology of the long nineteenth century, a media
ecology which includes poetry and the body as active components. From
William Wordsworth to I. A. Richards, the involuntarily responsive body
appears as a privileged site for querying the nature of poetic affect: the ways
in which readers and writers are moved and influenced by seemingly
immaterial language. And in stark contrast to the poetic automatism of
the Surrealists, which uses the mechanics of the body to connect with the
deep subconscious mind, nineteenth-century poetic automatism under-
stands the mechanics of the body itself as a source of creativity. For the
Romantics and the Victorians, that is, theories of bodily automatism are
used to question and even reassign the role of the mind in the production
and reception of poetry. In reconsidering automatism in nineteenth-
century poetics, I aim to demonstrate that models of how the body
interacts with poetry have long included elements that we tend to identify
first in modernism: automaticity, fragmentation, even mechanization.

Rather than begin in the early twentieth century, then, I trace a tradition
of autopoetics that is born in the Romantic moment of *Lyrical Ballads*,
when a growing awareness of the material mediation of poetic language
begins to articulate the stakes of the nineteenth-century's interest in poetry,
media, and automatism. The ballads themselves are deeply concerned with
questions of voice in print – aware, in other words, of the ways in which
print poetry must negotiate its media. These are crucial issues in any
history of poetics and mediation in the nineteenth century, and I discuss
them at greater length in the chapters that follow; indeed, the second
printing revolution provides the impetus for the new material poetics
I outline in this book. But Wordsworth's "Preface" to *Lyrical Ballads* also
exemplifies the complexity of the early Romantic attitude toward poetic
agency:

> For all good poetry is the spontaneous overflow of powerful feelings: and
> though this be true, Poems to which any value can be attached were never
> produced on any variety of subjects but by a man who, being possessed of
> more than usual organic sensibility, had also thought long and deeply. For
> our continued influxes of feeling are modified and directed by our thoughts,
> which are indeed the representatives of all our past feelings; and, as by
> contemplating the relation of these general representatives to each other, we
> discover what is really important to men, so, by the repetition and con-
> tinuance of this act, our feelings will be connected with important subjects,
> till at length, if we be originally possessed of much sensibility, such habits of
> mind will be produced, that, by obeying blindly and mechanically the

impulses of those habits, we shall describe objects, and utter sentiments, of
such a nature, and in such connexion with each other, that the understanding of the Reader must necessarily be in some degree enlightened, and
his affections strengthened and purified. (394)

Chapters One and Two contain a more sustained engagement with
Wordsworth's model of poetic agency, and with Romantic and Victorian
responses to it. For now, however, I refer to this founding moment in
Romantic poetics as a touchstone for the role of automatism in poetic
theory around 1800. In fact, the model of autopoetics I outline in this book
tends to operate in opposition to Wordsworth's depiction of poetry as
"recollected in tranquility" and regulated by habit (407). Yet even
Wordsworth depicts poetic agency as a complex intermingling of automatism and intent, sensibility and sense. He is careful to insist on the
necessity of mental action – thought – in modifying and directing our
sensations, and he clearly relies on association in order to describe how
thought can evolve into habit. His emphasis on "blindly and mechanically"
obeying habitual impulses can seem startling in a manifesto about poetic
sensibility: involuntary and automatic actions play a surprisingly important role in the seemingly spontaneous production of poetry.[9] Moreover,
Wordsworth's theory of poetic agency relies on an easy slippage between
producing and receiving poetry. The process of automatism and habit that
he describes moves through the first-person plural – the "we" refers
originally to poets who "describe objects" – and yet the same mechanisms
of automatism and habit dictate that the Reader "must necessarily"
respond in a certain way. Both writing and reading poetry appear, in
fact, to be in part involuntary. And the process depends upon the poet's
body itself as being "possessed of more than usual organic sensibility": even
the guiding force of habit is built upon an original physical responsiveness.

   In this book, I chronicle the nineteenth century's developing engagement with such a material and involuntary model of poetic affect, one that
develops in dialogue with the discourse of automatism I outlined above.
With the century's increasing interest in the automatic body, the structure
and direction provided by associationism – Wordsworth's "habit" – disappears, untethering the responsive body from the guidance of the mind
and leaving it at the mercy of a variety of dangerously random stimuli.
Organic sensibility as a trope for poetic inspiration in turn becomes
increasingly material – and increasingly embodied – throughout the century. Although the narrative I trace begins with the Romantics, it offers
a very different model of poetic inspiration than the one traditionally
associated with Romanticism – poetic inspiration as immaterial and deeply

expressive. Percy Shelley's *Defence of Poetry* is often taken to exemplify this model. Shelley defines poetry as "the expression of the imagination," privileged above other modes of artistic creation for its immediacy (23). Language, Shelley writes, is "a more direct representation of the actions and passions of our internal being":

> For language is arbitrarily produced by the imagination, and has relation to thoughts alone; but all other materials, instruments, and conditions of art have relations among each other, which limit and interpose between conception and expression. The former is as a mirror which reflects, the latter as a cloud which enfeebles, the light of which both are mediums of communication. (28)

Poetry has direct access to thought and passion, whereas other mediums of communication merely "enfeeble" and "reflect." What this means for poetic agency is that the poet himself is often at the mercy of the imagination, as in the metaphor of the Æolian harp: "Man is an instrument over which a series of external and internal impressions are driven, like the alternations of an ever-changing wind over an Æolian lyre, which move it by their motion to ever-changing melody" (23). Shelley's model links this metaphor of instrumentality – a form of mediation, one might add, despite his insistence on immediacy – to an extreme lack of volition on the part of the composing poet. "Poetry is not like reasoning, a power to be exerted according to the determination of the will," Shelley writes; "A man cannot say, 'I will compose poetry.' The greatest poet even cannot say it" (53). Emphasizing the involuntary nature of inspiration, Shelley's metaphor of the Æolian harp works to efface its own sense of mediation: "the very mind which directs the hands in formation is incapable of accounting to itself for the origin, the gradations, or the *media* of the process" (54). Minds direct hands here: Shelley's poetic instrumentality aspires to immediacy, insisting on the transcendence of the inspired mind even in its most involuntary expressions. This model assumes a hierarchy of muse over medium.

The history of autopoetics I trace runs alongside and in many ways counter to this more familiar poetic tradition, which aims to establish poetry as a means of unmediated or visionary expressiveness.[10] In this countertradition, we see a move away from the Æolian metaphor of immediate inspiration – and in its place we see a more pointed attempt to understand the automatic body as an actual material medium. William Johnson Fox, an influential reviewer of Tennyson's 1830 *Poems, Chiefly Lyrical*, literalizes the poet's body as a material Æolian harp: poets, he writes, "think and feel poetry with every breeze that sweeps over their well-tuned nerves" (211). What we see here that differs from Shelley is a model of poetic inspiration as being deeply material in nature, something that occurs in the body as much as in the mind. And again, the body that is figured here is one that is involuntarily responsive – and thus involuntarily productive of poetry. Even Keats, who so deeply conflates poetic agency with disembodiment ("A Poet is the most unpoetical of any thing in existence; because he has no Identity . . . . When I am in a room with People . . . the identity of every one in the room begins so to press upon me that I am in a very little time annihilated"), makes reference to the ways in which his own body is materially acted upon by poetry: "The faint conceptions I have of Poems to come brings the blood frequently into my forehead" (Letter to Richard Woodhouse, October 27th, 1818). The act of poetic composition, for Keats, is hardly one of agency: the "Poems to come" seem to exist already, waiting to be recognized by him, and marking their presence upon his very forehead. Unlike Shelley's muse, Keats's is unexpectedly entangled in the physical medium of Keats's body.

I argue that this poetic investment in the body as a physical and often involuntary medium for poetry – present even in the seeming immediacy of Romantic poetics – continues and evolves throughout the century. The automatic body which Wordsworth and Keats only ambivalently embrace becomes more and more central to Victorian poetic theory; by the 1860s, E. S. Dallas can make the bold claim that "imagination is automatic, and only automatic" (I: 260) and find more resistance to his notion of the unconscious than to the idea that poetry is peculiarly allied with it.[11] This trajectory is mirrored in many ways by the rise of physiological aesthetics, a development that runs parallel to the narrative of this book; while my focus is not on aesthetics per se, many of the developments in physiological and psychological science that contribute to the autopoetic tradition also figure prominently in the more well-traced history of aesthetic thought. Building on Carpenter's theory of "unconscious cerebration," for example, Dallas's "science of criticism" reflects the century's increasing drive to shift analysis of the aesthetic experience away from a narrative of poetic genius and toward a focus on reader response (I: 6). For evidence of the automatic workings of the imagination, Dallas turns to the same tales of language gone awry that appear in studies of memory throughout the nineteenth century.[12] His next step, however, is to assert that creativity and genius are likewise automatic. Rather than confining automaticity to the reception of literature, in other words, he associates it with literary production. These are moves that might seem out of place in traditional histories of critical thought.[13] Yet in the narrative I trace here, the century's turn toward physiological aesthetics reflects the growing conflation of muse and medium – the privileging of the curious automaticity of the material body – that underwrites the autopoetic tradition.

Poetic Materiality, Poetic Media

As the automatic body comes to figure more and more prominently in nineteenth-century poetics, poetic theory remains deeply engaged with developing theories of the materiality and automatism of the human body, theories that place the body within the media ecology of the nineteenth century. Post-McLuhan, of course, it is not hard to understand the ways in which the body is in dialogue with – or extended by – other media.[14] But the model of the automatic body I aim to uncover here suggests that the body's relationship to material mediation is not merely one of extension; instead the body itself is imagined to take on attributes of developing media, from imprinted retinas to phonographic larynxes. Literary scholars have recently turned their attention to the complex relationship between nineteenth-century literature and its multiplying media, focusing on technologies ranging from the industrial steam press to the magic lantern to the wireless telegraph.[15] Within this body of scholarship, however, the novel remains solidly at the center of the critical landscape. Shifting our attention to poetry alongside these same discourses of nineteenth-century media and technology affords a new perspective on the relationship of language to mediation and materiality in the period. We are prone, I think, to allow poetry to retain the mystique of immateriality and immediacy granted to it by New Criticism. I argue instead that poetry is peculiarly material, and that this peculiar materiality presents a special case in considerations of nineteenth-century media and literature.

What do I mean by the peculiar materiality of poetry? Part of this materiality stems from poetry's historic relationship to memory, as I briefly rehearse above (and which I will discuss more fully in Chapter One): its use of meter and rhyme to manipulate the automatic functions of memory. To fully answer this question, however, I want to return our attention to the media ecology of nineteenth-century Britain. The beginning of the century witnessed what Friedrich Kittler has demonstrated to be a media revolution that altered our interactions with language, both technologically and bodily: the growth of a mass print culture that resulted in the hegemony of silent reading practices. As a result of this technosomatic shift, Kittler argues, poetic theorists established an organicized model of composition-as-speech. "When defining Poetry they forgot, fundamentally, that the poetry in front of them has been written and printed," Kittler writes; such forgetting "made poetic writing so easy that philosophers could call it speaking. The philosophers also forgot that speaking is a technique of the body" (*Discourse Networks* 112). But this model of erasure – of a poetics that purports to forget its materiality – simplifies a more complex historical picture. The technological advances that occurred during the Romantic period also emphasized the ways in which mechanization underwrote print culture – and would continue to do so through the nineteenth century. Extraordinary technological changes of the early nineteenth century defined what Adrian Johns calls the "second printing revolution" and enabled the development of mass literacy and modern readership (390). 1814 witnessed the birth of the industrial steam press, but equally important, perhaps, was the invention of the papermaking machine, patented in France in 1799 and introduced into England in 1804; another key technological development was the advent of stereotyping, which allowed for the production and reproduction of identical pages of type. The mass literacy of the new modern readership, whose development depended upon technological changes that rendered language at once increasingly material and increasingly reproducible, provides the historical backdrop for my investigation of poetic automatism. And as this modern readership evolved, the developments in language-reproduction technology that followed throughout the century – telegraphy, stenography, phonography – were similarly interdependent on changing understandings of the body as a system for reproducing language, either in written or spoken form. In the chapters that follow, I consider the ways in which poetry borrows metaphors from other media – metaphors of printing, of inscribing, of excerpting, of reproducing sound – in order to claim for itself a special power over the eyes, ears, mouths, and hands of its readers and writers.

Indeed, poetry presents a special case in considerations of material media in the nineteenth century. Richard Menke has compellingly argued that the information system of Victorian realism relies in part on the fact that fiction discards the "formal markers" that set poetry apart from "everyday printed information" (4). Poetry, then, would seem to offer a different model of information. Celeste Langan and Maureen McLane – in a project that focuses on Romanticism but whose argument has implications for the century that follows – have suggested that we may understand early-nineteenth-century poetry itself as a medium, a medium in dialogue with other nineteenth-century media and especially with print. For Langan and McLane, Romantic poetry's hypermediacy – its "conspicuous marking of mediation" (242) – draws attention to its traces of materiality and embodiment even as it aspires to the status of immaterial information: its residues of orality and aurality, its strikingly visual indentations on the page. Indeed, throughout the century, poetry in print leans toward the virtual: essential sensory elements of its data – its residues of sound in meter and rhyme – are merely evoked. Poetry can be said to maximize its status as a medium among media, imagining itself (much like Menke's telegraphic realism) as a technology for the reproduction of language *and* drawing attention to itself as such. And Victorian (and Victorianist) debates about the nature of sound in poetry, especially in the burgeoning age of sound reproduction, extend the problem of poetic mediation beyond print and demonstrate its importance to nineteenth-century theories of media and information.[16]

If poetry is a particularly allusive medium – one that alludes to rather than represents information – this allusiveness is also echoed in its status as an especially fragmentable medium. Excerpted and collected in commonplace books and books of beauties throughout the century, poetic quotations proliferate outside of their original contexts. As David Allan and Barbara Benedict have documented, poetry was the most popular genre to appear in these collective genres – a popularity Allan attributes to the fact that "verse possesses certain intrinsic advantages for the note-taker, typically framing dense concentrations of thought and feeling in textual forms that are either relatively short or else are naturally divisible by stanza, speech, couplet, or line – and therefore almost inviting dismemberment and subsequent re-use." (141). For Allan, the hegemonization of the rhymed couplet throughout the Georgian period

> accentuated contemporary readers' sense that even the most substantial bodies of poetry could, in certain circumstances, be regarded simply as concatenations of epigrams, formed fortuitously by each pair of rhyming lines. Precisely because they seemed both unusually compact and effectively complete in themselves, textual subdivisions of this kind may have made it even more tempting for a reader to think of commonplacing them—in short, to imagine physically dismembering the writer's original words and appropriating parts of a poem for transfer and re-use elsewhere. (157)

Poetry, in combination with print culture, gained status as an easily fragmentable and even proto-plagiaristic medium. As Benedict points out, the anthology is "entirely a printed genre," embodying the shift from an oral to a print culture ("Paradox" 235). At the same time, collective genres like anthologies and books of beauties cultivate a new model of reading, one characterized by what Benedict calls "its rejection of linearity, its hospitality to a multiplicity of reading procedures, its invitation to readers to read nonteleologically" (249). Indeed, as I argue, Coleridge identified the "striking passage" – the fragment of poetry that pops up in the mind, unbidden – as a product of poetry's newly non-mnemonic status in print culture at the beginning of the century. This model of poetic mediation suggests that print poetry's excerptability grants it strange powers: easily fragmented and recollected, it still contains allusive connections to its larger contexts. Seemingly immaterial and detached units of poetry, in other words, contain within themselves links to the material and contextual information they seem to discard.

This brings me back to the problem of poetic autonomy – not poetic agency, as in the agency of the poet, but rather a kind of agency on the part of the material poem itself. While the word "autonomy" is occasionally used to describe Romantic poetry's attempt to distinguish itself from other forms,[17] I use the word here in a more material sense: when I write of a developing sense of poetry as autonomous, I mean to suggest that poetry itself becomes imagined to be able to act independently. It is as if, as nineteenth-century poetics attributes less and less agency to its human media – its readers and writers – it grants successively more agency to the material poem. In the autopoetics I outline here, poems and fragments of poems are reproduced – or, rather, reproduce themselves – on and in the bodies of their readers and writers. Striking passages attain a curiously material independence. For that reason, the problem of quotation, and particularly involuntary quotation, comes to play a key role in my argument. And quotation poses a particular challenge to the typically Romantic definition of poetry offered in Wordsworth's "Preface": as William Flesch writes, "in quotation the self or speaker or poet or ego utters words which do more than express the spontaneous overflow of his or her own feelings" (6). What constitutes this "more" that is actually expressed – what is added, or subtracted, from poetic agency and affect in quotation – is one of the questions this book works toward answering. Throughout the century, involuntary quotation figures prominently in theories of both poetic composition and reception.[18] From Coleridge to Kipling, we are asked to imagine our encounters with poetry as acts in which language – frequently other people's language – overwrites our own bodies and minds. And this works as well to further destabilize the distinction between writers and readers of poetry. Indeed, the poetics I describe manifests a logic of quotation that verges at times on a logic of plagiarism, a poetics hyperaware of its status as mediating and reproducing other people's words. Tracing this autopoetics back into the nineteenth century unsettles our easy conflation of such hypermediation with modernist aesthetics. When T. S. Eliot makes his famous assertion about literary tradition – "if we approach a poet without this prejudice we shall often find that not only the best, but the most individual parts of his work may be those in which the dead poets, his ancestors, assert their immortality most vigorously" (22) – it's not surprising that such a model of poetic inspiration as involuntarily reproductive also insists that the poet is "only a medium" (22, 28). What is surprising, however, is that such a signal statement of modernism relies so significantly upon Romantic and Victorian challenges to poetic agency.

In the chapters that follow, I outline the nineteenth century's increasing interest in learning to operate this bodily medium – and, in particular, in imagining how poetry may be used to act upon it. Indeed, I argue here that over the course of the century such a notion came to be seen not merely as threatening to organic theories of poetic production and reception but also as productive: the automatic body provides a new medium for transmitting and recording poetry. As such, theories of automatism develop a sense of a collective memory, a physical memory, that stores its own experiences and reproduces them. Readers and writers alike are drawn into this collective mnemonics, which depicts physical memory not as a causal or associative process but as a random and intertextual proto-database of language. At the same time, the drive to decontextualize has its own effects on the relationship of language to media and memory. John Durham Peters writes that "[e]very new medium is a machine for the production of ghosts" (139), and poetry's particular ghosts are inevitably present in these pages. When E. S. Dallas writes, in 1866, that all good poetry will "force the burial places of memory to render up their dead, will set innumerable trains of thought in motion" (I: 318), he links together two important elements in the autopoetic tradition: the surprising automaticity of poetic processes and the uncanny sense that these very processes trouble the boundaries between the material and the immaterial, the living and the dead. If poetry is peculiarly linked to memory, memory in turn is often linked to death. It is no coincidence that in each of my chapters, bodies and texts alike are haunted – by literal ghosts, often enough, but also by the material traces and allusions that linger around the edges of poetic language.

***

Structurally, this book explores the problem of poetic automatism from a variety of angles and perspectives. My goal is to trouble much of the received wisdom about poetic creativity and the very nature of poetry in the nineteenth century. I do so not by elevating obscure poets and texts but by targeting major figures in British poetic theory; in other words, my intention is not to *re*cover a genealogy of forgotten writers but rather to *un*cover an alternate and often unfamiliar strain of thought within an often familiar corpus. Although the narrative moves chronologically, however, this book is emphatically not a survey of poetry. Each chapter is organized around a specific aspect of the automatic body as it engages with the developing media of nineteenth-century poetry: vision and print in Chapter One, physical sympathy and mass readership in Chapter Two, oral culture and phonography in Chapter Three, and handwriting and telecommunication in Chapter Four. Within these chapters, the lines of connection I draw between discourses are not direct lines of influence. I want to avoid a technodeterminist reading of the relationship between poetry and media; my method is informed by approaches to media history that explore the cultural theories of mediation that coincide with or even anticipate the technological innovations that would seem to bring them into being.[19] I am less interested, that is, in arguing for the direct impact of certain technological shifts on certain poets than I am in investigating the shared discourses that contribute to the complexity of nineteenth-century accounts of poetic agency.

In this way my project is neither a work of book history nor of reception history but rather a cultural history of the idea of poetic agency and its relationship to material mediation. In effect, I find theories of poetry in both likely and unlikely places, in texts ranging from canonical criticism to analyses of sleepwalking. Poetry (along with poetic theory and criticism) and nonliterary prose are given equal weight in this book: I am chiefly concerned with how poetry was imagined to operate in nineteenth-century British culture, and I draw upon a diverse range of genres and forms in order to demonstrate the depth and breadth of the century's interest in problems of mediation and automatism. At the same time, my goals are not merely historicist: each chapter culminates in close readings of literary texts in order to demonstrate the stakes of a poetics so strangely invested in divesting its readers and writers of material agency. My methodology is therefore inspired by the complex logic of mediation I see at work in the texts I study. This is a logic that privileges circulation over origin, and over hierarchies of messengers and receivers. Nineteenth-century thinkers were interested in the ways in which shared language can disrupt traditional contexts – were intrigued, that is, by the very fact that fragments of poetic language can exist simultaneously in ordinary and extraordinary places. And more often than not, tracing the movements of this fragmented language (within the body and without it) proved to be as productive as finding its source. The autopoetics of the nineteenth century celebrates coincidence: simultaneity and spontaneity are the phenomena given special attention here, from the post-associationist philosophers to the analysts who attempted to interpret the allusive scripts of the SPR's automatic writers. In a way, I am attempting to take seriously their concerns and methods, in order to interrogate them but also to query their distance from our own.

In Chapter One, I lay much of the historical groundwork for the chapters that follow by outlining the relationship of poetry to both print media and physiology at the turn of the nineteenth century. I argue that Coleridge's theory of "striking passages" – excerpts of poetry that impress a reader instantaneously and then, subsequently, arise spontaneously in the mind – marks an historical shift in the relationship of poetry to memory, one linked explicitly to the invention of print culture and implicitly to physiological theories of hallucination. Coleridge's theory echoes Romantic physiologists who conceived of memory as material, physical, and imprinted; in particular, they sought to explain our strange liability to hallucination as visual memories decontextualized, relocated, and involuntarily recalled. Tracing the problem of the isolated, autonomous imprint – the striking passage – in Romantic poetry, poetic theory, and physiology, I argue that print culture reconfigured poetry's age-old mnemonic effects into a logic of visuality and mechanical reproduction.

Chapter Two contributes to the discussion of nineteenth-century poetry's relationship to the body a more explicit engagement with theories of sympathy – a central aesthetic concept in much recent work on the nineteenth century, and an important term in this book as well. Here I redraw a crucial moment in the history of thinking about sympathy by attending to the oddly neglected idea of "self-sympathy." In the 1830s, poetic theorists grappling with changes in science, technology, and society sought to define a new, modern poetry to fit the times. For such critics as William Hazlitt, William Johnson Fox, and Arthur Henry Hallam, the body became a crucial location for defining modern poetry: these writers treat the poet's relationship to his subject as a material encounter within the body. And while early-Victorian poetic theory seems to promote a super-agency on the part of the poet, who (as Fox writes of Tennyson) can "cast his spirit by strong volition" into the bodies of his subjects, I contend instead that the materiality imagined here requires the poet to perform involuntary acts of sympathetic action and reaction within his own body – to sympathize, that is, with himself.

Long before Arnold's formulation of Victorian poetry as "the dialogue of the mind with itself," we find critics in the 1830s suggesting that, in fact, poetry might be better termed "the dialogue of the body with itself."

The problem of voice and orality in Victorian poetry returns to the fore in Chapter Three. Here I map the period's strange conceptions of the speaking and listening body, using as a touchtone Tennyson's early poem "Morte d'Arthur" (1842) as it evolves into "The Passing of Arthur" (1869, 1873). Victorian theories of speaking and listening depict the interaction between the body's speaking apparatus (that is, the mouth) and its listening apparatus (the ear) as not productive but reproductive – phonographic, even. In doing so, Victorian physiological theory imagines voice as a surprisingly mechanical function. To whatever extent poetry's investment in sound is greater than that of prose, it is oddly a way of hearing with the mouth rather than the ear, a way of taking something silent and reproducing it in other mouths. I argue that in 1842, Tennyson was invested in exploring the body's ability to reproduce heard sound as spoken sound, and in reading aloud as a medium for transmitting and reproducing poetry; in the 1860s and 1870s, his interest turns toward phonography's ability to reproduce sound without the body and its implications for poetry as a medium for preserving voice. In other words, as the century leans toward the impending invention of Edison's phonograph, the problem of the disembodied and endlessly reproducible voice comes to figure prominently in Tennyson's revisions to his Arthurian epic.

Chapter Four examines the apotheosis of the nineteenth century's investment in autopoetics: in this final chapter, I turn to the phenomenon of spiritualist automatic writing in order to investigate the function of poetry in turn-of-the-century attitudes toward literary transmission. Spiritualist automatic writing revives and reconsiders the striking passage, fully realizing its model of other people's language as a powerful muse. This chapter draws on a wide archive that places literary representations of automatism (including Browning's "Mr. Sludge, 'The Medium'" and Kipling's short story "'Wireless'") alongside a large-scale late-Victorian experiment with poetic evidence: the Society for Psychical Research's experiments with automatic writing, in which multiple mediums were enlisted to channel the fragmented communications of the dead. In these experiments, poetic quotation is used as evidence for the existence of life after death – and this system of evidence relies on a network of information that travels from spirit to automatist and finally to interpreter, the SPR researcher who must identify and retrace the allusive data. The product of a century's worth of growing interest in the body as a machine that can involuntarily produce (and reproduce) language, spiritualist automatic writing practices allow us to see the degree to which tropes of automaticity and reproduction abut and often overlap with concerns about originality and creativity. Yet even more interesting is what they reveal about reception: they implicate bodily automatism in the pleasures of critical recognition.

In a brief conclusion, I follow the problem of poetic automatism into twentieth-century literary criticism. I argue that the SPR's seemingly esoteric or incidental experiments with poetic evidence – and the model of poetic information they display – are implicated in a far more influential experiment with decontextualized, collectively interpreted poetry: I. A. Richards's monumental study of close reading, *Practical Criticism* (1929). In introducing the founding practices of New Criticism, Richards demands that we respect the "liberty and autonomy of the poem" by overcoming our own dangerous tendency toward "stock responses." The development of this New Critical idea of a poem's – not a poet's – autonomy is, I argue, born of the nineteenth century's innovations in thinking about media. This is a media moment that comes to emphasize the materiality and reproducibility of poetry, its ability to reproduce itself and to act out of context. It does so precisely because of its status as uniquely fragmentable and yet also materially allusive. And its power comes from its direct autonomy over the human body, turning the bodies of its readers and writers alike into reproductive media. Richards, however, attempts to disqualify from poetic evidence the very allusions and "dangerously" random actions of poetry upon the body that granted it autonomy in the first place.

The autopoetics of the long nineteenth century thus comes to an end with Richards: he disentangles the autonomy of the poem from the automatism of the body, rejecting "stock responses" as valid components of poetics. He does this, of course, in an attempt to glorify the critic. In a way, this is a logical conclusion to my narrative: if poetic automatism destabilizes the agency of the poet in favor of the poem, New Criticism steps in again and asserts critical authority over the poem. But it does so by disavowing the slipperiness, the productive instability, of our interactions with poetry. In this light, my conclusion appears more counterintuitive: that the development of close reading – perhaps the critical tradition's fullest expression of interpretive agency – would have such deep roots in a nineteenth-century poetics of automatism. In restoring attention to the nineteenth century's investment in involuntary response as a valid form of engagement with poetry, perhaps we as critics might reevaluate the degree to which so-called stock responses can function as important avenues of poetic mediation.

CHAPTER I

Striking Passages
Vision, Memory, and the Romantic Imprint

The history of autopoetics I trace begins with the Romantic media moment of *Lyrical Ballads* – a moment in which the problem of poetic materiality comes to manifest the tensions between balladry and oral traditions on the one hand and the media demands of print and readership on the other. For scholars of Romantic poetics, Wordsworth and Coleridge's joint venture constitutes a signal moment in the emergence of a new, often nostalgic literary orality inevitably entangled with print.[1] The problem of the Wordsworthian ballad takes center stage in this model of Romantic poetry's material mediation: scholars from J. Douglas Kneale to Maureen McLane have identified in Wordsworth a deep attentiveness to the problem of voice in print and an attendant awareness of the ways in which print poetry must negotiate its media. However, I want to complicate our understanding of Romantic orality by approaching it from an oblique angle – by circumnavigating, as it were, the usual suspects of Wordsworth, balladry, and voice. This chapter uses the media moment of *Lyrical Ballads* as an entryway into what would appear at first glance to be an altogether different problem in the debate about poetic materiality: the relationship of print poetry to theories of vision and memory in Romantic science. The problem of imprintedness, I will argue, is a problem in common to both texts and bodies. By lingering over the Romantic imprint – a phenomenon neglected by our longstanding critical tendency to read Romanticism for its investment in the immaterial and the organic – we can begin to outline an alternate model of the relationship between bodies, poetry, and media.

Instead of beginning with Wordsworth himself, then, I begin with Wordsworth as he appears in Coleridge's *Biographia Literaria* – in particular, with a striking phrase Coleridge uses to critique his friend's poetic theory. According to Coleridge, the problem is this: Wordsworth, in his "Preface" to the 1802 edition of *Lyrical Ballads*, puts forth a theory of poetry – a poetics based in the real language of men – to which his own poetry does not adhere. "In short," Coleridge complains, "were there excluded from Mr Wordsworth's compositions all that a literal adherence to the theory of his preface would exclude, two-thirds at least of the marked beauties must be erased" (II: 106). Coleridge's objections to Wordsworth's theory are well rehearsed. But it is worth attending to how Coleridge describes these "marked beauties," for in doing so he raises provocative questions about the role of memory in poetic affect. Coleridge goes on to argue: "because the pleasure received from Wordsworth's poems being less derived either from excitement of curiosity or the rapid flow of narration, the striking passages form a larger proportion of their value" (II: 106). What is most intriguing here is that these "striking passages" find their own independent life in the memory of their reader. Many people confess, Coleridge writes, that "from no modern work had so many passages started up anew in their minds at different times" (II: 106). In fact, one of the striking aspects of these memorable passages is that they isolate themselves in the mind, arising "without reference to the poem in which they are found" (II: 106). This decontextualization (and subsequent relocation) of the passage indicates an historical shift in the relationship of poetry to memory, which, for Coleridge, is explicitly linked to the invention of print culture: "Before the introduction of printing, and in still greater degree, before the introduction of writing, metre, especially *alliterative* metre, (whether alliterative at the beginning of the words, as in "Pierce Plouman," or at the end as in rhymes) possessed an independent value as assisting the recollection, and consequently the preservation, of *any* series of truths or incidents" (II: 67). In an oral culture, the memorization of poetry was facilitated by its rhythmic consensus, its integrity as a "series." But this changes, Coleridge says, with the introduction of print. What happens, then, when poetry is memorized without the rhythmic context provided by regular meter? What happens when we memorize poetry by reading it from the printed page?

In this chapter, I will examine poetry's newly non-oral mnemonics as it is theorized in an unlikely context: Romantic studies of the physiology of hallucination. In Romantic science, hallucination is rewritten as a product of the natural workings of our sensory system – merely the result of visual memories printed on the retina and "renovated" so as to reappear. By their nature, hallucinations are removed from the realm of the supernatural and become instead a disorder to which any body is susceptible. As one text puts it, "the belief in apparitions, ghosts, and specters, is not only well founded, but that these appearances are perfectly natural, arising from secondary physical causes, and depending on circumstances to which all nations, all mankind, are equally liable" (Alderson 20–21). This naturalizing of hallucination, I will argue, depends on a newly physiological understanding of memory as a somatic repository imprinted with past sensory experiences. These sensory imprints are dangerously autonomous, often resurfacing without warning: any visual image, imprinted on our retina, may reappear before us even when the original object is absent. The hallucination, then, is an involuntary function of the physiology of memory. In fact, it seems to find new life (as it were) in people's bodies, which are depicted in these accounts as sites of inscription, passive texts that retain but do not quite contain their unruly impressions.

Just as Coleridge's "striking passages" possess an independent force that can "start up anew in the mind," hallucinations are theorized by physiologists in the early nineteenth century as sensory images decontextualized, relocated, and involuntarily recalled. And for these scientists, as for Coleridge, it is the materiality – the imprintedness – of the printed poem that best characterizes this strange power. Indeed, Romantic-era physicians and philosophers alike note the peculiar relationship of hallucination to memorization – and, in particular, the memorization of poetry. In these texts, spectral illusions are frequently linked with the materiality of reading and writing. Over and over again, hallucination seems to take as inspiration the materiality of the page, which seems to possess the memory (and thus, according to these materialist physiologists, the body) of its reader. These case studies repeatedly insist that the poetry being recounted – the "striking passage" that reproduces itself within its readers – possesses a kind of power that comes not from rhyme and rhythm but from the patterns of the printed page.

To some extent, then, this chapter contributes to a growing body of work that seeks to reconsider the traditional critical interpretation of Romanticism – and Coleridge in particular – as invested primarily in organic theories of voice and speech. Celeste Langan, for example, has suggested that Coleridge's "Christabel" enacts an explicit move away from orality as a medium of transmitting and recording meaning. Langan sees Coleridge's Romantic project "not in terms of a nostalgia for the 'oral' culture of the ballad but rather as an exploration of ballad meter as the sign of 'narration without a narrator,' as the sign of writing-as-citation rather than of speech" ("Pathologies" 148). Indeed, Coleridge's poetry (and his poetic theory) does much to challenge Wordsworth's easy equation of poetry with speech. But it also suggests more than a simple non-orality: Coleridge implies that poetry operates within memory in ways that are irregular, striking, and self-replicating – in other words, in sharp contrast to a Wordsworthian poetics of context, association, and recollection. In fact, Coleridge's poetic technology relies very much on a new understanding of memory as physiological, one that grows out of Enlightenment materialist philosophy and early Romantic medical science. Linda M. Austin identifies in this newly embodied memory a privileging of repetition and iterability over authenticity: "a mnemonic process governed by physiology is unbeholden to a recollected, cognitive past and can generate aesthetic pleasure that thrives, correspondingly, on copies and replicas" (3). Indeed, the process of hallucination as theorized by Romantic physiologists replaces the very question of authenticity (was that a real ghost that I just saw?) with a faith in the replicable (no, it's just an endlessly reproducible memory). In hallucination theory, sensory memory operates like print.

As this chapter progresses, I will consider Coleridge's poetic (and mnemonic) theory, which reveals his concern about the disruptive function of language within memory, before moving on to a discussion of similar problems in physiological studies of hallucination. Finally, I'll return to Coleridge's "supernatural" poetry – "Kubla Khan," "The Rime of the Ancyent Marinere," and "Christabel" – in order to examine its investment in the self-reproducing technology of the striking passage. In doing so, I will begin to outline a tradition of Romantic autopoetics that runs counter to the period's conventional investments in organicism and originality, one in which reverie and hallucination appear not as creative but as mechanical and reproductive. The writers I investigate here construct an idea of memory that relies on metaphors of imprinting and thus imagine both bodies and texts as hallucinatory, containing unruly traces of previous imprints. In both poetic theory and hallucination theory, the problem of the striking passage – the decontextualized, self-replicating excerpt – serves as a crucial space for investigating print culture.

The Despotism of the Excerpt: Print Culture and Poetic Agency

Hallucination and poetry have long been associated as the twin expressions of a Romantic investment in dreams and reveries. But this close relationship, I contend, has deeper and more profound roots in the decidedly undreamy workings of materialist physiology. Even Wordsworth's "Preface" – that paean to the mundane reality of poetic language – suggests that poetry itself arises from the same mental and physiological phenomena as hallucination. Like the specter-seer, who was haunted by what one medical text called "past feelings renovated" (Hibbert 66), Wordsworth's poet is "affected more than other men by absent things as if they were present" (400). This kind of strange detachment from external stimuli was, according to physiologists, a form of hallucination, but Wordsworth identifies it as merely a unique attribute of poetic genius: "the Poet is chiefly distinguished from other men by a greater promptness to think and feel without immediate external excitement" (404). Wordsworth's interpretation of this symptom differs from that of his medical contemporaries in part because he allows human agency to play a role in directing the process of memory. Inherent in Wordsworth's poetic theory is a commitment to recollection – an act of mastering the emotional affect of memory, a controlled and contextualized act of voluntary hallucination. Wordsworth famously explains: "I have said that Poetry is the spontaneous overflow of powerful feelings: it takes it origin from emotion recollected in tranquility: the emotion is contemplated till by a species of reaction the tranquility gradually disappears, and an emotion, kindred to that which was before the subject of contemplation, is gradually produced, and does itself actually exist in the mind" (407). Wordsworth's poet, working in tranquility, directs the "renovation" of his past feelings, steering what would be the unruly "overflow" of spontaneous hallucination into the controlled act of recollection. What makes Coleridge's critique of Wordsworth's "striking passages" so interesting, then, is that it undermines recollection, the very quality on which Wordsworth builds his theory of poetic genius. In fact, Coleridge locates the strengths of his former friend's poetry in an altogether different form of memory: the irregular, undirected, and decidedly un-tranquil autopoetics of the striking passage, which "starts up anew" in the mind. According to Coleridge, even Wordsworth's supposedly regulated, contextualized poetry possesses an independent force that is subject to what Wordsworth terms "infinite caprices" (404). In other words, he believes that Wordsworth himself has mistaken the true value of his poetry: his emphasis on tranquility and context are misguided. Instead, Coleridge identifies in Wordsworth's poetry an autonomous and disruptive power Wordsworth himself has overlooked.

Similarly, Coleridge devotes many pages of his *Biographia Literaria* to debunking Wordsworth's speech-based poetics, which is based on the central claim that the language of poetry must derive from the "real language of men" ("Preface" 390). For Coleridge, these pretensions toward orality, like his privileging of recollective powers, merely mislead Wordsworth (and his critics). Instead, Coleridge argues, Wordsworth's "beauties" – his best, most noteworthy, and most memorable phrases – are those passages in which he returns to his naturally "lofty" poetic diction

(*Biographia* II: 8). Yet Coleridge's distinction between poetry and speech is based as much on meter as it is on diction. He disagrees with his fellow poet's claim that meter is a necessary tranquilizer: for readers, Wordsworth fears, "there is some danger that the excitement may be carried beyond its proper bounds" (406). This, according to Wordsworth, is why we need the regulations of poetic rhythm: "the distinction of metre is regular and uniform, and not like that which is produced by what is usually called poetic diction, arbitrary, and subject to infinite caprices upon which no calculation whatever can be made. . . . [T]he Reader is utterly at the mercy of the Poet respecting what imagery or diction he may choose to connect with the passion" (404). Meter, then, guards against the caprices of memory and its associated emotions.

Coleridge vehemently rejects Wordsworth's claim that the arbitrariness of poetic diction leads to a dangerous situation in which the reader is "utterly at the mercy" of the poet. In the *Biographia* he exclaims:

> But is this a *poet*, of whom the poet is speaking? No surely! rather of a fool or madman: or at best a vain and ignorant phantast! And might not brains so wild and so deficient make just the same havock with rhymes and metres, as they are supposed to effect with modes and figures of speech? How is the reader at the *mercy* of such men? If he continue to read their nonsense, is it not his own fault? (II: 81)

Indeed, Coleridge's own theory of metrics implies that meter is itself *more* affective than language. "As far as metre acts in and of itself," he argues, "it tends to increase the vivacity and susceptibility both of the general feelings and of the attention" (II: 66). Meter, for Coleridge, possesses an independent force capable of leaving the reader "at the mercy" of the poet.

But Coleridge's next query – "If he continue to read their nonsense, is it not his own fault?" – is less definitively resolved, despite his best efforts in the *Biographia*. The relationship Coleridge posits between reader and poet, or at least between reader and poem, is hardly one of clearly defined boundaries, especially when meter is involved. As he wrote in a letter to William Sotheby in 1802, "*Metre itself* implies a *passion*, i.e. a state of excitement, both in the Poet's mind, & is expected in that of the Reader" (*Collected* II: 812). To be sure, Coleridge is always quick to reject philosophies that fail to allow for human agency, readerly or otherwise; but his statement here robs the reader of some of this agency. The metrical contract of "passion" and "excitement" that dictates the reader/poet relationship implies that readers may not have as much control over their reactions to the "havock" of rhyme and meter as Coleridge might hope –

and that, in "continuing to read their nonsense," readers may in fact not be at fault at all. The phenomenon of the "striking passage" Coleridge identifies in his friend's poetry suggests that fragments of a text, isolated within the reader's memory, may indeed leave the reader "at the mercy" of its disruptive mnemonics, just as the sensory system of a hallucinator is (according to Romantic physiologists) possessed by renegade memories.

Coleridge shares with his physiologist contemporaries an interest in the relationship of language to memory – particularly when either goes awry. He illustrates arguments about memory (in this case, in an attempt to disprove Hartley's theory of associationism) with tales of linguistic mysteries, just as Hibbert and Darwin recounted endless examples of ladies talking in their sleep, orators performing astounding feats of memorization, consumptive young men conversing suddenly in foreign tongues. Earlier I recounted Coleridge's widely circulated anecdote, originally printed in the *Biographia*, about a young German woman who becomes at once insane and multilingual while suffering from a nervous fever: "She continued incessantly talking Latin, Greek, and Hebrew, in very pompous tones and with most distinct enunciation. ... Sheets full of her ravings were taken down from her own mouth, and were found to consist of sentences, coherent and intelligible each for itself, but with little or no connection with each other" (I: 112–113). The problem, of course, is that the woman seems *not* to be the source of her own speech; and for that reason, perhaps, her speech lacks the kind of continuity of authorship one would expect from a single speaker. As a polyglot, she functions dangerously like a disorganized collection of excerpts, each of unknown origin and each bearing little connection to the next. The final diagnosis confirms this: the physician discovers that the young woman grew up in the care of a learned guardian who used to "walk up and down a passage of his house into which the kitchen door opened, and to read to himself with a loud voice, out of his favorite books" (I: 113). These excerpts, stored in her memory, transform the ailing girl into their unwitting mouthpiece; her orality is merely an involuntary response to – an extension of – these fragments of texts.[2]

Similarly, Coleridge's poetic theory suggests that there is something unholy, as it were, about the very idea of the excerpt – the passage of poetry dissociated from the larger context of the poem. Poetry, Coleridge insists, "is discriminated by proposing to itself such delight from the *whole*, as is compatible with a distinct gratification from each component *part*"; a "*legitimate* poem" is one "the parts of which mutually support and explain each other; all in their proportion harmonizing with, and supporting the purpose and known influences of metrical arrangement" (II: 13). Coleridge expects each component of a poem to participate in the creation of its larger context – to be, in other words, organic. He applauds astute critics for "denying the praises of a just poem ... to a series of striking lines or distichs, each of which absorbing the whole attention of the reader to itself disjoins it from its context, and makes it a separate whole, instead of an harmonizing part" (II: 14). The excerpt, then, is a problem in and of itself (precisely because it exists in and of itself): "striking lines" absorb the reader's attention and, acting with an uncanny degree of autonomy, "disjoin" and recontextualize themselves as independent.

That this autonomy is somehow inorganic – mechanical, even – is not lost on Coleridge, who acknowledges a growing trend toward this kind of disjointed reading as a result of the advent of print culture. Writing to Thomas Poole on 28 January 1810, he complains that the country's "love of reading" has been carried "to excess" by "Newspapers, Magazines, and Novels": "the Spectator itself has innocently contributed to the general taste for unconnected writing – just as if "Reading made easy" should act to give men an aversion to words of more than two syllables, instead of drawing them *thro'* those words into the power of reading Books in general" (*Collected* III: 281). Similarly, in the *Biographia,* he laments that "a shelf or two of BEAUTIES, ELEGANT EXTRACTS and ANAS, form nine-tenths of the reading of the reading public" (I: 48–49). Indeed, the rise of print during the Romantic period was paralleled by (and itself made possible) an obsession with excerpts. Print enabled the popular genre of "beauties" – collections of an author's most acclaimed passages, clipped from their original contexts – to replace the individual reader's commonplace book.[3] At the same time, the growth of the periodical press underscored this focus on excerpts, as reviews of poetry continued to extract and reprint passages from long poems; as Andrew Elfenbein notes, critical excerpting tended to highlight the same "beauties" as the collected editions, thus causing the content of the poem to fade before the privileging of selected excerpts (*Byron* 54). Yet it is not merely content but context that fades here: excerpts are detached from their original location as pieces of longer poems and are instead reprinted as isolated – and replicable – passages.[4] And indeed, the rise of the "beauties" genre can be seen not only as an expression of print culture's ability to excerpt and reprint but also as a response to its overabundance of material poetry: as the page (rather than memory) becomes the repository for poetry, it posits the unit of the passage as the fundamental unit of a poem rather than relying on what for Coleridge are the oral mnemonics of context.

This process of selective extraction is one that Coleridge clearly disdains, especially because of its effect of the memory. In fact, he insists that "the habit of perusing periodical works may be properly added to Averrhoe's catalogue of ANTI-MNEMONICS, or weakeners of the memory" (I: 48–49). Yet the striking passages Coleridge identifies in Wordsworth's poetry cannot be easily grouped into this category. They are not carefully collected in compilations of "beauties." In fact, they are not collected (or recollected) at all: they are disruptive and autonomous. For Coleridge, the striking passage possesses a power that – if anti-mnemonic in any way – tyrannizes the memory rather than simply weakening it. Readers are at the mercy not only of a passage's imagery and emotional affect but also of its formal aspects, its status as an unconnected and independent unit of text that proliferates dangerously in print culture.

Yet for Coleridge, the antithesis of this disconnection – *too much* connection – is equally, if less obviously, problematic. In the *Biographia*, he delineates his break with David Hartley's theory of association, which structures mental processes along chains of predictable and habitually associated ideas. Critics emphasize that Coleridge's disenchantment with associationism stems from the fact that it denies the individual mind agency: ideas are dictated by their connections to other ideas, leaving human life "divided between the despotism of outward impressions, and that of senseless and passive memory" (I: 111). Yet human agency is not the only issue at stake here. What Coleridge objects to most strongly is Hartley's theory that "every partial representation recalls the total representation of which it was a part" (ibid.) – in other words, that associationism rejects not only individual agency but also any individual isolation or fragmentation of ideas. While Coleridge critiques associationism as a rejection of subjective agency, he also implicitly recognizes that (equally problematically) it models an overly organic self: that it allows, as it were, a despotism of the whole at the expense of the fragment. In Hartley's philosophy, the laws of association dictate predictable connections between ideas, privileging in particular an inviolable connection between part and whole. Association, while dictatorial, is surprisingly organic; there are no truly disconnected ideas, and this troubles Coleridge. While he may reject the "despotism of outward impressions," Coleridge's own theory of memory seems to allow for the despotism of the *inward* impression – the ability of a fragmented memory to become independently active. By rejecting Hartley's claim that the "partial" idea always refers back to the whole, he admits a kind of independent agency on the part of the excerpt, the very kind that allows Wordsworth's poetry to "start up anew in the mind."

It seems, then, that Coleridge recognizes the autonomy of the striking passage as an important element in poetic affect and effect. Perhaps the reader is indeed at the mercy of the poet (or the poem), but not for the reason that Wordsworth suggests: the problem doesn't lie in poetic diction, which wreaks havoc with associations, but rather with the striking passage that operates *outside* of the mechanics of association. The conclusions Coleridge draws about the garrulous German girl suggest, indeed, that memory is far trickier than Wordsworth's poetic theory might admit. He deduces that this "authenticated case furnishes both proof and instance, that reliques of sensation may exist for an indefinite time in a latent state" (I: 113); it is, in fact, "even probable, that all thoughts are in themselves imperishable" (I: 114). Here, Coleridge acknowledges that the strange case functions not merely as an anecdote about insanity but as evidence of a fundamental aspect of human physiology, one that would allow these undying sensory impressions to live on even in the sanest of people. Indeed, both the problem (that "reliques of sensation" linger in latency) and the evidence it relies on (that excerpts from printed books move from pages to people by unpredictable routes, and that they reproduce themselves uncontrollably) are precisely the terms on which physiologists sought to understand the materiality of hallucination in the early nineteenth century. These terms, I will argue, rely on a newly materialist understanding of the relationship of language to memory, one that emphasizes its visibility (and reproducibility) by employing metaphors of print technology to explain the process of hallucination.

The Imprinted Body: The Physiology of Hallucination

David Brewster's 1832 *Letters on Natural Magic*, one of the period's definitive texts on hallucination and other deceptive visual phenomena, sought to explain the science behind the supernatural.[5] Stripping contemporary "magic" of its glamour, Brewster uses his expertise in optics to reveal the physiological causes of certain spectral phenomena. Brewster's science is deeply committed to a materialist understanding of the mind-body relationship. Responding to fellow physiologist Samuel Hibbert's claim "that the pictures in the 'mind's eye' are more vivid than the pictures in the body's eye," Brewster proposes "to go much further, and to show that the 'mind's eye' is actually the body's eye, and that the retina is the common tablet on which both classes of impressions are painted" (49). The retina is deliberately figured as a medium:

> This wonderful organ may be considered as the sentinel which guards the pass between the worlds of matter and of spirit, and through which all their communications are interchanged. The optic nerve is the channel by which the mind peruses the hand-writing of Nature on the retina, and through which it transfers to that material tablet its decisions and its creations. The eye is consequently the principal seat of the supernatural. (10–11)[6]

Brewster's depiction of the retina – literally, here, the retainer of images – deploys a powerful metaphor of vision as inscription (and, in particular, writing). This metaphor is called upon to explain the problem of spectral illusions, in which "we find the retina so powerfully influenced by external impressions as to retain the view of visible objects long after they are withdrawn" (37). The mediacy of the retina, then, is complex. It is a reproductive medium rather than simply a medium of transmission, one that not only retains impressions but also replicates them. Moreover, these impressions are unruly. For Hibbert, whose 1824 *Sketches of the Philosophy of Apparitions* was perhaps the most influential of all such studies, "any past impression of the mind never becomes, as it were, extinct" (284). These undying impressions are etched into our sensory pathways, creating a permanent record of our past physical experiences – experiences which, when revivified, can repossess the body (and, thus, the mind) with "recollected images of the mind" that seem as immediate as reality (v). Spectral apparitions are recollected, then, not in tranquility (as Wordsworth would have it) but in the dangerously mechanical systems of our sense organs. Memories here are physical: they are printed on the body, and they may reappear, unbidden. The body literally carries with it its perceptual past.

This materialist understanding of physical memory as a reproductive medium underwrites most Romantic studies of hallucination. The Romantic craze for ghost-debunking began in earnest in 1813 with the publication of Manchester physician John Ferriar's seminal *Essay Towards a Theory of Apparitions*. Over the next few decades, scientists, philosophers, and storytellers took up the problem, drawing upon the burgeoning science of physiology in a collective attempt to debunk the supernatural.[7] Ferriar's essay is generally credited with popularizing the word "hallucination" in the English language (Castle 55); for Ferriar, this term included "all delusive impressions, from the wandering mote before the eye, to the tremendous spectre, which is equally destitute of existence"

(95). Ferriar's essay is also notable because it republished the groundbreaking testimony of a German bookseller and philosopher, Christoph Nicolai, who claimed to have suffered from phantasms for many months during the year 1790 – a disorder which he identifies as the result of having ceased to perform his regular blood-letting.[8] What made Nicolai so interesting, it seems, was his certainty that his spectral visitors were "nothing but the consequence of nervous debility, or irritation, or some unusual state of the nervous system" (164). Indeed, Nicolai's account insists upon a radical materialism, one that calls upon the workings of physiology to explain phenomena that had previously been understood only in spiritual terms.[9] This is, in fact, the very basis of Ferriar's argument: evidence of ghosts, which used to be offered as testimony of the soul's immortality, was no longer irreconcilable with scientific materialism. If we could only recognize these apparitions as hallucinations, Ferriar maintains, we would be freed from the fears and terrors roused by superstition, and "a ghost would be regarded in its true light, as a symptom of bodily distemper, and of little more consequence than a head-ach" (138). In this way, memory becomes physical – and, simultaneously, oddly dysfunctional.[10]

By relocating the ghost to the body's sensory apparatus, then, Romantic studies of hallucination emphasize the status of the perceiving body as a material medium that is printed upon, literally, by sensory experience. In many ways these studies are a natural extension of Enlightenment theories of mind: seventeenth- and eighteenth-century thinkers strove to understand creation not as some ineffable mystery but rather as entirely reducible to cause-and-effect relations well within the comprehension of human reason. As Allison Muri has argued, central to this discourse was a model of the body that was increasingly revealed to rely on automatic processes.[11] Descartes in 1641 depicted the human body as a kind of mechanical extension of an immaterial soul, though in his schema the mechanical body was merely evidence of God's exquisite workmanship; later writers reached the more disturbing conclusion that the automatic processes of the body might operate without any kind of incorporeal motivation or divine governance.[12] Hallucination theory thus builds upon a long tradition of imagining the human as a kind of automaton. At the same time, however, Nicolai's account of the mediating body – like Coleridge's – poses a direct challenge to one of the dominant eighteenth-century models for understanding this increasingly automatized body: associationism. Associationism grounds the dangerously automatic body in predictable patterns of association: ideas and memories follow certain rules and are, as such, never completely unconnected or autonomous.

In contrast, Romantic studies of hallucination suggest that, rather than operating according to the laws of association, "past feelings" are not so much "renovated" as "self-renovating" – that these renegade imprints operate autonomously, following no law but that of their own self-replicating processes. They are, it seems, genuinely random and disconnected. Nicolai's testimony in 1803 thus analyzes his own hallucinations:

> After frequent accurate observations on the subject, having fairly proved and maturely considered it, I could form no other conclusion on the cause and consequence of such apparitions than that, when the nervous system is weak and at the same time too much excited, or rather deranged, similar figures may appear in such a manner as if they were actually seen and heard; for these visions in my case were not the consequence of any known law of reason, of the imagination, or of the otherwise usual association of ideas . . . . (167)

Unable to identify any method to his madness, Nicolai can only conclude that the derangement of his bodily system is, in fact, the only law in operation.[13] Drawing on Enlightenment theories of the automatic body but rejecting the comforting predictability of associationism, Nicolai's testimony insists that the bodily medium is involuntarily reproductive, at the mercy of its unruly impressions.

Inherent in studies like Nicolai's is an understanding of the mnemonic impression as at once physical and autonomous. Like the young German woman in Coleridge's anecdote, we are all susceptible to the decidedly disorderly workings of memory – the return not of the repressed but of the impressed, as it were. Mental agency only extends far enough to allow the hallucinating man or woman to observe, but not control, the renovated impressions. The physicality of memory is inherently passive, as Nicolai testifies:

> I afterwards endeavoured, at my own pleasure to call forth phantoms of several acquaintances . . . but in vain. For however accurately I pictured to my mind the figures of such persons, I never once could succeed in my desire of feeling them *externally* . . . . The phantasms appeared to me in every case involuntary, as if they had been presented externally, like the phenomena in nature, though they certainly, had their origin internally. . . . I was in general perfectly calm and collected on the occasion. (168)

Here we have, it seems, an example of Wordsworth's poetic theory in practice: a man, already highly sensitive to external impressions, recollecting them in "calm and collected" tranquility. And yet, clearly, these attempts at recollection fail. Nicolai is unable to reassemble his memories voluntarily; instead of a resuscitated sensation that builds into its associated emotion, he instead achieves an eerie emotional disconnect. A calm and passive observer of his own possession, Nicolai makes no claims toward regulation or control: he is unable to direct the content (or context) of his hallucinations.

Like Coleridge and his striking passages, then, physiologists of hallucination display a deep interest in the phenomenon of disruptive memory. Like Coleridge, too, these texts suggest that language – both in the mouth and on the page – is a crucial piece of the puzzle. When Dugald Stewart critiques, in 1792, "the Memoria Technica of Mr. Grey, in which a great deal of historical, chronological, and geographical knowledge is comprised in a set of verses, which the student is supposed to make as familiar to himself as school-boys do the rules of grammar," he suggests that memory is not reducible to mnemonic rhyming strategies (453). However, the studies of hallucination and disordered memory that became so prevalent merely two decades later suggest that the problem of putting memory into language (and language into memory) may, in fact, be central to the problem of memory itself. It seems impossible, in these texts, to discuss memory and its behavior without drawing on tales of linguistic anomalies like Coleridge's raving German polyglot. Memory is deemed to be awry when language is awry: hallucinators, madmen, and somnambulists all demonstrate their disorders by speaking, reciting, or reading in ways that would seem unnatural (or supernatural), were it not for hallucination theory's account of the body as an unruly collection of imprints.[14] It comes as no surprise that William Hamilton, presenting his *Lectures on Metaphysics* at Edinburgh University in 1836–1837, lists "Talents for eloquence [and] poetry" as the first two signs of memory disorder in his discussion of madness (237). Language may no longer be the key to directed mnemonics, as Coleridge and Stewart suggest, but it is prime real estate for the kind of disruptive memory that underlies hallucination.

If Nicolai's testimony was instrumental in establishing the reproductive mediacy of the body in studies of hallucination, another case study of a celebrated ghost-seer helps to illustrate the central role that language plays in hallucination theory – the uncanny relationship between the imprinted body and the imprinted page. This ghost-seer is Brewster's "Mrs. A.," the wife of "a man of learning and science" (and herself of "high character and intelligence"), who suddenly becomes subject to a series of strange optical and aural illusions (46). Despite Brewster's frequent assurances that Mrs. A., a true rationalist, "was convinced that she had seen a spectral apparition like those recorded in Dr. Hibbert's work, and she consequently felt no alarm or agitation" (41), there is still something oddly haunted about her story. In fact, Mrs. A. seems to be a victim of that despotic excerpt, the striking passage. Her hallucinations are preceded by an act of memorization and repetition: "Having an excellent memory, she had been thinking upon and repeating to herself a striking passage in the *Edinburgh Review*, when, on raising her eyes, she saw seated in a large easy chair before her the figure of a deceased friend" (44). Although physiology texts like Brewster's generally insist that hallucinations are the result of a (temporarily) diseased sensorium, here, instead, Mrs. A. is gifted with an excellent memory; in fact, she is able to recount entire passages of text. In this way, her memorization is an act that is paralleled by the status of her body, which has been (according to Brewster's theory) imprinted with experiences. She has been "struck" by the *Edinburgh Review* – just as Wordsworth's readers are struck, according to Coleridge, by autonomous, dislocated fragments of his poetry – and thus she repeats printed texts just as her body-as-printed-text repeats its own impressions.

What is most interesting here is that Mrs. A.'s hallucinatory disorder is linked especially to her memorization of poetry. Brewster describes her mysterious nocturnal elocutions: "She is subject to talk in her sleep with great fluency, to repeat long passages of poetry, particularly when she is unwell, and even to cap verses for half an hour together, never failing to quote lines beginning with the final letter of the preceding one, till her memory is exhausted" (47–48). Of course, physicians and philosophers alike have long recognized the peculiarly close relationship between hallu-cination and the memorization of poetry. Erasmus Darwin's 1796 treatise *Zoonomia*, for example, recounts the tale of a young girl seized with what Darwin calls a "wonderful malady": for an hour a day she becomes stuck in a state of reverie, following a series of convulsions. Darwin writes that, in these reveries, she "repeated whole pages from the English poets.[15] In repeating some lines from Mr. Pope's works, she had forgot one word, and began again, endeavouring to recollect it; when she came to the forgotten word, it was shouted aloud in her ear, and this repeatedly, to no purpose; but by many trials she at length regained it herself" (162). Like a stuck record, then, this girl seems to be possessed by the poetry she has memorized. Mrs. A. is in many ways similar to Darwin's reverie-stricken girl, and yet her hallucinated poetry isn't stuck like a record – in fact, it's stuck in a different medium entirely. Although Mrs. A. verbalizes her memorized poetry this time, not merely "repeating it to herself" (as she did with the *Edinburgh Review*), she does so in a way that draws attention to the visibility of the poem: each line, we are told, begins with the *letter*, not the sound, of the previous line's conclusion.[16] She is hallucinating the visual image of the words on a page; she is reading, as it were, in her sleep. This is the alphabetization of Friedrich Kittler, but with a twist: Kittler argues that printed letters (mediated through the mother's mouth) aid in the positing of a primary orality, but this is a primary visibility re-inscribed on the medium of the body, for whom the production of oral poetry exists only as an uncontrollable (and problematic) side effect.[17]

For Langan, who writes of the hallucinatory "glamour" of print, the connection between poetry and hallucination would be unsurprising – "the extraordinary indentation of printed lines, which might be thought to call attention to the medium of print, actually conjures its disappearance" ("Understanding" 63). But here print doesn't disappear, doesn't efface itself in the process of hallucination but instead guides its very structures. Unlike traditional Romantic philosophies of poetic memorization, which insisted that sound and rhythm were necessary mnemonic devices, these hallucinated poems are based explicitly on printed texts. Like Mrs. A. herself – a letter, a fragment of a word – the poetry she memorizes signals its attention to the letter on the page. The physiology of hallucination, which insists on the materiality of visual perception, leads in this case to a kind of visible memory – and a memorizing body that is at the mercy of its often fragmented memories. In Romantic hallucination theory, these memories are irregular and autonomous; detached from their original context, they are literally relocated (and repeated) on the retina. Like the "striking passage," the memorized poem is an impression – an imprinting – that can reproduce itself autonomously.

To be sure, the act of reading has long been the subject of anxiety and debate, as it threatened to foster unhealthy and overactive imaginations. Indeed, the phenomenon of Mrs. A.'s "striking passage" from the *Edinburgh Review*, which seemed somehow to prompt her hallucination, is repeated over and over again in these texts that seek to address the science of the specter. One of Walter Scott's oft-quoted anecdotes from his popular *Tales of Demonology and Witchcraft* recounts the story of a man who is visited by the ghost of Lord Byron after reading about his death:

> Not long after the death of a late illustrious poet, who had filled, while living, a great station in the eye of the public, a literary friend, to whom the deceased had been well known, was engaged, during the darkening twilight of an autumn evening, in perusing one of the publications which professed to detail the habits and opinions of the distinguished individual who was now no more. (38)

The deceased poet who, we are told, had "used to fill the eye" of the public, is shortly to make an appearance in the eye of his living friend, prompted – perhaps – by the act of reading. Similarly, Robert Paterson's essay "On Spectral Illusions" (published in the *Edinburgh Medical and Surgical Journal*) examines a case in which a man hallucinates the ghost of a dead sailor. "I was engaged in reading," he writes, "for a considerable time after the rest of the family had retired for the night, and after I had finished my book," he looks up to find a ghost in his room (84). But here, the usual association between reading matter and hallucination is unclear; like Mrs. A., whose memorization of the rather prosaic *Edinburgh Review* prompted a ghost to appear before her, this hallucinator was merely reading "Tytler's Life of the Admirable Chrichton" (84).[18]

What these studies suggest, in fact, is a far deeper connection between hallucination and print than could be explained by traditional narratives of reading and reverie. In these texts, writing provokes hallucination nearly as often as reading. This might give us pause: surely the writer retains a kind of creative agency that the passive reader never claims. But what these studies imply is that language itself – whether you are producing it or merely receiving it – is peculiarly linked with the act of hallucination. And this especially true for language *on paper*. Paterson, for example, writes that he was visited by a "renovated" impression – the image of a dead man laid out on a board, which he had witnessed some days earlier – reappearing before his eyes: "I had been employed for a few days in writing on a professional subject, and it so happened, that, of a forenoon when thus engaged, on raising my eyes from the paper, the vision of the dead stranger stood before me, with a distinctness of outline as perfect as when I first saw him extended on a board" (86). Henry Holland's *Medical Notes and Reflections* recounts the story of an old man who begins to experience strange aural hallucinations: "there came on the singular *lusus* of two voices, seemingly close to the ear, in rapid dialogue, or rather repetition of phrases, unconnected with any event of present occurrence, and almost without meaning" (221n). Like Coleridge's striking passages, these phrases are detached from any context and repeated involuntarily. And, though they purport to be aural or oral in origin – "voices, seemingly close to the ear" – Holland's next few sentences reveal their uncanny ties to the printed page: "In the evening, while seeking to read, similar voices seemed to accompany him, as if reading aloud; sometimes, getting on a few words in advance, but not beyond what the eye might have reached; sometimes substituting totally different words; the whole having the effect of distinct speech from without, and being entirely beyond control of the will" (221n).

These voices are, emphatically, involuntary and external; yet they are linked to the act of reading, of transforming printed text into speech. In fact, as Holland is careful to point out, the primary organ of hallucination here is the eye: while the voices play with the written text, they cannot move beyond "what the eye might have reached." The relationship between body and text – between the eyes and the words on paper – is the fundamental problem that interests these writers.

It is not, then, merely a casual association between reading and imagination that links language and hallucination so firmly in these texts. Instead, perhaps, what draws these physiologists to stories of reading and writing has more to do with the fact that they share with hallucination an understanding of impressions, of printing, on the senses or on the page – hypermediated texts (and bodies) that draw attention to their own materiality and to their status as objects that contain unruly impressions. Indeed, these texts highlight the media – the book, the page, the letter – that seem to prompt hallucination. "It was when laying down his book," Scott writes, that Byron appears (38); Paterson's apparition is there when he raises his eyes "from the paper." Ferriar describes the hallucinations that occur while sleeping by offering as examples the "Author," who "enjoys the delight of perusing works of infinite wit and elegance, which never had any real existence," and the "Bibliomane," who "purchases illuminated manuscripts, and early editions on vellum, for sums so trifling, that he cannot conceal his joy from the imaginary vendor" (17–18). In an essay in *Blackwood's* titled "The Spectre-Smitten," written by Samuel Warren (a barrister and Master in Lunacy), a man haunted by a spectral hallucination is prompted to hire an amanuensis with the intention of dictating a romance; later, he declares that he and his specter are going to copy some tales into Greek or Latin verse in a "large, bold, round hand" – specifically emphasizing the visible, material form of writing (247). "L. M.," responding to Nicolai, begins his tale by explaining that "a slight defect of memory was perceived in forming the phrases for dictating a letter" (290); later, he actually hallucinates "books, or parchments, or papers containing printed matter," the writing on which appears varyingly in "manuscript type" and "printed type," and afterwards, "instead of being erect, they were all inverted or appeared upside down" (294). Over and over again, hallucination seems to take as inspiration the materiality of the page – and what's on the page, it seems, is less important than the material fact of the page itself.

The effect of this materiality, moreover, is oddly contagious. In these studies, the printed page seems to replicate its own status –

"imprintedness" – on the body. John Abercrombie's *Inquiries Concerning the Intellectual Powers* recalls the story of an actor who, stepping in to replace someone on short notice, learned an entire role perfectly in one night: "he lost sight entirely of the audience, and seemed to have nothing before him but the pages of the book from which he had learned it" (82). Similarly, Paterson describes the strange case of a man whose sensory system remakes his world in the image of the printed page:

> He became aware that the pages of all books appeared to him to be divided into two colums [sic]. This was especially annoying to him when he perused his larger print Psalm-book, which he knew well from long and frequent perusal not to be divided unto columns. This illusion was at first alone confined to the pages of his books, but soon everything that he looked at presented a dark indefinite line dividing it into two halves (79–80).

The illusion, it seems, is catching: what begins on the page soon spreads beyond it, until the man's body interprets all visual stimuli as printed matter. The text, then, not only replicates itself mechanically as print but it effects the same replication within the physical sensorium. That sensory memory operates the way it does – with autonomous, detached imprints that "renovate" themselves – only makes it more susceptible to the mechanics of the striking passage.

As the case of Mrs. A. intimated, moreover, poetry has a special role to play in this Romantic reconfiguration of memory. Just as reading printed matter seems to provoke the kind of passive, imprinted state that leads to hallucination, so too does the composition of poetry suggest a strangely disordered memory. In hallucination theory, the ability to write or recite verse is consistently associated with *un*natural ability, even with the loss of any conscious agency. Poetic genius itself is figured as a symptom of (or susceptibility to) hallucination; Ferriar, for example, writes: "Unquestionably, the temperament which disposes men to cultivate the higher and graver species of poetry, contributes to render them susceptible of impressions of this nature" (63). Indeed, poetry appears in these studies as a dangerously self-replicating impression to which the (temporary) poet must surrender. Whereas in an oral culture, poetry was accorded a special status as a mode of active memorization, in print culture poetry appears to exemplify the disordered workings of this newly passive mnemonics. Some accounts involve the composition of poetry under strangely unnatural circumstances, much like Coleridge and his opium-induced "Kubla Khan."[19] But most often, the poetry is associated less with loss of consciousness and more with a temporary gain in mnemonic powers. Hibbert cites one Dr. Willis: "My memory acquired all of a sudden a singular degree of perfection. Long passages of Latin authors occurred to my mind. In general I have great difficulty in finding rhythmical terminations, but then I could write verses with as great facility as prose" (77). Unlike Wordsworth's theory of emotions "recollected in tranquility," this is poetry recollected in sleep, or madness, or some state in between.

In these studies, hallucinators' memories are oddly overflowing with poetry. Abercrombie notes that "[t]hey in some cases repeat long pieces of poetry, often more correctly than they can do in their waking state" (219); he also tells of a ghost-seeing gentleman who heard "long speeches that were occasionally made, some of which were in rhyme; and he distinctly remembered, and repeated next day, long passages from these poetical effusions" (261). Hamilton quotes a Mr. Flint, suffering from fever: "I was informed that my memory was more than ordinarily exact and retentive, and that I repeated whole passages in the different languages which I knew, with entire accuracy. I recited, without losing or misplacing a word, a passage of poetry which I could not so repeat after I recovered my health" (238).[20] And the most famous Romantic hallucinator of all, Thomas De Quincey, traces both poetic memorization and composition to the possessive forces of oddly autonomous language:

> Passages in Latin or English poets which I never could have read but once, (and that thirty years ago,) often begin to blossom anew when I am lying awake, unable to sleep. . . . [W]ords revive before me in darkness and solitude; and they arrange themselves gradually into sentences, but through an effort sometimes of a distressing kind, to which I am in a manner forced to become a party. (116–117)

Like Mrs. A., De Quincey calls attention to the visible materiality of his hallucinated poetry, found in the words that "revive" themselves and force him to become a passive accessory to their positively un-tranquil self-arrangement.

Coleridge's Mechanical Enchantments

In Romantic hallucination theory, imprints on the body and imprints on the page are both hallucinatory: they are disruptive, detached from their original contexts and endowed with self-replicating autonomy. Rejecting associationism's promise of predictability, Romantic studies of hallucination depict the body as a material medium capable of involuntarily and mechanically reproducing randomized fragments of language, especially poetry. In other words, they imagine the body as operating within the particular media ecology of Romantic print culture. We can find this hallucinatory mechanics at work in Coleridge's poetry as well. For Coleridge, as I demonstrated above, the problem of the striking passage is inherently linked to print culture, which promotes a kind of "Reading made easy" based on "unconnected writing" (*Collected* III: 281). In a way, this is a problem of fragmentation, of excerptability – and as such it's necessary to consider the relationship between those two terms. Fragmentation is at this point a recognizably Romantic trope, and Romanticist criticism (from Marjorie Levinson's new historicist approach to Susan Wolfson's formalist one) has long taken Coleridge as exemplary of the period's fascination with fragments[21] – a strategy that, as Levinson argues, uses poetic incompleteness to liberate writers from the "idea of purposiveness" and the related pressures of burgeoning commodity culture (213). Langan, however, raises the concern that previous scholarship fails to explain what this formal choice might have to do with the subject matter of Coleridge's poetry ("Pathologies" 129). By reexamining this trope in the context of the striking passage, revealing its inherent ties to the material mechanics of memory and print, I hope to reconsider those formal qualities that are also his subject matter: problems of fragmentation and involuntary repetition. I am interested in the ways in which the striking passage is underwritten not by incompleteness – the traditional mode of the Romantic fragment – but rather by decontextualization. Andrew Elfenbein argues that our critical tendency to emphasize organic development as a master trope for the literature of the period leads us to frequently ignore the "rise of the excerpt" as an important historical context: the "larger cultural demand for the instantaneous, synchronic bit that could be easily consumed" (*Romanticism* 169). Coleridge's interest in fragmentation may challenge traditional readings of Romanticism as invested only in organicism, but it also suggests that poetic fragments are peculiarly potent when they are, like excerpts, tied to the decontextualization and reproducibility of the striking passage.

For Coleridge, the fragmented writing that lends itself to "Reading made easy" threatens to introduce a dangerous tendency toward mechanical repetition of thought. Coleridge sneers at what he considers to be an unimaginative reading public; writing of circulating libraries, he contends that this sort of mass consumption cannot fairly be called reading: "Call it rather a sort of beggarly daydreaming . . . the whole *materiel* and imagery of the doze is supplied *ab extra* by a sort of mental *camera obscura* manufactured at the printing office, which *pro tempore* fixes, reflects and transmits

the moving phantasms of one man's delirium, so as to people the barren-
ness of an hundred other brains" (*Biographia* I: n48). Here, print and optics
are conflated into one reproductive technology, one that threatens to
spread the contagion of "beggarly daydreaming" mechanically – and one
which, it might be added, Coleridge takes full advantage of in his enthu-
siastic italicization.[22] Reading, it seems, can be a means of transferring
delirium to other brains, of replacing active mental activity with passive
replication. And elsewhere, Coleridge implies that this contagion of material language is linked particularly to print culture: "the passive page of
a book, by having an epigram or doggrel tale impressed on it, instantly
assumed at once loco-motive power and a sort of ubiquity, so as to flutter
and buz in the ear of the public" (*Biographia* I: 60–61). The page, formerly
"passive," becomes endowed with a self-reproducing autonomy by its
imprint.

Traditional readings of Coleridge emphasize his anxieties regarding
mechanization. Jerome Christensen, for example, takes Coleridge's injunction, "be not *merely* a man of letters" (*Biographia* I: 158), as a "statement of
his most literal fear": "Once he has been lost to print," Christensen writes,
"the man becomes a creature of the printing press, neither person nor
thing, and subject to endless, mechanical reproduction" (31). Yet, despite
his anxiety, Coleridge makes far more use of this contagious technology
than this critical tradition admits. Coleridge's poetic practice depends (as
does his poetic theory) precisely on an understanding of memory that relies
on the mechanics of print. Like the physiology of hallucination – and like
the striking passage – Coleridge's poems find their power in the involuntary reproduction of imprinted memory; or, as his obituary in the
Edinburgh Review remembered it, in "the mechanical enchantments of
his versification" (Merivale). In so doing, they call into question the
distinction between readerly passivity and authorial agency by implicating
both in the mechanics of the striking passage.

There is, perhaps, no better place to explore the problem of poetry and
memory than Coleridge's "Kubla Khan." Frequently labeled as a fragment,
one might argue that the poem is – according to Coleridge's own account
of its composition – more rightfully an excerpt, a passage taken from
a larger (if imaginary) piece. Written in 1797 after the poet ingested
a small dose of opium, "Kubla Khan" raises questions about the relationship of poetry to memory – questions that, like those asked by physiologists
of hallucination, revolve around issues of agency and autonomy, creativity
and reproduction.[23] And, as it is in fact a tale of hallucination itself,
Coleridge's strange vision is likewise preceded by an encounter with

a book: in his prefatory notes to the poem when it was finally printed in 1816, Coleridge explains that he had fallen asleep while reading Samuel Purchas's description of Xanadu (522). For three hours, he remained in a sleep ("at least of the external senses") while he composed ("if that indeed can be called composition in which all the images rose before him as *things*, with a parallel production of the correspondent expression") almost three hundred lines of poetry. When he awoke, he began writing down what he remembered, intending to transcribe the "distinct recollection of the whole," but was unfortunately interrupted, after which he was never able to recall the rest of the poem (522). Coleridge, like the hallucinating poets of the physiological studies, insists on his own passivity: the poem possesses a kind of autonomous agency, one that co-opts his creative powers to its own end.[24]

But this is no Romantic reverie of inchoate thoughts and dreamy, half-conceived imagery, despite the fact that it has been traditionally read as such: take, for example, Susan Eilenberg's claim that "Coleridge's words live a ghostly existence in exile from both stable subjects and stable objects, unsure of their relation to things in themselves" (x). Rather, Coleridge insists on the materiality of his ideas and their concrete relationship to words: "images" are "things," and the poetry that describes them (their "correspondent expression") seems similarly extant. Critics, in fact, faulted Coleridge for deriving language directly from his dream rather than simply finding inspiration there. The *Augustan Review* remarked scathingly on "the liberality of Mr Coleridge's muse, who, in the short space of three hours, brought, not a train of poetical ideas, to be afterwards embodied in appropriate verse, but a corps of well-appointed able-bodied lines, ready, without further training or discipline, for the service of Messrs. Bulmer and Co., Cleveland-Row" (18). "Kubla Khan," in other words, is simply too much like print, too ready for mechanical "service" at the printing-house. Like Mrs. A., Coleridge seems to be hallucinating poetry that is already written.

And, in a way, he nearly is: he notes that he "fell asleep in his chair at the moment that he was reading the following sentence, or words of the same substance, in 'Purchas's Pilgrimage': 'Here the Khan Kubla commanded a palace to be built, and a stately garden thereunto'" (522). But Coleridge's implication that it was the "substance" of the words that mattered, rather than the actual words themselves, proves to be disingenuous. Compare the opening lines of the poem ("In Xanadu did Kubla Khan / A stately pleasure-dome decree" [1–2][25]) with the opening of the actual sentence from Purchas: "In Xaindu did Cublai Can build a stately pallace" (qtd. in

Wu 522). The first line of the poem is a near-verbatim repetition of what he had been reading, as if the sentence had taken hold in his sleeping brain and written out the rest of the poem by itself. Unlike Eilenberg, then, I read Coleridge's words as in fact quite sure of their status as words on a page.

The model of composition-as-hallucination presented in "Kubla Khan" suggests that Coleridge saw the suspension of authorial agency – the involuntary reproduction of language that you did not create – as part of the process of composition. In a way, Coleridge's theory of "striking passages" depicts plagiarism as a species of authorial hallucination: the sudden and involuntary appearance of someone else's words inside your head, or even inside your text. For although Coleridge was in many ways skeptical of the kinds of passive reading promoted by print culture, he also appreciates – and even aspires toward – its particular brand of materiality, which promotes the kind of involuntary recollection exemplified by the striking passage. During one of his early stints at the *Morning Post* in 1800, he writes in a letter that he is proud of the contagiousness of his words in print:

> it is not unflattering to man's Vanity to reflect that what he writes at 12 at night will before 12 hours is over have perhaps 5 or 600 Readers! To trace a happy phrase, good image, or new argument running thro' the Town, & sliding into all the papers! ... Then to hear a favorite & often urged argument repeated almost in your own particular phrases in the House of Commons – & quietly in the silent self-complacence of your own Heart chuckle over the plagiarism, as if you were grand Monopolist of all good Reasons! (*Collected* I: 569)

Coleridge imagines his words – his "happy phrases" and "new arguments" – as autonomous and mobile, "running" through the town and "sliding" into papers with a will of their own.[26] The pleasure he takes in this "grand Monopoly" of language stems from the fact that it provokes involuntary repetition in his readers. And this tendency toward involuntary repetition extends as well to readers of his poetry, according to William Hazlitt, who reviewed "Kubla Khan" in the *Examiner* on 2 June 1816: he notes that readers "repeat these lines to [them]selves not the less often for not knowing the meaning of them" (349). Coleridge's poetry – like Wordsworth's striking passages – achieves a kind of mnemonic autonomy detached from context, source, and even meaning.

To establish this grand monopoly, Coleridge exploits the new physiological understanding of memory and its uncanny relationship with hallucination. Like Mrs. A. and her fellow hallucinators, Coleridge finds inspiration in the unruly materiality – the self-replicating "imprintedness" – of the printed page, which reproduces its hallucinatory effects first in Coleridge's poetry and then in the minds of his readers. Indeed, this newly physiological paradigm of mnemonic imprinting suggests that memory becomes collective in the very process of losing its claims to recollection. Coleridge's dream of a grand monopoly imagines an act of literary transmission that installs vicarious memories in its readers, memories that replicate and transmit themselves as possessive and material imprintings. And it suggests that some degree of literary effectiveness can be achieved by ceding authorial agency to the self-replicating autonomy of print.

It is in the original "Rime of the Ancyent Marinere," published as the first poem in the first edition of *Lyrical Ballads* (1798), that we can fully witness Coleridge's experimentation with the problem of collective and imprinted memory.[27] Written originally to complement Wordsworth's tales of "ordinary life" by providing "dramatic truth" of the supernatural (*Biographia* II: 6), this haunted poem garnered praise and condemnation alike from its numerous critics. Complaining of Coleridge's inconclusive vacillation, Hazlitt delivers this judgment: "he seems to 'conceive of poetry but as a drunken dream, reckless, careless, and heedless, of past, present, and to come'" (5: 166). This particular fault – that of disregarding the proper divisions of temporality – is clearly troubling for Hazlitt, but its shiftiness in this regard is also, I would argue, one of its deliberate strengths. The "Rime" questions the idea that memory is progressive and contextual; instead, it posits a disruptive (and highly visual) form of memory that possesses the body in order to reproduce itself. And the Ancient Mariner himself, forced into involuntary repetition, embodies this new mnemonics. He is a hallucinator, the passive victim of a wandering imprint that has an autonomous, and physical, agency: "Forthwith this frame of mine was wrenched / With a woeful agony, / Which forced me to begin my tale – / And then it left me free" (611–614). This telling necessarily turns into a *re*telling: "Since then, at an uncertain hour, / Now oft-times and now fewer, / That anguish comes and makes me tell / My ghastly adventure" (615–618). This involuntary repetition is, explicitly, irregular. The Mariner is fixed in repetition, evacuated of agency; as Wordsworth complained, "he does not act, but is continually acted upon" ("Note" 390). But this propensity for repetition does not end with the mariner: the narrator of the "Rime" is also possessed by it, and phrases are repeated verbatim throughout the text (for example, the phrase "He cannot chuse but hear" occupies lines 22 and 41). Even individual poetic lines display a kind of stuttering internal repetition:

"Alone, alone, all all alone, / Alone on the wide wide sea" (224–225). The tale involuntarily returns to and repeats its past expressions, as if it is both text and reader, source and repetition.

That this repetition aspires to – or at least intimates – the status of speech is, I would argue, also deliberate. Margaret Russett has noted that "a 'residual' version of sound serves as the alibi for a poetics grounded in the reproducibility of print" (776); and, indeed, sound and speech operate as a poetic red herring, an alibi of immateriality in a poem that ultimately stakes its claim as print.[28] Although the Mariner is, to be sure, an involuntarily speaking narrator, the wedding-guest (to whom the Mariner teaches his tale) denies that the affective power of the story lies in listening. Rather like Wordsworth, the misguided Mariner repeatedly insists that his "strange powers" are, in fact, "speech" (620): "Listen, stranger!" (45 and 49), "Listen, oh stranger, to me!" (204), "Listen, oh listen, thou wedding-guest" (360). It is up to the wedding-guest to correct him: "'Marinere, thou hast thy will! / For that which comes out of thine eye doth make / My body and soul to be still'" (361–364). What commands the acquiescence of the listener is not, in fact, the Mariner's speech: it is the power of his *eye*. This emphasis on visibility is similarly evident at the beginning of the tale, as the Mariner's first attempts to manually arrest the wedding-guest "with his skinny hand" are brushed aside (13); in the next stanza, however, the Mariner "holds him with his glittering eye – / The wedding-guest stood still, / And listens like a three years' child: / The marinere hath his will" (17–20). The poem, in other words, seems to be mocking those critics who would attempt to find in this poem an affective power based in speech. Instead, it insists that its power to arrest its readers, to have its will with them, derives from its material visibility.

In this way, the Mariner himself assumes the status of a striking passage: he communicates involuntarily, repeatedly, and visually. And the poem, too – with its deliberate textual archaisms in the first version, its explanatory marginalia in the final – intentionally presents itself primarily as a printed page. The revised version, which situates the poem within the pseudo-antiquarian tradition of Scott, makes it impossible to read the text as a simple transcription of an oral ballad; it merely embeds the poem in another layer of textuality. As Jerome McGann notes, the glosses draw specific attention to the text as an "imitation of a culturally redacted literary work" (51), each of whose layers are assigned a pseudo-historical specificity: the ballad's language dates it to the fifteenth century, while the editorial glosses imitate the style of the late 1600s and early 1700s (41). Yet the archaic language of the first "Rime" makes an even more critical distinction between antiquarianism and actual archaic *spelling*: if the tale were, as many critics have read it, deliberately hearkening back to an oral original, the spelling – the arrangement of letters on a page – would not need to be archaic; if it is meant to recall an ancient folktale, that folktale – like the forgotten stanzas of "Kubla Khan" – is somehow already written. McGann's reading of the "Rime" as "an evidently *mediated* text" is useful here: "each redaction specifies and calls attention to the series of distinct epochal (that is, ideological) interpretations through which the poetic material has been evolving" ("The Meaning of the Ancient Mariner" 57). But this reading does not register the central importance of print to the structure of the poem's textual format – a format that is itself historically specific to the era of print culture. Coleridge is imitating a *book*.

Despite its pretenses toward orality, then, the "Rime" is a creature of print. And the Mariner himself, arising unexpectedly in improper contexts and possessing the sensate body of his listener, an uninterested wedding-guest who nevertheless "cannot chuse but hear" (22): his enchantment, too, springs from his status as print. The Mariner operates not only as a hallucinator but as a hallucination – a "past feeling renovated," a renegade memory. At work in this poem we can see the mechanics of Coleridge's hallucinatory autopoetics: the "Rime" draws inspiration for both its form and its content from the Romantic reconfiguration of the mnemonic imprint.

The Metrics of the Striking Passage

If, as I've been arguing, involuntary repetition in Coleridge's poetry is inspired by the printed page, his most celebrated fragment poem would seem to challenge this notion. "Christabel" – a poem expressly about possession and involuntary repetition – is famous for its pre-print circulation via recitation, its complex relationship to orality. And yet, if we consider the effects of reading the printed version of the poem alongside its more famous history as an oral version, we can see that Coleridge builds into the printed page a new kind of involuntary repetition, one that – like "Kubla Khan" and the "Rime" – draws attention to itself as autonomous and mnemonically disruptive. In other words, "Christabel"'s striking, possessive power is not reducible to its orality. Both its content and its form seem to allegorize the hallucinatory power of the printed page: its unique ability to self-replicate verbatim, to enforce involuntary repetition.

During the poem's long circulation in manuscript form, "Christabel" prompted both hallucination (Shelley claims to have had a horrible vision of a woman with eyeballs for nipples) and repetition (it spawned dozens of imitations, many of which were partial plagiarisms). The poem was famous for its "striking" power – and that uniquely physical word is indeed the verb of choice, over and over again, for people describing their experiences with "Christabel." The most famous case of this strike is the case of Walter Scott, who admired in the "striking fragment called Christabel" its new, "singularly irregular structure of the stanzas" (qtd. in Russett 86). Scott found Coleridge's metrical experimentation so compelling that he was inspired to adopt a disconcertingly similar style for his widely read 1805 poem *The Lay of the Last Minstrel.* That he managed to compose and publish his poem ten years before Coleridge's original ever saw print, was, of course, a source of anxiety for Coleridge's friends, who feared he would be viewed as a plagiarist. The fact that Coleridge was, in fact, prone to plagiarism – repeatedly borrowing ideas and phrases, especially from his favorite German philosophers – sits oddly with his also famous claims to originality.[29] Indeed, the tale of "Christabel"'s contagiousness itself contains echoes of Coleridge's own dream of a "grand Monopoly" of enforced plagiarism. The poem, Russett writes, "creates an authorial personality by possessing and reproducing itself in others" (90).

In a letter of 27 October 1805, Dorothy Wordsworth acknowledged that the similarity between "Christabel" and the *Lay* "must strike every one who is acquainted with the two poems, and I fear it is to be accounted for by Mr Scotts having heard Christabel repeated more than once" (632). That she locates the source of the problem in the poem's repetition is telling. Indeed, this repetition functions in Dorothy Wordsworth's account like a contagion, spreading throughout the literati: "Coleridge gave a Copy of Christabel to a Mr Stoddart who used to recite it at Edinburgh ... and once he did so at W Scott's house, who being very much struck with it desired him to repeat it again, and, as he told us, he himself after this could repeat a great deal of it" (633). But this repetition, which begins for Scott as intentional, soon becomes unintentional as the poem's possessive mnemonics presses Scott into its service: Scott's only fault, according to Dorothy Wordsworth, is that "having been exceedingly delighted with C's poem he was led by it insensibly into the same path" (632). The poem is given the authority here; Scott is merely a passive mouthpiece (or, rather, amanuensis) for its reproduction, led "by it" into a recreation *of* it.[30] As Russett notes (85), Dorothy Wordsworth's account casts Scott in the role of poor Christabel, entranced by the sorceress Geraldine into an unconscious mimesis, the "forced unconscious sympathy" of Coleridge's poem (597). Indeed, Geraldine – like the poem itself – is able to self-replicate. Christabel, after witnessing Geraldine's bizarre (albeit momentary) facial transformation into a serpent ("the lady's eyes they shrunk in her head, / Each shrunk up to a serpent's eye" [572–573]), falls victim to the very kind of involuntary repetition that commanded the "insensible" plagiarism of Dorothy Wordsworth's Scott:

> So deeply had she drunken in
> That look, those shrunken serpent eyes,
> That all her features were resigned
> To this sole image in her mind,
> And passively did imitate
> That look of dull and treacherous hate.
> And thus she stood in dizzy trance,
> Still picturing that look askance
> With forced unconscious sympathy   (589–597)

And Christabel is not alone in her passive imitation. Just as the poem's heroine becomes the medium for automatic repetition, the narrator, too, is subsumed by it, forced to repeat lines over and over again.[31] This is a characteristic of the poem that the *Augustan Review* criticized, complaining about its "constant repetition" (24). Disruptive memory, in the form of the repeated line, thwarts narrative progress; at the same time, its fragmented state gives it a kind of autonomy that provokes – in Scott, at least – involuntary repetition.

But the poem's self-reproducing powers were not, according to its critics, limited to Scott alone. Byron had praised "Christabel" publicly – calling it "that wild and singularly original and beautiful poem" (3: 486) – but he had also borrowed from it in his "Siege of Corinth." While he, like Scott, was quick to acknowledge Coleridge's original as his inspiration, his praise was soon repeated nearly as often as the poem itself. William Roberts, writing for the *British Review*, dismisses the question of who plagiarized whom: "With this question we shall not trouble ourselves: where two are afflicted with an epidemic it is of little importance which caught it of it other, so long as *we* can escape the contagion" (66). He is, perhaps, reading the situation more astutely than he thinks, for the "striking" poem did seem to provoke a kind of epidemic of plagiarism. But Roberts seems to have caught another contagion – that of incessantly repeating Byron's famous praise of "Christabel," "that wild and singularly original and beautiful poem," which is quoted verbatim four times within the short review. Like the ubiquitous and locomotive printed phrase that, Coleridge complained, continues to "flutter and buz in the ear of the public," the language of "Christabel"'s reviews seem oddly repetitive in itself.

If any passage in "Christabel" itself assumed such autonomous locomotion, it was without a doubt the opening lines of the poem, which very nearly did acquire the kind of "ubiquity" Coleridge claimed to despise.[32] Almost every negative review – and there were many – saw fit to reprint at least the first thirteen stanzas, ridiculing its gothic imagery and its grotesquely mundane details. Most importantly, however, this repeated excerpt seems to be a rallying cry for those who wished to ridicule Coleridge's "new" meter – for meter, indeed, was the focus of his critics' disdain. In particular, they were fond of repeating the lines with the most difficult rhythms, challenging their readers to find any semblance of regularity in the oddly measured lines. The *Academic*'s reviewer declares: "it will ever be a secret to all but himself [Coleridge], how the two following lines, for example, may be accentuated so as to have the same regular metre; 'Ah, well-a-day!' / 'And didst bring her home with thee in love and in charity'" (340). Just as the reviews themselves participated in the replication of these irregular passages, so too are readers asked to continually repeat them, presumably out loud, playing with the accents – letting the strike of the meter itself, rather than its syllabic context, dictate the rhythm of each line. But this kind of repetition, this privileging of accent (strike) over syllabic regularity (context), is exactly what Coleridge intends: the odd, disruptive mechanics of hallucination and the striking passage.

In his introduction to the poem, Coleridge justifies his metrical experimentation, noting that the meter "is not, properly speaking, irregular, though it may seem so from its being founded on a new principle: namely, that of counting in each line the accents, not the syllables. Though the latter may vary from seven to twelve, yet in each line the accents will be found to be only four" (*Complete* 215). Coleridge's "new principle" is meter that lacks metrical consensus. What had been the regular "strike" of meter, the tranquilizing rhythm of Wordsworth, has become an independent strike: one that fixes permanently but irregularly; one that is decidedly reproducible and even self-reproducing. Like the odd, irregular mechanics of hallucination, Coleridge's metrical strike is repetitive but unruly. Its repetitions, moreover, are exaggerated when reading from the page. Unlike learning the poem by ear – a process that, as we have seen, prompted its own kind of imitation – reading the poem from the page transcends imitation entirely. Consider Scott, hearing the poem recited and then repeating it himself: he would have no question about how to deliver the metrical stresses because Mr. Stoddart, the poem's mouthpiece, would have already made the decision. Scott would merely imitate Stoddart reciting Coleridge. But this oral-aural imitation vanishes when the reader is confronted only with the printed poem and Coleridge's injunction to deliver four beats per multi-syllabic line. Instead of copying the sound, the silent reader must test each line to see where the requisite four beats may fall. Take, for example, the much-maligned third line, the unexpected brevity of which disrupts the galloping anapests of the first two eleven-syllable lines:

> 'Tis the middle of night by the castle clock,
> And the owls have awakened the crowing cock;
> Tu—whit! —— Tu—whoo!
> And hark, again! the crowing cock,
> How drowsily it crew. (1–5)

Doling out one accent to each of the four syllables in the third line, as Coleridge's "new principle" demands, almost always requires a second pass through the line.[33] The galloping reader who takes the phrase in iambs will suddenly find herself at the end of the line, with no text left to accent; only by repeating the line is she likely to give each nonsense-syllable its equal stress. As Langan notes, "It is not via orality, but by rereading," that "Christabel"'s meter becomes pleasurable ("Pathologies" 146). But I want to argue that more than rereading is at work here. Like Darwin's young woman, who is deaf to the voices of her friends attempting to aid her recitation, the reader of "Christabel" cannot merely repeat what is heard but must return repeatedly to the text in order to transform it into sound.

As Coleridge himself explains, the "accents will be found" to be four – but it may require some experimentation on the part of the reader. Thus the poem's metrical experimentation – its disruptive irregularity – is self-replicating just as the actual lines of the poem are repeated in the process of the experiment. The reader's agency is invoked only to replicate the text's, to find the proper irregularity dictated by the text itself. In this way the printed text compels both decontextualization and repetition, and thus it provokes a more fragmented reading experience – a more fragmented form of compulsive repetition – than did the contagiously oral version, in which the rhythm of the individual lines would come pre-interpreted for you, ready to be merely echoed. And Coleridge's metrical experiment in "Christabel" is decidedly *not* recollective: it is repetitive without the coherence implied in "collection." It remains fragmented, repeating only on a line-by-line basis: when each segment is done, the irregular count begins anew, with no reference to the syllabic content of the surrounding lines. "Christabel," far from being an orally contagious poem, actually operates on the principles of the striking passage. Even its "new principle," that of metrical experimentation based on the accent rather than the syllable, relies on this new relationship of poetry to memory.

This is a relationship that privileges the excerpt – the striking passage – over narrative completeness and context. And as in the physiological studies of hallucination, in which poetry is strangely linked to disordered memory and involuntary repetition, "Christabel"'s autopoetics also privilege the agency of the textual machine over that of the reader (or poet). The poem limits the reader's agency to the act of "renovating" the words on the page. As Hazlitt complained, the passivity of the poem's characters is echoed in the enforced passivity of the reader: "The mind, in reading it, is spell-bound" (349); the reviewer for *The Times* concurred that reading the poem induced "thought-suspending awe" (891). And this mental submission on the part of the reader is tied to the poem's fragmented state. In fact, the positive reviews of the poem tended instead to appreciate "Christabel"'s incompleteness, suggesting that it makes the poem more memorable: Josiah Conder wrote in the *Eclectic Review* that "we are much mistaken if this fragment, such as it is, will not be found to take faster hold of the mind than many a poem six cantos long" (566). Similarly, a reviewer for *The Times* (thought by some to be Charles Lamb[34]) argued, "we know not whether the fragmental beauty that it now possesses can be advantageously exchanged for the wholeness of a finished narrative. In its present form it lays irresistible hold of the imagination" (891).

If Coleridge asks, in the *Biographia*, "How is the reader at the mercy" of such imaginative despotism, his own poetry provides a compelling answer: it exploits the connection between memory and print, revealing both to be autonomous, fragmented, and self-replicating. In print culture, poetry's age-old mnemonic quality is disrupted and reconfigured into a logic of visuality and mechanical reproduction. The laws of rhythm and rhyme that were understood to structure oral poetry find their strength in numbers, their context as part of a series; the same is true for memory, which – according to Enlightenment theory – only operates within predictable chains of causes and effects that link every memory to some path of association. But the late-Romantic construction of a new, physiological memory – a sensory memory that operates on the basis of permanently revivable impressions – imparts an autonomous and disruptive agency to each individual mnemonic imprint. Similarly, in print poetry, "striking passages" are no longer mnemonically associated with their larger context via regular meter and rhyme: they become repetitive and irregular, just like the detached and disruptive sensory imprints that are the stuff of hallucination. And when meter *is* involved in memory, as Coleridge suggests, it possesses a dangerously independent force, one that disrupts and co-opts the structure of memory rather than easing its already predictable processes.

The phenomenon of the striking passage exemplifies the newly formulated relationship between poetry and memory in Romantic culture. In so doing, it shifts the burden of agency from the individual to the textual machine: the passage that arises "anew in the mind," "without reference to the poem in which [it is] found," is primarily textual – like Mrs. A.'s hallucinated poetry, "Christabel"'s meter, and the Ancient Mariner himself. And this is Coleridge's "grand Monopoly": his recognition that printed language enacts a kind of collective memory, an enforced plagiarism through which vicarious memories replicate themselves in other people's bodies. In other words, this is reading, but a kind of reading based on the striking passage. Unlike traditional models that figure Romantic poetics as a deep encounter between two selves who recognize each other through the medium of print – print that then dissolves in the process of reading – the striking passage suggests an alternate model for Romantic poetics: a non-humanist, non-subjective model based on the expansion of print and its effects on ideas of memory. In this model, material print *doesn't* dissolve in the process of reading. Instead, it draws attention to its own mediacy.

CHAPTER 2

Internal Impressions
Self-Sympathy and the Poetry of Sensation

The autopoetics of the striking passage emphasize the unexpected and often autonomous materiality of the imprint. For Coleridge, as well as for his medical contemporaries, the phenomenon of the striking passage complicates distinctions between readerly passivity and writerly agency by showing readers and writers alike to be at the mercy of material language. Yet if, in debates about material poetry and its relationship to the body, poetic excerpts are imagined to be increasingly autonomous, this tendency is mirrored by a growing interest in the mediacy of the body in the production and reception of poetry. Vision was my focus in the previous chapter; here, I turn to the internal workings of sensation in the nineteenth-century body in order to explore the period's intensifying concerns about what it means to be an agent of poetry in an age of materialism. This very concern is raised by William Hazlitt in his 1818 *Lectures on the English Poets,* which attempt to offer a definition of poetry. Hazlitt's definition makes clear that his commitment to materialism is less ambivalent than Coleridge's: in his lecture, he depicts the body as mediating – in a surprisingly physical sense – the production of poetry. Yet what is striking about Hazlitt's theory of poetic agency is that it models a way of being with poetry that in fact has very little to do with agency:

> The best general notion which I can give of poetry is, that it is the natural impression of any object or event, by its vividness exciting an involuntary movement of imagination and passion, and producing, by sympathy, a certain modulation of the voice, or sounds, expressing it. (*Complete Works* 5: 1)

Hazlitt's theory of poetry is built upon a favorite term of the late eighteenth and nineteenth centuries (and, recently, of scholars of that period): sympathy. But the sympathy to which Hazlitt here refers is not the sympathy we know. It is not emotional, mental, or imaginative, and it does not involve entering into the feelings of another person. Instead, it is a kind of

58

sympathy that operates within the self – a predominantly physiological sympathy between different parts of the body. The "involuntary movement of imagination and passion" that we might identify as sympathetic is, in Hazlitt's formulation, only the precursor to sympathy. And that sympathy itself results in not emotional but physical affect: "a certain modulation of the voice." This is, in other words, a sympathy in which the body responds to itself – and in which the imagination is figured as part of this involuntary physical system.

The physiological sympathy that Hazlitt describes, then, differs from the interpersonal sympathy of eighteenth-century philosophy: Smith and Hume offer models of sympathy in which community, social feeling, and morality depend upon the ability to imagine or feel yourself into another person's situation.[1] Hazlitt's sympathy, instead, depicts a startlingly internal affair. Yet his seemingly unfamiliar use of the word "sympathy" to depict physiological processes would in fact have been very familiar to his contemporaries. Indeed, Hazlitt was parodied by critics for relying too heavily on such a materialistic understanding of the poetic process. E. S. Barnett and William Gifford, writing for the *Quarterly Review*, satirized his use of the key terms "impression" and "sympathy":

> The impression, of which Mr. Hazlitt talks, is an impression producing by sympathy a certain modulation of sounds. The term sympathy ... [in] a physiological sense, is used to denote the fact, that the disorder of one organ produces disorder in the functions of certain other parts of the system. Does Mr. Hazlitt mean, that the impression produces the modulation of sound essential to poetry, in a mode analogous to that in which diseases of the brain affect the digestive powers? (426)

Barnett and Gifford ridicule Hazlitt's autopoetics, then, not merely because it is so seemingly automatic, but because it relies upon a grossly physiological understanding of sympathy. What is notable about this "physiological sense" of sympathy is that, rather than enacting an imaginative movement out of the self, it is limited to operating within the confines of the physical body. In fact, the idea of internal, physiological sympathy – which the *OED* defines as a "relation between two bodily organs or parts" in which "disorder, or any condition, of the one induces a corresponding condition in the other" (1b) – rose to prominence in medical books of the early 1600s, although the concept itself dates back to Galen (Clarke and Jacyna 102–107). The term was still current in the Romantic era, which found scientists actively attempting to parse the sympathetic relationship between the brain and the body; as the influential physiologist John Bostock wrote in the mid-1820s, physiological sympathy was understood to act as an "intermediate between the mental and physical powers" (753). This self-mediating process is the sympathy to which Hazlitt makes recourse in his definition of poetry.

The growing body of critical literature on sympathy has, by and large, focused on its interpersonal effects – on the ways in which individuals can be made to imagine themselves feeling someone else's emotions. For scholars of the nineteenth century, sympathy in this sense has become a key term in discussions about Victorian theories of reading, and reading the novel in particular. At the forefront of this criticism is a concern with the way readerly sympathy can be seen to affect social and interpersonal dynamics: Thomas Laqueur and Martha Nussbaum, for example, have suggested that novel-reading develops "sympathetic passions" (Laqueur 180) and thereby encourages social action on behalf of poor or marginalized groups; Audrey Jaffe, on the other hand, argues that novelistic sympathy is based on a highly visual system of spectacle and representation, in which subjects are transformed "into spectators of and objects for one another" (8); Rachel Ablow identifies sympathy as the "psychic structure" under-lying Victorian models of both reading and marriage, where wives and novels alike are expected to cultivate sympathy (2); and most recently, Rae Greiner has argued that the realist novel is "devoted to representing the exertions of sympathetic labor so as to hone readers' sympathetic powers" (12). For all their considerable differences, critics in this tradition focus on the sympathetic susceptibility of the reader and depict reading as an imaginative and interpersonal process.

Moreover, these studies of interpersonal sympathy revolve around a crucial issue of readerly agency – or what is really a lack of readerly agency, for the reader is conceived as the passive subject of the text's sympathetic manipulations in a model reminiscent of Wordsworth, as I discussed in the previous chapter.[2] Kirstie Blair – one of the few critics to write on sympathetic affect in poetry, and one of the few to focus on physiology – argues that sympathy might happen "on a physiological level if the rhythm of a poem draws the reader into participation in a bodily sense, affecting blood and health," and she records the Victorian anxiety that readerly sympathy "might be pathological, creating illness or instabil-ity" (17); Adela Pinch, in her study of interpersonal emotions, notes that "literary affects threaten to enter the reader immediately and entirely" (86); Kate Flint traces the history of the Victorian concern about female readers' "vulnerability to textual influence, deaf and blind to all other stimuli" (4). According to this critical tradition, the sympathetic process was understood to be a method for readerly interpellation or conscription – a way for writers to infect, possess, and incorporate their readers, whether for good or for ill. Reading rendered the reader dangerously permeable, unstable, and passively sympathetic. Our critical literature on sympathy, in other words, tends to use it to explain the ways in which readers were absorbed, as it were, into a text's emotional or ideological structure.[3]

That nineteenth-century thinkers were obsessed with the effects of sympathy on readers is, then, a generally (and rightfully) accepted fact. But if we attend to Hazlitt's model of sympathy as an internal, bodily process – a process I will be calling self-sympathy – we can see that readerly absorption was only one of the concerns in nineteenth-century debates about literature and sympathy. Sympathy was understood to be at work in poetic production as well as reception; in fact, it was thought to be central to the physiology of the poet. This is crucial to my intervention: our critical tendency to study readership and authorship as discrete and ultimately dissimilar practices means that we are prone to overlook the surprising structures they share. In dismantling the equation of sympathy with permeability, the writers I discuss here re-envision the relationship between poets and readers, imagining them both as guided by the workings of their own involuntarily responsive bodies – bodies that respond not to each other but to themselves. This leads to my most substantial claim: that attending to the physiological concept of self-sympathy enables us to rewrite our critical understanding of nineteenth-century concerns about the automatic responsiveness of the body. According to the autopoetics of self-sympathy, such responsiveness doesn't threaten to dissolve the self: rather, it substantiates it.

Self-sympathy is an especially important term for poetic theory starting around 1830, when critics were beginning to identify a new and modern "poetry of sensation," defined in opposition to a Wordsworthian poetics of reflection. Wordsworth thus provides a natural touchstone for this chapter, which aims to expand upon the stakes of Hazlitt's materialist definition of poetry and its considerable physiological connotations. Broadly, I will consider physiological theories of self-sympathy alongside two signal state-ments of early-Victorian poetic theory: William Johnson Fox's and Arthur Henry Hallam's influential reviews of Tennyson's first solo volume, *Poems, Chiefly Lyrical*. For critics like Hazlitt, Fox, and Hallam, the body of the poet – rather than that of the reader – is the crucial location for defining modern poetry. And what is perhaps most striking, for present purposes, in their conception of that poetry is that they understand the relation between the poet's body and his poetic subjects – from Mariana to the Merman – as dramatizing the internal workings of self-sympathy. That is, for Fox and Hallam, the relationship of poets to their subjects has the nature of an encounter within the body, an encounter in which the poet is asked to embody (and sympathize with) a multiplicity of selves. Long before Matthew Arnold's formulation of Victorian poetry as "the dialogue of the mind with itself," we find critics in the 1830s suggesting that, in fact, it might be better termed "the dialogue of the body with itself."

Sympathetic Bodies: The Internal Science of the Self

As critics such as Jason Rudy and Kirstie Blair have shown, Victorian poetry is remarkable for its engagement with contemporary theories of embodiment. Rudy notes that "[p]oetry has always, in various ways, been associated with bodily experience," but "the Victorians' all-out engagement with a poetics of the body" is uniquely informed by early-century developments in physiology (7). As we can see in Barnett and Gifford's sarcastic response, this physiological turn, which Hallam would soon dub "the poetry of sensation" (and which I'll discuss at greater length later), incurred the disdain of conservative critics, who insisted that poetry should "focus on ideals, not physiological sensations" (Rudy 52): surely the digestive workings of the intestines should be incompatible with the lofty ideals of poetry. And yet, in nineteenth-century physiology, even seemingly involuntary bodily processes affected mental activity – and vice versa – within the body's system of complex sympathetic reactions. Physiological sympathy within the self was invoked in the nineteenth century to explain both the relation between the parts of the body (including the brain) and the body's responses to all that was external to it. These relations were understood to be problematic, even obscure, and the concept of self-sympathy both recognized that difficulty and tried to clarify it. In a way, these writers were grappling with the same problem that Noel Jackson addresses in his study of Romantic science and sensation: "I want to ask," Jackson writes, "what kind of knowledge we acquire when we attend to our own sensation" (106). But where Jackson is interested in locating sensation outside of the self – in showing how ideas of sense and sensation lead to a mode of consensus, upon which a social or political order could be constructed – I'm attending to the questions posed by nineteenth-century theorists who aimed, instead, to query the nature of sensation that exists only *within* the self. In self-sympathy, this inward attention leads not toward commonality but toward particularity, even isolation.

By the 1820s and 1830s, the theory of association – the eighteenth century's favorite philosophy of mental phenomena – was in decline, and self-sympathy presented a new model for theorizing the (often involuntary) inner workings of the material body.[4] In this model, the mind is embedded in a body composed of multiple systems, and self-sympathy governs how these systems interact. Bostock, in his widely read *Elementary System of Physiology* (1824), writes, "One of the most distinguishing peculiarities of the animal frame, unlike any thing that we behold in inanimate nature, is the connexion subsisting between different parts, which we term sympathy" (760–761). The theory of self-sympathy proposes to explain these mysterious connections, but in doing so often leaves the logic of cause and effect unclear. William Pulteney Alison, for example, explains in his influential essay on sympathy for the 1826 *Transactions of the Medico-Chirurgical Society of Edinburgh* that "Sympathetic Effects" occur when "any particular impression, made on one superficial nerve, is immediately and almost uniformly followed by a particular action of a distant set of muscles, or of bloodvessels, or by a particular alteration of the heart's action" (167). Alison's model of physiological self-sympathy does not disavow the original external impression, the one made on a "superficial" nerve. But its focus is on the internal processes that follow: the processes by which the body internally reproduces that external effect. We see the same focus in a medical treatise by Caleb Hillier Parry, who offers as an example of sympathy the fact that, "in inflammation of the liver, a pain is sometimes felt on the top of the right shoulder" (209). Here the original impression is the inflammation of the liver; it is still the active agent that prompts the "second effect" of sympathy, but any original external influence that may have rendered the liver inflamed is unimportant. Thus when John Elliotson (later famous for his mesmeric demonstrations) defines sympathy in his 1835 *Human Physiology* as "the affection of one part of the body directly by the affection of another," he confidently declares that this happens "through vital agency alone" – meaning, in the parlance of the day, through an internal mechanism of the body (452).[5] In physiological self-sympathy, then, the body appears as a kind of machine – a medium – for transmitting and replicating internal impressions.

These sympathetic reactions function within a kind of system, analogous to the nervous system, which (Bostock argues) unites "all the several parts and functions of the animal machine into one connected whole, each portion of which may, to a certain extent, feel the impressions that are made upon every other portion" (761). This mechanistic system governs a wide variety of bodily processes:

the general uniformity in the motion of the two eyes; the secretion of milk by the mamma, consequent upon parturition; the convulsive contraction of the diaphragm which produced sneezing, as caused by the irritation of the nerves belonging to the mucous membrane of the nostrils; pain in the head occasioned by a certain condition of the stomach; imperfect vision from a morbid state of the intestinal canal. (762)

Bostock's list of examples moves slyly from the incontrovertible toward the more theoretical; the uniform movement of our eyes is a less mysteriously sympathetic connection than the relationship between vision and a "morbid" intestine. But these mysterious relationships form the core of physiological theories of sympathy: the body that is modeled here is made up of multiple, seemingly unrelated yet jointly functioning bodily systems. As a popular encyclopedia of 1835 explains (in language that underscores the theory's materialist basis), "The human body is composed of several parts or systems, which serve particular purposes, and perform distinct offices" – and the fact that they all work together "to one general end" is as remarkable as the inner workings of the steam engine (Chambers 57). Although the nervous system provided a useful heuristic analogy for self-sympathy, physiologists were careful to insist that the two were distinct. Sympathetic responses, Alison writes emphatically, "cannot be explained by the connections of the nerves of the sympathizing parts" (170). Bostock concurs:

> There is scarcely any action which we perform, or any part that is moved or affected, but the motion or affection influences other parts, besides those primarily acted upon. In some cases this evidently depends upon mere contiguity, in others we can trace a direct vascular or nervous communication, and it may be frequently referred to association. But there are instances where none of these causes seem to be applicable, where the parts are distant from each other, where there has been no repetition of the actions, so that they cannot have acquired an association with each other, and where there seems to be no direct communication through the medium either of the vessels or of the nerves. (760)

Later in the century, this sympathetic system would in fact be discarded in favor of a true nerve-based physiology; but in the decades leading up to the Victorian period proper, self-sympathy served to explain physiological processes that could no longer be explained by associationism and that were not yet under the purview of neurology.[6]

Self-sympathy around 1830, then, provided a newly physiological model for understanding how the disparate systems of the body function as a united whole. And unlike associative or nerve-based processes, self-sympathy was particularly useful in explaining seemingly random relationships between parts of the body that possessed no habitual relationship or nervous connection. As might be expected, the brain was thought to play a role in this process, but physiologists argued over the extent of its influence. While some writers asserted that the brain was necessarily the apex of the self-sympathetic system, any hierarchical model of sympathy was hotly contested. Elliotson notes that "the condition of the peculiar functions of certain parts of the brain exercises very powerful influence upon every part of the body," listing as examples "blushing under anger or shame, paleness, polyuria, and diarrhoea, under fear, erections under desire" (454), but he is quick to dismiss the idea that the brain is thus the primary actor in self-sympathy. The brain and the nerves, he writes, "stand exactly in the condition of all other sympathising parts":

> When sympathetic pain is felt, brain and encephalo-spinal nerves must be required, the latter to communicate and the former to take cognizance of the sympathetic condition of the part in which the sympathetic pain is felt. But this is not an agency of the brain, chord, or encephalo-spinal nerves in sympathy: a sympathetic change first occurs in the part, and this is then felt by the encephalo-spinal system. (458)

Elliotson's model denies the "agency of the brain" in self-sympathy; what is more, it demotes mental action to a kind of secondary effect, the ability to feel or "take cognizance of" the sympathetic change that "first occurs" in some part of the body. In other words, the mental faculties are relegated to a position of passive observation.

What these theorists depict, in varying degrees of extremity, is an understanding that the majority of self-sympathetic actions are unconscious,[7] conducted by the body's automatic responsiveness rather than by any form of mental activity or volition. In this way, the theory of physiological self-sympathy builds on the eighteenth-century discourse of sensibility. At the same, time, however, it departs from this tradition in important ways. Sensibility depicts a body that is acted upon by emotion, involuntarily responsive and subject to the pervasive influences of the external world. But in the tradition of sensibility, this involuntary responsiveness results in imaginative movement outside of the self. James Chandler's work on the subject rightly identifies at its heart a focus on transport, on "the sympathetic movement of going beyond ourselves" ("Languages" 25). John Brewer likewise describes late-eighteenth-century sentimentality as "a new literary technology" with an "ability to transport the reader, to transform the relations between authors, texts and readers"

(35). While self-sympathy shares with sensibility an emphasis on embodied passivity, its movements are not interpersonal. In these physiological studies, sympathy does not transport the imagination out of the self but rather turns the self – the body, even – into a medium for reproducing an internal movement. Self-sympathy, in other words, is not the openness to external inspiration that we find in sensibility, but rather a kind of internal, bodily reproduction of a material event whose source is lost, obscured, or unimportant. In the interaction of self-reproducing stimulus and sympathetically responsive medium, something is created that turns inward on itself at the very moment that it appears to gesture at, or refer to, an external source.

Samuel Taylor Coleridge noted this internalizing move in his writings on the problem of physiological self-sympathy. In "On the Passions" (1828), he speculates about the body's ability to produce emotion simply from internal sources:

> The influence of the Stomach on the Eye and of the Eye (as in seasickness) on the Stomach is known and admitted – but are not Tears analogous (however ludicrous it may appear at the first thought) to the watering of the Mouth? Is there not some connection between the Stomach & the lachrymal Ducts? One or the other must be true, as the copious weeping and intense passion of Grief during Sleep, which on waking proves to be heartburn or a pain at the pit of the Stomach. (qtd. in Gigante, *Taste* 89)

Here Coleridge's musings take him from strictly physiological data (the relationship between the eye and the stomach) toward a consideration of the implication of mental processes in self-sympathy (the relationship between grief and the stomach). What he offers in conclusion is a model of the body in which emotion – intense grief, a passionate response to some kind of external experience – is revealed to be the result of a self-sympathetic response not to heartache but to heartburn. Elsewhere Coleridge offers a characteristically bizarre example of the seemingly cerebral (and agential) process of writing being overwritten, as it were, by physiological self-sympathy:

> I have myself once seen (i.e. appeared to see) my own body under the Bedcloaths flashing silver Light from whatever part I prest it – and the same proceed from the tips of my fingers. I have thus written, as it were, my name, greek words, ciphers, etc. on my Thigh: and instantly seen them together with the Thigh in brilliant Letters of silver Light. ... I deduced from the Phaenomenon the existence of an imitative sympathy in the nerves, so that those of the Eye copied instantaneously the impressions made on those of the Limbs. (Letter to Thomas Boosey, Jr., May 20, 1817; *Collected Letters* 731)

In Coleridge's account, physiological self-sympathy allows writing to bypass semantic content, the body literally reproducing a meaningless collection of words on itself rather than transmitting them to an external medium. Coleridge acts as a kind of passive witness to his own body here; in so doing, he implicates the mind as a system that exposes sympathy between other systems, even if it has no control over this process it observes.

Indeed, although the physiologists whose work Coleridge is engaging here similarly worked to disavow the agency of the mind, they recognized that this seemingly passive role – that of the observer, the one who attends to or registers sensation – can be a crucial actor in the internal interactions of self-sympathy. For if one example of self-sympathy is the impression, undirected and involuntary, of one internal organ felt on another, another example is the impression on an internal organ or bodily part caused by our attention to it. Physiologists of the period were particularly intrigued by the effects of voluntary attention on involuntary physical processes like salivation, digestion, and circulation.[8] Henry Holland, in his *Medical Notes and Reflections*, is careful to differentiate this kind of self-sympathy from sympathy with an external source: "Where indeed the attention is excited by external impressions, it is perhaps but another name for sensation itself," he writes; but this is different from "that voluntary act by which the consciousness receives, as it were, a local direction, and is by effort retained for a time in this state" (47). This is another kind of internal impression, differentiated explicitly from the external kind; but this internal impression requires effort. It is a voluntary act of self-sympathy. Holland suggests that his readers attempt a kind of self-experiment:

> [D]irection of consciousness to the region of the stomach creates in this part a sense of weight, oppression, or other less definite uneasiness; and when the stomach is full, appears greatly to disturb the due digestion of the food. It is remarkable how instantly under such circumstances the effect comes on; a fact readily attested by experiment which every one may make for himself. (66)

This directed self-sympathy can have more profound material effects on the body: hysteria can be explained as attention gone awry (70), as can hypochondria, in which focusing "morbid intensities on certain organs, creates not merely disordered sensations, but also disordered actions in them" (69). Holland suggests to the reader that "a single limb, or portion even of a limb, may be taken for experiment; and a peculiar sense of weight and restlessness, approaching even to a cramp, be produced by urging the attention expressly upon it" (67). Active attention, then, can set into motion the involuntary reactions of self-sympathy without any kind of external excitement or instigation. In other words, attention can cause the body to respond to itself in the absence of external stimuli.

What is more, Holland argues that this phenomenon – involuntary responses within the self-activated by the self – may be occurring even when we think we are sympathizing with something external. Take, he suggests, the example of "an expected impression on some part of the body, producing, before actually made, sympathetic sensations or movements in other parts which are wont to be thus affected by the impressions in question" (51). In this example, the external influence is completely erased; attention can stimulate sympathy exactly as an external impression would. Or take the science of animal magnetism – an extreme version of interpersonal sympathy, in which the body is susceptible to the directed attention of another person. Holland argues that the mechanism of self-sympathy is actually at work here:

> I doubt not that certain of the results of animal magnetism are to be explained by reference to these facts. In some instances, where I have seen the magnetizer perform his operations on a limb, and then inquire as to the feelings created in it, the sensations expressed by the patient were such as might readily be created by the solicitation of the question. (68n)

The magnetizer profits from the workings of self-sympathy here: the patient attends to her own body, and in doing so she instigates an internal impression, of which the magnetizer then claims to be the cause. Instead of an example of the permeability of the material self and its susceptibility to the conscious will of another, Holland finds evidence of the self's impermeability, its susceptibility only to its own attention. In the schema of physiological self-sympathy, the self is a closed circuit; what seemed to come from without, albeit mysteriously, in fact has its origin internally.

Solipsism and Sensation: Late-Romantic Materialist Poetics

One answer to the question of what it means to sympathize with yourself, then, is that the self is the *only* person with whom it can sympathize. This is intimated too in Hazlitt's definition of poetry as an "involuntary movement," already internal, that excites "by sympathy" a specific bodily response. And that definition places the body's relationship with itself at the heart of the poetic impulse. Whatever external event or emotion may inspire a poetic reaction, it is far less important than the *impression* of that event and the body's sympathetic response to that impression. Given these physiological facts, then, the poet's task is "to prolong and repeat the emotion, to bring all other objects into accord with it, and to give the same movement of harmony, sustained and continuous, or gradually varied according to the occasion, to the sounds that express [the emotion]." This, Hazlitt says, "is poetry" (5: 12). He identifies a unifying impulse in poetry – a desire to make the world over from the inside out, to "bring all other objects into accord with" an internal impression. Instead of an open, porous body, we have a closed, resonating one. Hazlitt's poetic materials are located inside the self, and the process of poetry is, in a way, a process of letting that self-impression overwrite the external world.

It is easy to see how the physiological model of self-sympathy might be useful to poetic theorists like Hazlitt, second-generation Romantics grappling with Wordsworth's theory of composition put forth in the 1802 "Preface" to *Lyrical Ballads*. Indeed, there are important ways in which Wordsworthian poetic theory engages with the same complex model of the self-sympathetic body we find in the physiological studies I have discussed. For Wordsworth, a poet is chiefly defined by the ability to describe sensations and emotions long after the original external triggers have disappeared: "from practice, he has acquired a greater readiness and power in expressing what he thinks and feels, and especially those thoughts and feelings which, by his own choice, or from the structure of his own mind, arise in him without immediate external excitement" (400). Like Wordsworth's theory of composition, self-sympathy seeks to privilege the ability to evoke feeling without external excitement. And yet Wordsworth retains a strong emphasis on association, habit, and mental agency, all of which are missing from the physiological model of self-sympathy (and, as we shall see, from the poetics of sensation). For physiologists like Holland, instead, the effects of attention do not arise (as Wordsworth writes) from "practice," or from "choice"; they do not arise from "the structure of [one's] own mind." It is not that attention allows you to rebuild an emotion at will, but rather that attention creates an involuntary sensation itself. And these sensations – these internal impressions – are not Wordsworth's "thoughts and feelings"; instead, they are direct physical effects: weight, restlessness, cramp, disordered sensations, even disordered actions. In other words, the self-sympathetic autopoetics at work in Hazlitt's theory of poetry, like the autopoetics of the striking passage in Coleridge, resist Wordsworth's privileging of context and association by attending instead to the involuntary and the disruptive.

Like Holland's physiological theory, Hazlitt's materialist theory of poetry is at once a direct extension of and challenge to first-generation Romantic poetic theory. Wordsworth identifies an internal source for poetic affect in *Lyrical Ballads*: "the feeling therein developed gives importance to the action and situation, and not the action and situation to the feeling" (394–395). And yet Hazlitt's model of self-sympathetic poetry strikingly elides the agency of thought so central to Wordsworth's theory. "Poems to which any value can be attached were never produced on any variety of subjects but by a man who, being possessed of more than usual organic sensibility, had also thought long and deeply," Wordsworth insists:

> For our continued influxes of feeling are modified and directed by our thoughts, which are indeed the representatives of all our past feelings; and, as by contemplating the relation of these general representatives to each other, we discover what is really important to men, so, by the repetition and continuance of this act, our feelings will be connected with important subjects, till at length, if we be originally possessed of much sensibility, such habits of mind will be produced, that, by obeying blindly and mechanically the impulses of those habits, we shall describe objects, and utter sentiments, of such a nature, and in such connexion with each other, that the understanding of the Reader must necessarily be in some degree enlightened, and his affections strengthened and purified. (394)

Wordsworth's poet allows his internal impressions to overwrite his external situation, to be sure. But for Wordsworth, this operates along the laws of association, building "habits of mind" through "repetition" in order to forge permanent connections between emotions and subjects. In other words, Wordsworth is not interested (as Hazlitt is, and as these theorists of self-sympathy are) in explaining the disparate, non-habitual and seemingly random connections between elements of the body that are not under the direct control of thought. The "organic sensibility" that will evolve into the central principle of sensation poetry is here tempered by and subservient to the powers of mind.

For Hazlitt, on the other hand, a materialist theory of poetry suggests that Wordsworthian reflection is too weak, too indirect, to serve as the primary building block for poetry – or, for that matter, for sympathy. In "Self-Love and Benevolence" (1828), he associates "reflection" with unsuccessful attempts to imagine yourself into someone else's body. And such attempts will always be unsuccessful, he writes, because other people's physical sensations are entirely inaccessible to us: "A door of communication ... is locked and barred by the hand of Nature and the constitution of the human understanding against the intrusion of any straggling impressions from the minds of others. I can only see into their real history darkly and by reflection" (20: 174). For Hazlitt, the boundedness of our bodies renders interpersonal sympathy physically impossible: "I have no nerves communicating with another's brain, and transmitting to me either the glow of pleasure or the agony of pain which he may feel at the present moment by means of his senses. So far as my present self or immediate sensations are concerned, I am cut off from all sympathy with others" (20: 173). This fact of physical isolation underscores the prominence of internal sympathy in his theory of poetry: if true communion with other people's sense experiences is impossible, poetry must act within the self. Indeed, Hazlitt emphasizes self-sympathy's physiological basis in order to focus on the body's relationship with itself. This allows him to recast the body as the central medium of poetry – the space in which the poet can, as he writes, "prolong and repeat" an impression and "bring all other objects into accord with it." He is not interested in sympathy as an imaginative movement out of the self, but rather as a means of understanding movement within the self.

As such, the physicality of self-sympathy serves an additional purpose for Hazlitt: it resolves another problem posed by the materiality of the embodied self. He shares with writers like Holland a concern about the cohesion of a self made up of multiple, seemingly disparate elements. Holland suggests that self-sympathy helps to unify the workings of a dangerously multiple body. Hazlitt, though, seeks in his theory of self-sympathy not merely the cohesion of bodily organs but the cohesion of the self across time. He prizes the continuity he traces between himself in the past and himself in the present: as he notes in "A Farewell to Essay-Writing," "looking back to the past," he is "surprise[d]" to "find [him]self so little changed in the time" (17: 316). This is important for Hazlitt: how can he retain access to his past experiences when the physical impressions of the present quickly fade into mere memory? As in "Tintern Abbey," where Wordsworth's younger self is inaccessible to him, Hazlitt is afraid that time will divorce himself from his own past. But the sympathy that operates within the self – the process by which impressions are internalized, harmonized, prolonged – makes these multiple experiences physically accessible. This provides the temporal constancy that Hazlitt craves: "This continuity of impression," he writes, "is the only thing on which I pride myself" (17: 318). Attempts at interpersonal sympathy may be thwarted because, as he explains in "Self-Love," "there is no link of connection, no sympathy, no reaction, no mutual consciousness . . ., in a mechanical and personal sense" (20: 174). But such sympathy *is* available within the material self, at once mechanical and personal: he writes that "there is a real, undoubted, original and positive foundation for the notion of self to rest upon; for in my relation to my former self and past feelings, I do possess a faculty which serves to unite me more especially to my own being" (20: 174). While sympathy may not assist Hazlitt in accessing other people's sensations, then, it does enable him to hold multiple versions of himself – past and present – together in one body. Sympathy does not transport him out of himself; instead, it returns him to himself.

I have been emphasizing the remarkable degree of attention paid by key Romantic writers to sympathetic processes *within* the self. Nineteenth-century theorists of literature like Wordsworth and Hazlitt were interested in more than just interpersonal sympathy. Physiological self-sympathy modeled a materialist body that acted as a sympathetic medium, in a counterintuitive sense of the word: rather than enabling sympathetic movement out of the self, it depicted sympathy as an attentiveness to internal sensation. And this physiological model of self-sympathy is uniquely important for poetry because, in the 1830s, "sensation" came to be a key term in debates about the poetic process – and especially in evaluations of Tennyson, who was seen to exemplify a new and modern school of poetry: the "poetry of sensation." Arthur Hallam identifies this school – which he also calls the "cockney school" – as originating with Leigh Hunt and developing with Shelley and Keats before finding its apotheosis in the future laureate (1831: 617). For Hallam, the poetry of sensation is explicitly pitted against the Wordsworthian "poetry of reflection":

> It is not true . . . that the highest species of poetry is the reflective; it is a gross fallacy, that because certain opinions are acute or profound, the expression of them by the imagination must be eminently beautiful. Whenever the mind of the artist suffers itself to be occupied, during its periods of creation, by any other predominant motive than the desire of beauty, the result is false in art. (616)

Hallam condemns the act of reflection as a dangerous form of mental "occupation," one that distances the poet from his original sensory experiences. Instead of reflection, Hallam requires his new poet to remain attuned to "those emotions which are immediately conversant with the sensation" (617). And for Hallam (as well as for Hazlitt) sensation is an unexpectedly solipsistic phenomenon, one that turns the self inward rather than outward: "So vivid was the delight attending the simple exertions of eye and ear, that it became mingled more and more with their active trains of thought, and tended to absorb their whole being into the energy of sense" (617). Hallam's poet uses the sensate body as the medium of poetic production. The poet of sensation, in other words, is asked to build his poetry out of the Wordsworthian "spontaneous overflow of powerful feeling" without Wordsworth's second, reflective step: recollecting those feelings in tranquility ("Preface" 407). Where Wordsworth writes, in 1802, that "our continued influxes of feeling are modified and directed by our thoughts" (393), Hallam in 1831 wants to discard the mediating agency of the mind in favor of an immediate and embodied experience. Indeed, such attempts to define this new and modern sensation poetry contain the seeds of early Victorian aestheticism. In refuting "reflection," critics like Hallam at once expand upon and exceed first-generation Romantic models of poetic genius. The poetry of sensation, as we shall see, takes as its source an explicitly material and sensate body. And yet the model of sensation these critics adopt does not seem to open the poet's body to external influence; it does not seem to move the poet out of himself. Rather, these critics suggest that sensation is in fact an internal impression, one that returns you sympathetically to yourself. Such a self-sympathetic (and highly physiological) model of sensation is central to important early reviews of Tennyson's poetry, to which I now turn.

Oversympathetic Poets: W. J. Fox's Internal Explorers

William Johnson Fox's 1831 essay in the *Westminster Review* – the first review of Tennyson to be printed in a major quarterly magazine – is at once a paean to the poet's ability and a manifesto for a newly modern, material poetics. "The machinery of a poem is not less susceptible of improvement than the machinery of a cotton-mill," Fox writes; "There is nothing mysterious, or anomalous, in the power of producing poetry, or in that of its enjoyment; neither the one nor the other is a supernatural gift . . . . It may be a compound, but it is not incapable of analysis" (213). For Fox, the best modern poets are attuned to the material workings of the mind. Unlike Hallam, Fox acknowledges the importance of "reflection" in Tennyson's poetry: he demands that poets write with attention to "mental philosophy," or what elsewhere he calls "the real science of mind" (213).[9] Yet Fox's version of "mental science" (215) is, like Hallam's poetics of sensation, a far cry from Wordsworth's tranquil reflection on past emotions. Instead it asks the poet to use the mind as a tool to extract subject matter for his poetry. A poet, he writes, may use "moral dissection" – what he calls "the application of the logical scalpel" – to find "some of the finest originals for his pictures; and they exist in infinite variety" (215). It is inside, he suggests, that a poet may find his subject. Fox's materialist theory of poetry centers on an almost medical attentiveness to the inner workings of the bodily machine. His praise of Tennyson links poetic skill with a kind of embodiment: he lauds the poet for his ability to "personate anything he pleases from an angel to a grasshopper" (215), which he does by taking "their senses, feeling, nerves, and brain" (216) and making "the feeling within generate an appropriate assemblage of external objects" (217). Fox's Tennyson is imagined to interact with the body of his poetic subject in a remarkably physical manner. Coleridge's lectures on Shakespeare make similar claims,[10] but Fox's materialism allows him to imagine this embodiment as strikingly physiological, even articulating the specific organs his poet must adopt. He imagines a poet whose job is not to reflect on past sensations, not to recollect emotion in tranquility, but rather to survey the automatic material workings of imaginary bodies and minds.

Indeed, Fox's focus is not merely on physiology. He is particularly interested in exploring the body's systems of involuntary responsiveness and interconnection – its self-sympathetic processes, in other words. For Fox, the body of the modern poet represents a material instantiation of an Æolian harp, a prominent Romantic metaphor for poetic inspiration used to depict the poet as a passive instrument of the muses. Coleridge, for example, describes his own composing brain operating in a similarly passive manner: "Full many a thought uncall'd and undetain'd, / And many idle flitting phantasies, / Traverse my indolent and passive brain" ("The Eolian Harp" ll. 39–41). Coleridge goes on to ask, "And what if all of animated nature / Be but organic Harps diversly fram'd, / That tremble into thought, as o'er them sweeps / Plastic and vast, one intellectual breeze . . . ?" (ll. 44–47). Fox transforms this poetic metaphor of "organic Harps" into a physiological one, but he retains much of the Romantic meaning. Poets, he writes, "think and feel poetry with every breeze that sweeps over their well-tuned nerves" (211). In place of the Grecian instrument Fox gives us the poet's body, strung not with harp-strings but with nerves.[11] He argues that poetry depends upon the physiological sensitivity of the poet, rather than his imaginative capabilities – and it is this physiological sensitivity that will, according to Fox, guarantee the contin- ued production of poetry in the seemingly unpoetic modern age:

> So far as poetry is dependent upon physical organization; and doubtless it is to some extent so dependent; there is no reason why it should deteriorate.

> Eyes and ears are organs which nature finished off with very different gradations of excellence. ... *Poeta nascitur* in a frame the most favorable to acute perception and intense enjoyment of the objects of sense. (211)

The ideal poet, Fox writes, possesses not a mental capability but a physical "frame" that renders him uniquely able to perceive and enjoy sensations. For Fox, the body is the instrument of poetry, and in many ways its role is one of passive respondent.

It is this seeming physiological passivity that got Fox into trouble with the conservative press, who were (as Jason Rudy notes) intent on demonizing the poetry of sensation (51). For these critics, Fox's substitution of the poet's body for the harp was an embarrassing example of what critic John Wilson (writing as Christopher North) called "Cockney materialism" (124) – vulgar, overly sensual, passively sympathetic to external influences. In particular, Fox's contemporaries were alarmed that his physiologically based definition of poetry required a disturbing looseness of the physical self, a kind of corporeal permeability, on the part of the poet. When Tennyson "personate[s] anything he pleases from an angel to a grasshopper," adopting "their senses, feeling, nerves, and brain," the poet seems to be in danger of losing his own body in a kind of hyperactive sympathy with another. Indeed, in a way, this is a problem of extreme interpersonal sympathy: if the poet's very body is susceptible to "every breeze" (or external influence) it encounters, what kind of agency does the poet possess? And if he adopts another body, what happens to his own? This threat of material dissolution disturbed Fox's critics. Wilson – whose scathing rebuttal of Fox appeared in *Blackwood's* in May of 1832 – vociferously objected to the implication that Tennyson must lose himself in sympathy with Mariana or the Merman in order to write from their point of view. Wilson labeled Fox's theory "a perfect specimen of the super-hyperbolical ultra-extravagance of outrageous Cockney eulogistic foolishness" (124) and accused him of promoting a poetics of sensual passivity). Wilson objects most strongly to the idea that Tennyson must relinquish his individual agency; the poet, he argues, should retain a sense of physical selfhood even as he masquerades as another, lest he risk a dangerous (and emasculating) dissolution. Wilson offers an example from mythology – a peculiar one, perhaps – to prove the indissolubility of the self: "Was not Jupiter still Jove – aye, every inch the thunderous king of heaven, whose throne was Olympus – while to languishing Leda the godhead seemed a Swan?" (113). In Wilson's mind, poetry should be an act of supreme, even superhuman control. Indeed, his primary complaint about Fox's definition of poetry is precisely that it disavows the primacy of the creative will. He claims to refuse to "define poetry, because the Cockneys have done so," but he goes go so far as to make this assertion: "every thing is poetry which is not mere sensation. We are poets at all times when our minds are makers" (109). A poetics based merely on physical sensation, Wilson insists, is one that threatens to dissolve into sympathetic passivity. Instead, Wilson exalts the agency of the mind.

To be sure, sensual passivity plays a large role in Fox's theory. Fox himself recognizes that this kind of sympathy, the same remarkable sympathy he so admires in Tennyson, threatens a loss of self: "Mr. Tennyson has a dangerous quality in that facility of impersonation . . . by which he enters so thoroughly into the most strange and wayward idiosyncrasies of other men. It must not degrade him into a poetical harlequin" (223). Wilson's view of passivity, however, is too restricted, too ungenerous. He interprets this physical passivity in the context of interpersonal sympathy – as a kind of dangerous and unmanly permeability to external influence that threatens to undermine the agency of the self and the mind. Yet if we consider Fox's depiction of physiological passivity in terms of self-sympathy, we can see that he shares with Hazlitt a belief that the sympathetic, internal workings of the body in fact make up the self – and that these internal workings, in turn, make up the content of Tennyson's poetry. For Fox, it seems, the passive workings of internal physiology are precisely the material of poetry: they are the landscape the poet must survey. In one striking passage his Tennyson is an internal explorer, literally climbing around inside the physiology of his subject: "He seems to obtain entrance into a mind as he would make his way into a landscape; he climbs the pineal gland as if it were a hill in the centre of the scene; looks around on all objects with their varieties of form, their movements, their shades of colour, and their mutual relations and influences" (215).[12] This model of the poet could not be further from the passive, breeze-blown harp; here, Tennyson is out conquering new worlds, climbing hills, surveying properties. Even more interesting is the object of his activity. He does not use the traditional method of inter-personal sympathy to assume another body – he does not imagine himself into his subject's "situation," as Adam Smith terms it (2), or recreate emotions as the Wordsworthian "translator" of Lyrical Ballads (395) – but rather abandons external circumstances altogether and attends instead to the "mutual relations and influences" that exist inside his subject's cranium. Even the "landscape," that most external of images, is relocated internally.

Fox's model of sympathy, then, is an odd and complex one: the poet's sympathetic process is triggered not by engaging with the external land-scape of imagined context, but rather with a very internal landscape of physiological selfhood. The poetic act of identification that seems like interpersonal sympathy is complicated by the fact that, of course, the Merman (perhaps most obviously of all Tennyson's subjects) does not actually exist. There is no real otherness, no interpersonal communication, no external mind to struggle into. And yet the poetic process Fox describes is one of physiological identification. According to Fox, Tennyson does not mean to attend to external influences; what he must do is attend to the (imaginary) body's internal reactions, and this attention prompts the self-sympathetic responses that give rise to poetry. And, in a way, Tennyson himself – rather than any external "breeze" – is the active agent to which the body responds. In order for the poet to initiate the passive sensations that Fox claims structure his poetry, he must voluntarily attend to the involuntary workings of his subject's body. Fox writes of "The Merman" that "one seems to feel the principle of thought injected by a strong volition into the cranium of the finny worthy, and coming under all the influences, as thinking principles do, of the physical organization to which it is for the time allied" (216). Fox's physiological language – a "strong volition" being "injected" into the merman's "cranium" – only emphasizes his main point: that any "thinking principles" are dependent upon the "physical organiza-tion" of a particular body, and that self-sympathy is the means by which this poetic process takes place. Moreover, this self-sympathetic process is set into motion by the attention – the injection of thought – of the inhabiting poet. In this bizarre double internalization, Tennyson's volition injects thought into the head of the imaginary Merman, which allows his thought to become allied with this very differently organized body. In other words, the self-sympathy that we witness in the poem is the Merman's, which Tennyson, as poet-agent, creates in language. He repre-sents the process of self-sympathy as the content of the poem.

And this, Fox implies, is the only way to build such content – the only way, perhaps, to access the external. Again, contrary to Wilson's objec-tions, Fox's poet is not passively permeable to external influence. Externality is clearly secondary, only accessible from an internal perspec-tive. Fox depicts the process of internal observation as a process of making the world over from the inside out: there is no external world to speak of unless, or until, it is accessed from the perspective of the body. When Tennyson climbs atop the pineal gland and surveys the internal landscape of his subject, he gains access to the "mutual relations and influences" of the body reacting to itself and to its surroundings. This inhabitation is necessary in order to perceive not only the subject's body but also his or her environment. He praises Tennyson for the thoroughness with which he builds a whole world out of a "single germ." "Mariana," for example, is an exploration of "but one feeling, the variation of which is only by different degrees of acuteness and intensity," and which is matched by "the ruinous, old, lonely house, the neglected garden, the forlorn stagnation of the locality" (219). In each of his poems, internal information is used to generate the external world:

> He has created a scene out of the character, and made the feeling within generate an appropriate assemblage of external objects. Every mood of the mind has its own outward world, or rather makes its own outward world. (217)

Here, Fox more materially instantiates Wordsworth's well-known claim that in good poetry "the feeling therein developed gives importance to the action and situation, and not the action and situation to the feeling." Rather than internal feeling generating importance, Fox depicts internal feeling as generating actual external objects. In other words, Fox's Tennyson builds from the inside out, using not his own responsiveness as inspiration but his survey of the internal and involuntary responses of the imaginary body he has adopted.

Fox suggests that the poetic ideal of sympathizing with another person, of embodying an imagined or imaginary perspective, is far from the first-generation-Romantic model of the creative process. Fox's ideal poet is protean, to be sure – much like Coleridge's Shakespeare of the *Biographia* – but this imaginative shape-shifting is startlingly material and physiological. Fox suggests that the most productive perspective for sensation poetry is not the view from someone else's eyes, but rather the view inside their body. What is more, his model of the creative imagination does not move the poet out of the self to sympathize with another but rather moves the poet further and further into his own mind. The kind of embodied sympathy that leads to poetic expression, for Fox, is not a material open-ness to the external world; it is an attentiveness to internal materialities.

Unsympathetic Readers: Arthur Hallam's Inner Libraries

In its emphasis on the dangerous passivity of the Victorian reader, Victorianist criticism of sympathy has overlooked the ways in which the poet was likewise an object of anxiety regarding the involuntary sympathetic responsiveness of the body. Fox's poetic theory – and Wilson's response to it – has allowed me to reevaluate the problem of sympathy in poetic production: the poet, not just the reader, threatened to be undone by material sensations. But Fox's poetic theory also suggests that the workings of the self-sympathetic body can act as a medium for the production of poetry: as with the autopoetics of the striking passage, the involuntary workings of self-sympathy interrogate the role of agency and volition within poetic composition. As the striking passage does, self-sympathy works to dismantle critical distinctions between writers and readers. If Fox's model of the poetry of sensation shows self-sympathy at work within Tennyson himself, in Arthur Hallam's model, self-sympathy offers a similarly radical way of conceptualizing Tennyson's reader. Like Fox, Hallam is interested in the question of what it means to sympathize with oneself, and the model of physiological self-sympathy provides a means for him to explore the problem of the poet-reader relationship. Poetry, he suggests, is born of an act of unique self-sympathy – so unique, in fact, that interpersonal sympathy is nearly impossible. In Hallam's model, excessive readerly sympathy is not the problem; rather, he sees readers as impermeable to interpersonal influence. But reading, too, can be imagined as a self-sympathetic action, one that draws its strength from that very impermeability.

Hallam first introduced Tennyson to the world as a "poet of sensation" in August of 1831, when he published "On Some of the Characteristics of Modern Poetry" in the *Englishman's Magazine*. As I discussed above, Hallam depicts his friend as part of a lineage of poets attuned to their unique sensate responses to the world: "their fine organs trembled into emotion at colours, and sounds, and movements, unperceived or unregarded by duller temperaments" (617). It's worth considering these lines again in light of the question of agency; the self-sympathetic process Hallam describes here, as Jason Rudy points out, seems to be primarily passive. Rather than letting the poet's brain "actively interpret sensory data as he goes along," Rudy contends, "Hallam emerges as a radical figure . . ., allowing the brain to take a passive role while sensory experience plays out howsoever it may in the human body" (58). In this way, Hallam's depiction of poetic production is closely aligned with physiological theories of self-sympathy, which refocus attention on the automatic workings of the sensate body. Hallam is also closely aligned with fellow poetry critics Hazlitt and Fox in his emphasis on internal impressions: the original "impulse from external nature" is quickly passed over as Hallam focuses on the internal effects of the "fine organs trembl[ing] into emotion," which resonate within the body until they "absorb their whole being into the energy of sense" (617). Hallam's vision of the poet of sensation draws attention to the role of the body in mediating the production of poetry.

If the poet's individual body is the medium by which sensation may be turned into poetry, however, such an emphasis on individual embodiment also creates an impediment for the poet of sensation. As with Hazlitt's model of the self, Hallam's poet is cut off from sympathy with other people. This is due in part, Hallam explains, to the quality of his sense organs: poets (and poets alone) are gifted with a unique set of physical characteristics. Such a physiological-poetic elite is destined to be under-appreciated by the public simply because their sensations are equally elite. "How should they be popular," Hallam asks, "whose senses told them a richer and ampler tale than most men could understand, and who constantly expressed, because they constantly felt, sentiments of exquisite pleasure or pain, which most men were not permitted to experience?" (618). It is, I think, not coincidental that concerns about sensation poetry arise at the same time as concerns about mass readership as an ever-growing and anonymous body of potential critics. Hallam, who abhors the masses, happily posits a physiological barrier between the ideal poet and his innumerable readers – a barrier that he employs to explain why poets should not be concerned with public response. Writing of Wordsworth's assertion that "immediate or rapid popularity was not the test of poetry," he argues that "it was the truth, and it prevailed; not only against the exasperation of that hydra, the Reading Public, whose vanity was hurt, and the blustering of its keepers, whose delusion was exposed, but even against the false glosses and narrow apprehensions of the Wordsworthians them-selves" (616).[13] Hallam demonizes the Reading Public, suggesting that its very multiplicity of experience – its many-headedness, as it were – gives it no genuine vantage-point from which to relate to the unique poet. Poets and readers, he implies, should not expect interpersonal sympathy to underwrite their relationship in any easy way. Uniqueness, rather than commonality of experience, defines poetic production.

Poets of sensation are especially isolated from the growing body of readers, then, by their inaccessibly fine physiology. But Hallam is dubious of claims toward true interpersonal sympathy in general. In his Smith-inflected essay "On Sympathy," read to the Cambridge Apostles on December 4, 1830, Hallam argues that even interpersonal sympathy arises out of a self-based (but not self-interested) process of self-sympathy: "How, how can the soul imagine feeling which is not its own? I repeat, she realizes this conception only by considering the other being as a separate part of self, a state of her own consciousness existing apart from the present, just as imagined states exist in the future" (137). Like Hazlitt, then, Hallam uses self-sympathy as a model for maintaining the self through time; and also like Hazlitt, he sees this contiguous self as isolated and impermeable, capable only of sympathizing with others by sympathizing with itself. This has formidable implications for any potential theory of reader-poet sympathy – especially the involuntary, all-absorbing readerly sympathy that appears most prominently in our critical discussions of the subject. For Hallam, readerly sympathy is far from involuntary. To be sure, he strictly denies that any "barrier between these poets and all other persons" could be insurmountable (618); but it is the reader, not the poet, who must work to overcome this potential barrier: "Every bosom contains the elements of those complex emotions which the artist feels, and every head can, to a certain extent, go over itself in the process of their combination, so as to understand his expressions and sympathize with his state. But this requires exertion; more or less, indeed, according to the difference of occasion, but always some degree of exertion" (618).[14] In particular, the action necessary for the reader to perform is an act of forced interpersonal sympathy, a kind of inhabitation of the poet's interior processes: "it is absolutely necessary *to start from the same point*, i.e., clearly to apprehend that leading sentiment in the poet's mind" (618, emphasis original). Hallam insists that such an act of willed inhabitation is physical – it is "never *physically* impossible," he writes – but he complains that "this requisite exertion is not willingly made by the majority of readers" (618–619, emphasis in original). Although his reader is participating in a kind of interpersonal sympathy, it is not the interpersonal sympathy we know, where the reader is passively (and often dangerously) influenced by every text she encounters. Nor is this a sympathetic relationship along the lines of the eighteenth-century tradition of sensibility, in which (as Brewer writes) sentimental storytelling "was believed to set in train the sympathetic reaction that proliferates sensibility, uniting narrator, narrated and listener/reader" (29). Instead, the reader is positioned outside the text – outside the poet's body, even – and must work to gain access to it. Hallam's construction of sympathy relies on the premise that the boundary between poem and reader is nearly impermeable – that the reader is not automatically susceptible to the interpersonal sympathies of the reading experience.

I want to turn now to Tennyson's poetry itself – the poetry that Hallam includes in his review – and look at both the poems themselves and at Hallam's treatment of them, for here we can see the stakes (as well as the rewards) of his model of readerly impermeability. Hallam reproduces in his text three of Tennyson's poems in their entirety: "Adeline," "Oriana," and "Recollections of the Arabian Nights," all poems that have failed to attract much attention from twentieth- and twenty-first-century critics. Like the more widely discussed "Mariana," these poems are highly repetitive in structure, choosing to expound upon moods or refrains rather than advance plotlines or develop trains of thought – we might call them "anti-conversation" poems, poems whose deep recursivity stands out even within the lyric tradition. These are poems that move in, not out. And in keeping with self-sympathetic resistance to outward movement, each of these particular poems depicts failures of (and dangers inherent in) interpersonal sympathy. Two of the poems Hallam reprints focus in particular on attempts to imagine the interiority of a mysterious and inaccessible woman, thus invoking tropes of femininity that (as Kathy Alexis Psomiades has persuasively argued) will play an influential role in the development of aestheticism, and which come to fruition more famously for Tennyson in "The Lady of Shalott."[15] In these early poems, however, the reader is never granted access to the interior lives of these mysterious women. Neither is the poet: he remains firmly outside the impermeable boundaries of his subjects' selves. In "Adeline," the speaker encounters a "[f]aintly smiling" woman (l. 2) and spends the next sixty-four lines speculating as to the cause of her mysterious expression. The slow-moving refrain alternates its questioning, first asking "Wherefore those dim looks of thine, / Shadowy, dreaming Adeline?" (ll. 9–10), followed by a repetitive variation: "Wherefore those faint smiles of thine, / Spiritual Adeline?" (ll. 19–20). Adeline, he says, is "beyond expression" (l. 5), and it is the very faintness and dimness of her looks and smiles that arouse the speaker's curiosity. But Tennyson lets the speaker's postulations – what amounts to a list of guesses and speculative queries, including "Lovest thou the doleful wind, / When thou gazest at the skies?" (ll. 49–50) and "Hast thou heard the butterflies, / What they say betwixt their wings?" (ll. 28–29) – remain in the form of unresolved questions. Adeline remains a "[m]ystery of mysteries" (l. 1), despite the speaker's multiple attempts to access her interiority. And these attempts, the poem hints, seem to require a kind of sacrifice of the speaker's own interiority. "Thy rose lips and full blue eyes / Take the heart out of my chest," the speaker complains (ll. 7–8). Yet his heart has nowhere to go, no welcoming interior with which to sympathize. The reader is left with the uncomfortable and unresolved image of physical sacrifice in the name of an unachievable interpersonal sympathy.

"Oriana," however, goes further: it acknowledges the violence inherent in "Adeline"'s model of sympathetic identification. In "Oriana," attempts at accessing another person's interiority prove not only fruitless but dangerous, a means of forcibly entering into another person's heart or chest. The poem depicts the tragic death of the speaker's love at his own hand – by way of a "bitter arrow" that "went aside" (l. 37) – and queries the lady in a manner similar to "Adeline": "Whom wantest thou? whom dost thou seek, / Oriana?" (ll. 71–72). But here Tennyson proposes a difficult answer to the problem of Adeline: the speaker knows what's inside Oriana, and it's himself – or his proxy, the arrow: "Within thy heart my arrow lies, / Oriana" (ll. 80–81). This sentiment of forceful inhabitation is foreshadowed in an earlier stanza, in which the speaker tells us that

> The damn'd arrow glanced aside
> And pierced thy heart, my love, my bride,
> Oriana!
> Thy heart, my life, my love, my bride,
> Oriana! (ll. 41–45)

The altered repetition is telling. In the final two lines of the stanza, the list of definitions that has served to describe Oriana – "thy heart, my love, my bride, Oriana" – is pierced, as it were, with the presence of the speaker: "Thy heart, *my life*, my love, my bride, Oriana!" Attempting to make her life his, it seems, lies at the heart of the tragedy. In a way, the poem depicts a violent attempt to get inside another person, to access their interiority, to claim their life as one's own. Like "Adeline," "Oriana" ends with the collapse of interpersonal sympathy, with the poet assigning feelings to the dead woman ("Oh happy thou that liest low" [l. 84]) and swearing that he "dare not think" of her [l. 93]. If Hallam insists that true interpersonal sympathy is "never *physically* impossible," his choice of poems suggests that this model of physical inhabitation might have violent consequences.

In contrast to the model of reading as a dangerous and difficult act of interpersonal sympathy, however, Hallam offers an alternative: the right kind of reader, he implies, only needs to sympathize with him or herself. Hallam is happy to dictate who should read Tennyson's poems – to suggest the qualities that separate a successful individual from the hydra of the reading public. He writes: "We have spoken in good faith, commending this volume to feeling hearts and imaginative tempers, not to the stupid readers, or the voracious readers, or the malignant readers, or the readers after dinner!" (628) – the last group, possibly, in danger of oversympathizing with their digestive tracts. But when Hallam prepares his reader for an encounter with an individual poem – one of the ones he reprints in his review – he offers a different set of criteria. Prefacing Tennyson's "Recollections of the Arabian Nights," Hallam exclaims: "What a delightful, endearing title! How we pity those to whom it calls up no reminiscence of early enjoyment, no sentiment of kindliness as toward one who sings a song they have loved, or mentions with affection a departed friend!" (621). The poem, he implies, appeals to those who possess a specific set of memories, which are activated by the new poem. Indeed, like the more celebrated "Mariana," "Recollections" relies on intertextuality: it makes direct reference to another pre-existing text. But "Recollections" goes much further than "Mariana" in that it takes the act of reading as its content. What is more, it depicts this textual encounter – which is masked as an exotic scene of transport out of the self – as simultaneously a move deeper into the self and into the self's past. The poem's opening stanza charts this recursive movement:

> When the breeze of a joyful dawn blew free
> In the silken sail of infancy,
> The tide of time flow'd back with me,
> The forward-flowing tide of time;
> And many a sheeny summer-morn,
> Adown the Tigris I was borne,
> By Bagdat's shrines of fretted gold,
> High-walled gardens green and old;
> True Mussulman was I and sworn,
> For it was in the golden prime
> Of good Haroun Alraschid.

Tennyson purposefully muddles the temporality of the reading experience: the "tide of time," generally "forward-flowing," reverses its course and flows backward – "back with me," the speaker explains, emphasizing his own presence. Indeed, the vision of Arabia offered by the poem consistently foregrounds the subjective experience of the speaker. The journey the poem depicts is not a singular event but a recurring one, that bears the speaker down the Tigris on "many a sheeny summer-morn." The movement is one of returning to a place in memory. *We* are not there, not now; rather, Tennyson gives us a passive dummy subject that places us in the past while fully acknowledging its past-ness: "it was in the golden time / Of good Haroun Alraschid," the speaker repeats.

As he will later do with other intertextually referential poems such as "The Lotos-Eaters" and the *Idylls of the King*, Tennyson in "Recollections" asks his reader to return to and expand upon previous reading experiences. And this request is, I think, not lost on Hallam. His review celebrates the poem's intertextual drive by emphasizing – in his depiction of Tennyson's ideal reader – the necessity of this recursive and reading-based movement inward, toward reminiscences of "early enjoyment," beloved songs, and departed friends. In fact, Hallam continues, the poem's strength lies not in its ability to transport the reader out of herself, but rather to return her to herself: "The scene is before us, around us; we cannot mistake its localities, or blind ourselves to its colours. That happy ductility of childhood returns for the moment" (623). What Hallam's reader encounters is the experience of her own childhood; and familiarity of image, rather than alterity or originality, is what prompts this experience. In a way, Hallam expects of the reader the same continuity of self that Fox expects of his poet: *still it is herself in the poem*, as Fox would say, and her own memories are what allow her to access fully its seemingly exotic setting. The reader in Hallam's formulation does not so much attempt the tedious exertion of interpersonal sympathy as turn inward toward her own memories and recollections – as does Hazlitt as he attempts to hold himself throughout time together – in an act of self-sympathy.[16]

What is more, Hallam implies that the reader's suitability to any particular poem depends on his or her previous reading experiences. If one has not read the original *Arabian Nights*, one has no inner landscape, as it were, with which to sympathize when reading Tennyson's poem. Hazlitt's discussion of self-sympathy in "A Farewell" expresses a similar sentiment: "I have the same favourite books, pictures, passages that I ever had," he writes; "I may therefore presume that they will last me my life . . . . This continuity of impression is the only thing on which I pride myself" (17: 318). Reading, it seems, *makes up* the self by giving the reader the interiority on which she can draw in her subsequent reading experiences. This is evident too in Hallam's introduction to "Oriana":

> Have we among our readers any who delight in the heroic poems of Old England, the inimitable ballads? Any to whom Sir Patrick Spends, and Clym of the Clough, and Glorious Robin, are consecrated names? Any who sigh with disgust at the miserable abortions of simpleness mistaken for simplicity, or florid weakness substituted for plain energy, which they may often have seen dignified with the title of Modern Ballads? Let such draw near, and read the Ballad of Oriana. (624)

Here Hallam dictates *who* should "draw near" to read Tennyson's poem; but the "who" is defined not by a sensibility or impressionability but rather by a set of reading memories that can be activated, or reactivated, in this new setting. "Oriana" does not require the reader to sympathize with

Tennyson, or with his speaker, or even with its tragic heroine; it does not require projecting the self-sympathies outward; it is not, according to Hallam, a strange new mental landscape that requires exertion to access. Instead, it is as familiar as the reader's own inner library. In other words, Hallam imagines Tennyson's readers not as impressionable, highly permeable sympathizers but as self-sympathizers. Reading is not an original impression, an external impression, but rather a secondary internal reaction to something that already exists within the self. In fact reading is what makes up the self; it does not undo it but rather it gives the reader her own inner landscape from which to build toward outward worlds.[17]

As this chapter draws to a close, I want to consider the broader implications of the autopoetics of self-sympathy and internal sensation I've been working to outline. Why was it useful for poetic theorists to draw upon a model of sympathy that operates entirely within the self? Why was it important to define a poetry of sensation at this moment – and, more to the point, why was that poetry of sensation built not upon a model of the body as open to external influence but rather on a model of embodiment deeply invested in internal impressions? While the poetry of sensation may not ultimately represent the full scope of the Victorian poetic imagination, in the 1830s it marked a conspicuous attempt to define a modern poetics. This generation of writers faced an ever-increasing awareness of the body's material automatism, which often could be seen to threaten the notion of the agential self. And this posed a crucial problem for a model of poetics still deeply indebted to a Romantic model of sensibility: if we don't have control over our body's involuntary responses to the world, how can we safely draw upon on our own responses to create poetry? And how can we rely upon readers to respond appropriately? What we find in Fox and Hallam is an attempt to define a poetry of sensation that celebrates the benefits of returning to the material self (and specifically the material body), not in order to gauge its responsiveness to external stimuli but rather to observe and expand its responsiveness to itself. In the face of an ever-increasing, and largely anonymous, reading public, these writers seek to shore up the boundedness of the individual. While a poetics of sensation would seem – like the threateningly interpersonal sympathy that has been the focus of recent work in Victorianist criticism – to undermine the agency of the self, it in fact recasts automatism as part of the creative process: poetic agency can result from passively attending to the involuntary interactions of the body. In so doing, sensation poetry transforms the material body of the poet, alongside that of the reader, into the medium of poetry. Both Fox and Hallam use self-sympathy to substantiate their assertion that modern poetry should make the world over from the inside out. And yet this overwriting takes physical sensation, rather than imaginative reflection, as the starting point. In this way the autopoetics of self-sympathy delineated by these writers suggests a radical move away from imagined community and toward a kind of resonating, materially productive solipsism.

CHAPTER 3

Listening with the Mouth
Tennyson's Deaths of Arthur

In the first chapter, I raised the question of orality only to bypass it in order to explore the visual mechanics of the striking passage. Yet if the nineteenth-century body was understood to be capable of automatically reproducing poetry, one crucial mechanism for such reproduction was, of course, the human voice. There is perhaps no better place to consider the autopoetics of voice than the germinal text of Tennyson's endlessly revised Arthurian epic, the "Morte d'Arthur." The 1842 poem is peopled with speakers and listeners. It is missing, however, the most famous speaker of the poem's later incarnation: Bedivere, the aged knight of "The Passing of Arthur," who narrates the story of the King's death. While Bedivere has an active role to play in the "Morte," he is not its narrator; when the story is first given to his charge, in Tennyson's revised version in *The Holy Grail and Other Poems* in 1869, he narrates as "no more than a voice" (3). This Bedivere seems the fitting culmination of a nineteenth-century obsession with a lost culture of orality – an obsession that stems, arguably, from James Macpherson's Ossian poems of the 1760s. As print culture rose to prominence, the story goes, the poetic imagination seized on the figure of the aged, ghostly bard whose voice is all that remains of an ancient oral tradition. Katie Trumpener describes the role of the Ossianic bard in pre-print culture: "For nationalist antiquaries, the bard is the mouthpiece for a whole society, articulating its values, chronicling its history, and mourning the inconsolable tragedy of its collapse" (6). Indeed, Tennyson's tragic Arthurian epic deals heavily in mourning, in recognition of loss, and Dafydd Moore argues that the "Morte," along with "The Passing of Arthur," depicts poetic transmission along Ossianic lines by establishing a powerful nostalgia for a lost oral culture. The Ossianic bard is dead, and the printed page contains only the traces of his orality.

For Tennyson, the Arthurian legend is doubly laced with loss: his first engagement with Arthurian mythology, the "Morte d'Arthur," was composed in the early 1830s after the death of Arthur Hallam. And yet the

"Morte"'s relationship to loss – to the process of death and the potential for resurrection – is more complicated than scholars such as Moore suggest. I want to argue, instead, that Tennyson is less interested in any primary orality than he is in the question of the transmission of voice, as it moves both from text to reader and from speaker to listener. And this question, for Tennyson, does not center on an ancient tradition of orality: it is a question about modern media and mediation, about the technology of poetry and its relationship to the body in the nineteenth century. Victorian critic R. H. Hutton noted of Tennyson, in 1871, that "[n]o poet ever made the dumb speak so effectually" (372). This claim might apply, it seems to me, not only to Tennyson's ability to give voice to his characters but to his ability to give voice to silent things – both people and pages – and to make them come alive with his speech.

In this way Tennyson's evolving depictions of voice and listening in his Arthurian elegies engage a broader debate in both Victorian and Victorianist criticism, a debate about the function of voice in printed poetry in general. At bottom, the question at stake goes something like this: in print culture, is poetic voice a production of orality, of textuality, or of something in between? The hypermediacy of Victorian poetry – ever aware of its status as print – is a particularly rich lens through which to explore this debate. Eric Griffiths, in his influential exploration of the "printed voice" in Victorian poetry, argues that voice is both present and absent – a spectral voice, one that exists in the mediation of aural and oral:

> Whatever else poetry may be, it is certainly a use of language that works with the sounds of words, and so the absence of clearly indicated sound from the silence of the written word creates a double nature in printed poetry, making it both itself and something other – a text of hints at voicing, whose centre in utterance lies outside itself, and also an achieved pattern on the page, salvaged from the evanescence of the voice in air. (60)

Even in print culture, Griffiths argues, poetry is invested in sound – but the nature of this sound is in dispute. In a way, Griffiths's theory is a midpoint in the debate about the function of voice in printed poetry: scholars such as Walter Ong and Ann Banfield argue that a primary orality underwrites (underspeaks?) print culture, whereas Yopie Prins, Margaret Linley, and others reject the assumption that "poems are transcriptions or prescriptions for voice" (Prins, "Voice Inverse" 45), taking the Derridean stance that textuality is the primary medium and voice merely a metaphor.

Prins and Linley also move beyond textuality, however, to investigate Victorian poetry's relationship to media beyond print. If poetry is on some level a place to explore the problem of unspoken voice – of voice that operates without sound, of sound that comes from something silent – this is an inherently mediated voice, a voice whose origin is disputed or even unknown. Poetry, according to Prins and Linley, negotiates the *re*production of sound in print culture rather than its actual production, and in this way it is useful to consider poetry not only in the context of print culture but also in the context of phonographic culture. "Victorian poetry," Linley writes, "could be a precedent for the 'experience of sound disconnected from its source' that Gillian Beer suggests is novel to the history of the world with the invention of radio" (539). Prins makes a similar argument: "Victorian poems circulated as 'acoustic devices' for the mediation of voice, preceding and perhaps even predicting the sound reproduction technologies that emerged in the course of the nineteenth century" ("Voice" 44). Poetry, indeed, takes something silent and puts it in other people's mouths and ears, and in this way is a kind of reproductive technology of its own.

It is to this discussion – of Victorian poetry as a technology for reproducing sound – that this chapter contributes. It does so by reviving and putting in conversation (so to speak) two key concepts I've worked to outline in the previous chapters: the disruptive mechanics of the striking passage and the material resonance of the self-sympathetic body. In assessing poetry's relationship to sound reproduction, I will argue, we must consider not only the traditional media of phonography, stenography, and telephony but also the speaking apparatus of the human body, which – in Tennyson's day – was a primary medium for poetry. In the Victorian period poems were read aloud, they were listened to, they were memorized and recited and repeated. And the processes by which the body reproduced sound were the subject of much analysis by physiologists, elocutionists, and poets alike. What is most interesting to me is that nineteenth-century theories of speaking and listening depict the interaction between the body's speaking apparatus (the mouth) and its listening apparatus (the ear) as not productive but reproductive – phonographic, even. In doing so, Victorian physiological theory imagines voice as a surprisingly mechanical function, one that exemplifies a central phenomenon this book has worked to uncover: the increasing entanglement of theories of the production of language with theories of its reception. In the Victorian automatic body, speech is dependent on listening; the full contours of Victorian orality, in other words, are only visible when examined alongside aurality.

What does this mean for Tennyson's "Morte d'Arthur"? In this chapter I map the changing conceptions of the speaking, reading, and listening body alongside Tennyson's evolving depictions of the death of Arthur in order to explore Tennyson's investment in the body as a suitable medium for reproducing poetry. The physiological automatism that underlies Victorian theories of listening and speaking seems, in 1842, to allow poetry to use the body to resurrect sound from the page and to reproduce it in other bodies. Poetry acts on the mouth via the ear and the eye, and even via the page: it is a technology in which "voice" is secondary, automatically activated by the body. But this construction of voice as automatic – of the mouth as a reproductive technology – threatens, later in the century, to abolish the body altogether. As the "Morte" evolves into the "Passing," it abandons mouth in favor of sourceless voice.

The Reader's Voice in Victorian Britain

The "Morte d'Arthur" (along with its frame poem, "The Epic") was first published in Tennyson's 1842 *Poems*; it would later reappear as "The Passing of Arthur" in *The Holy Grail and Other Poems* (1869) and finally serve as the closing poem in his Arthurian epic, *The Idylls of the King*, in 1873. It is this final incarnation – his conservative poet laureate in his habitual stance of deep mourning, nostalgic for the lost nobility of King Arthur's court – with which we are most familiar. It is this final incarnation, too, that is by far the least incarnate. The original "Morte" differs strongly in this regard: rather than mourning the loss of an ancient poetry, it investigates the materiality of modern poetry and its relationship to its communicative media. This is a complicated problem, as Linley writes: "The embodied voice of poetry that is born in the era of the printing press is neither wholly mechanical nor animate but both simultaneously. . . . [The spirit of voice] returns, as the written sign of voice and in acts of reading aloud, as an organic (though technologically enhanced) prosthesis for the machine-made word" (539). The "Morte d'Arthur" and its frame poem, which depicts an act of reading aloud, is invested in exploring the role of the embodied voice as a medium – an organic prosthesis, as Linley terms it – for modern poetry.

Tennyson's Arthuriana of 1842 is deeply concerned with the tangibility of poetry in the present day. In place of the bodiless Bedivere of the "Passing" – to whom I'll turn later in this chapter – Tennyson's "Morte" gives us a narrator with a palpably modern presence. Rather than present his epic tale of Arthur's death as part of an ancient oral tradition, as he does in the final *Idylls of the King*, Tennyson here chooses to anchor his "faint Homeric echoes" (38) firmly in the present day: in its frame narrative of "The Epic," the "Morte" is read aloud by the poet Everard Hall as he sits with friends on

Christmas Eve. Indeed, this concern about anchoring is inherent to the frame narrative. The parson, fretting about the "general decay of faith" (18), bemoans that "there was no anchor, none / To hold by" (20–21). But the other listeners – the host, Francis Allen, and the unnamed narrator – offer the poet as a kind of anchor: "I hold by him," Francis says, clapping a hand on Hall's shoulder (22). A poet, even one who writes antiquated epics, can serve as a material anchor in the modern world. Poetry, too, has a tangible presence in the "Morte." But Tennyson is specific about the kind of materiality – the kind of media – that gives poetry its tangibility. In a letter to the Duke of Argyll in 1859, Tennyson recalls having once written a poem about the quest of Lancelot (one of his earliest attempts at an Arthurian theme): written in "as good verse as I ever wrote – no, I did not write, I made it in my head, and it has altogether slipt out of memory" (*Memoir* II.125). The difference between writing and simply conceiving (making it in one's head), it seems, is that the latter may "slip out of memory," unrecorded and thus lost forever. But writing is no guarantee of permanence, either. Written poetry is material, subject to material loss: Everard Hall's twelve-book Arthurian epic has been burnt by the poet as "[m]ere chaff and draff" (40). Only one book remains: "'I,' / Said Francis, 'picked the eleventh from this hearth / And have it: keep a thing, its use will come" (40–42). In "The Epic," eleven books have disappeared forever, gone because their mode of transmission – writing – is gone.

The poetry Tennyson celebrates in the "Morte," then, is *not* the poetry of a lost orality, of an Ossian-style bard whose voice died with print culture; instead, it is a distinctly modern epic whose transmission depends on written language.[1] The book that remains is a "thing," a material item with a "use" that comes with its keeping. What is lost, in Tennyson's scenario, is not the voice of an ancient bard but the text of a modern poet. To be sure, if Tennyson's epic takes written language as its primary medium, he remains ambivalent about its reliability as a mode of cultural transmission and retention in the modern age. But by framing the almost-lost "Morte" with "The Epic," Tennyson suggests an equally modern way of interacting with this culture of the written word: reading aloud. Once Francis produces the rescued eleventh book, Everard Hall entertains his friends by reading aloud from the rescued manuscript:

> the poet little urged,
> But with some prelude of disparagement,
> Read, mouthing out his hollow oes and aes,
> Deep-chested music, and to this result.   (48–51)

This is no lost voice that must be captured by print; it is a lost text that must be transformed into voice.

In "The Epic," such voice is modern: a way of transforming the "faint Homeric echoes" of ancient heroic poetry into something accessible, something vital to the nineteenth century. The modernity to which the "Morte" aspires is a modernity that redrafts a seemingly pre-modern orality into the service of a new, text-centric literary culture. Indeed, as much recent scholarship has revealed, nineteenth-century British culture was highly vocal. It was during the nineteenth century that poetry recitation became a staple of the education system, as Catherine Robson has convincingly demonstrated.[2] Outside the classroom, orality remained very much alive during the Victorian era, even with the rise of print culture. As David Vincent writes, "the sound of the human voice was magnified rather than quelled by the mass production and distribution of prose and verse. The simple relationship between the faceless publisher and the soundless reader was disrupted by men and women reciting, singing, shouting, chanting, declaiming and narrating" (201).[3] The popularity of reading aloud was due in part to economics and education: the working classes, many of whom were illiterate, relied upon oral readers to gain access to the information circulated in print; even those who could read were unlikely to be able to afford to own books or subscribe to periodicals, so funds for these media were often split among groups and communities, who then shared with each other by reading aloud. Changing constructions of middle-class families, too, played a role, as husbands and wives were expected to read to each other and, in turn, to their children. Although oral reading practices existed long before the Victorian era, burgeoning mass readership in the nineteenth century meant that Tennyson and his contemporaries were particularly interested in the relationship between reading aloud and print culture. Ivan Kreilkamp argues that the 1830s saw "a shift in the 'imagined community' of readers" away from a public sphere of print and toward "the emerging Victorian public identified with a mass readership that read novels in public and out loud" (97, 98). Tennyson, indeed, would have expected the practice of reading aloud to be one prominent way his poetry was disseminated.

That this practice was dependent on the body is illustrated too by Everard Hall's highly embodied voice, "mouthing out" his "deep-chested music." Indeed, alongside its remarkable vocality, the Victorian era witnessed a growing interest in the sciences of sound, an interest that made reading aloud not merely a practice but an object of study. At the time of Tennyson's composition of the "Morte" and its frame poem, British scientists were beginning to query the physiological mechanisms of speech, voice, and hearing (see Picker 8). Reading aloud – along with its related activities of speaking and listening – was understood to be a bodily process, one that engaged both the mind and the muscles. In fact, unlike the silent reading practices that came to be the subject of much concern later in the century, reading aloud was considered to be a healthy form of exercise in the early 1800s. Late-eighteenth-century literacy theory had promoted it as a suitable alternative to actual physical exercise:

> the action of walking, in which the effort required causes the blood to circulate, prevents the bodily fluids from coagulating, and wards off illnesses and feelings of weariness. During any rainy or unhealthy weather, or when we are ill, we have to take refuge in reading aloud as a substitute for the pleasures and benefits of a walk in the open air. (qtd. in Wittman 298)[4]

By the mid-nineteenth century, such vocal exercises were recommended to everyone from mothers at home to clergymen practicing their sermons. "To young ladies," *Chambers's Edinburgh Journal* reported in 1844, for example, "the habit of reading aloud has much to recommend it. As mere exercise, it is highly beneficial on account of the strength and vigour which it confers on the chest and lungs" ("Reading" 248).[5] Like Tennyson's Everard Hall, Victorian readers-aloud were very much aware of the role of their bodies as communicative media.

Indeed, if the body was seen as a communicative medium, the voice was seen as a kind of instrument. In *The Physiology of the Senses, Voice, and Muscular Motion,* translated into English in 1848, Johannes Müller claims that "the human organ of voice is a reed-instrument with a double membranous tongue" (1023). Such an instrument was dependent upon the reader's physiology, which came to be seen as a medium for transmitting and communicating written language. But these human media, of course, could be faulty – and this was a source of anxiety for writers who wanted to dictate the dissemination of their texts. Tennyson himself noted that proper reading of his poetry depended, in fact, on the reader's physiology: in "Maud," he explained, "[s]ome of the passages are hard to read because they have to be taken in one breath and require good lungs" (*Memoir* I: 395). In fact, the poet laureate was admired for his own set of lungs, as well as for his readerly prowess. Philip Collins rates him as "[o]ne of the most memorable and powerful of readers-aloud" and notes that he was known for his intoning style of recitation, much like Hall and his "hollow oes and aes" (4).

To that end, Tennyson was concerned with poetry's ability to reproduce in other bodies sounds written for his own. A shy man who refused to speak or lecture in public, he was nevertheless known to entertain at dinner-parties with lengthy recitations of his own work, which, he felt, could only be properly "read" in his own voice. Friends recount Tennyson's anxious contention that no one "save himself can read aloud his poems properly" (*Memoir* I: 395), and Hallam Tennyson recalls his father bemoaning the possible misinterpretations of "Boadicea," which he "feared that no one could read except himself, and wanted someone to annotate it musically so that people could understand the rhythm" (I: 459). While he admits that his individual body may indeed provide the best vocal medium for his poetry, he attempts to overcome the problem of different voices – different bodily instruments – by standardizing the textual medium. He imagines poetry as a multimedia experience, one that depends on a combination of written word and individual body. This multimediacy is indicative of the kind of modern poetry to which the "Morte" aspires: a poetry that, while text-based, enlists the human body (and, particularly, its mouth) in its communicative system.

In the "Morte" – which, as Hallam Tennyson tells us in his memoir of his father, was one of the poet's favorite poems to read aloud (II: 133) – Arthur is brought to life again by this same combination of text and human body. At the end of Hall's reading, Tennyson tells us, his audience "Sat rapt: it was the tone with which he read— / Perhaps some modern touches here and there / Redeemed it from the charge of nothingness" (277–279). The narrator explains that the poem's "modern touches" helped make it present to the audience; but so did the presence of a reader-aloud, a man (rather than a book) whose voice – "the tone in which he read" – kept his listeners enraptured. Everard Hall's poetry moves from the page to the listener via the instrument of the human body, and it lingers with the narrator long into the night as he dreams of Arthur's return. What Tennyson imagines for us as an ideal scene of poetic communication, then, relies on an interaction of text and vocalizing body: a written manu-script is brought to life by an oral reader. Unlike the orality of the Ossianic tradition – a primary orality that is dead and yet resurrected on the page – Tennyson gives us a construction of orality that is necessarily secondary, following a prior textuality. In this way, Tennyson in 1842 aligns himself with physiological theories of the time, which presented voice itself as a reproductive technology. I turn now to these theories in order to demonstrate the ways in which Tennyson's concern about the role of readerly voice in printed poetry – its role as a communicative and yet not originary medium – participates in a larger Victorian debate about the nature of speech and listening.

A Vocal Embrace: The Physiology of Listening

Tennyson's depiction of reading aloud is as much concerned with listening as it is with speaking: the problem of communicative voice necessarily depends upon proper reception as well. Musical annotation may help to communicate the rhythm of poetry, but another kind of annotation could be necessary when reading to a group of listeners. Collins notes that Tennyson, when reading aloud, "had the endearing habit of telling his hearers what to admire particularly" (4); R. C. Lehmann, in his 1908 *Memories of Half a Century*, remembers a party given by George Eliot "to *hear Tennyson read*" (emphasis original):

> I had at first some little difficulty in accustoming myself to his very marked Northern dialect, but that done I thoroughly enjoyed the reading. He would interrupt himself every now and then to say quite naively, 'We now come to one of my best things. This has been tried before me, but not successfully,' and so on. [. . .] We were spell-bound, and he seemed to enjoy it so much that his son had at last to make him stop by reminding him of the lateness of the hour. (132; qtd. in Collins 4)

Lehmann's account draws attention to the fact that voice, far from being standardized, is in fact highly individual, qualities like a "very marked Northern dialect" falling differently on different listeners' ears. Moreover, Lehmann reminds us that merely listening does not guarantee proper attention. In a way, Tennyson's public readings of his own work are annotated with instructions for his listeners, reminding them what to attend to, what to appreciate, what to contextualize. This verbal high-lighting – which Collins calls "endearing" and Lehmann labels "quite naïve" – can also be read as a deliberate attempt to control his listeners' responses to (and interpretations of) his texts.

Tennyson's verbal annotations draw attention to a topic often over-looked in critical discussions of speech and voice: the problem of the listener. For the Victorians, the listening audience – while it may fail to pay proper attention to the nuances of the reader's expression – was, like the speaker or reader, highly embodied. Indeed, physiologists themselves were interested in both speaking and listening as physical experiences.

William Carpenter, lecturing in 1875, laid bare the role of physiological mechanism in every aspect of the speaker-listener relationship:

> What am I doing at the present time? – endeavouring to excite in your minds certain ideas which are passing through my own. How do I do so? – by means of my organs of speech, which are regulated by my nervous system; that apparatus being the instrument through which my mind expresses my ideas in spoken language. The sounds I utter, transmitted to you by vibrations of the air falling upon your ears, excite in the nerves with which those organs are supplied certain changes which are propagated through them to the sensorium, that wonderful organ through the medium of which a certain state of consciousness is aroused in your minds; and my aim is, by the use of appropriate words, to suggest to your minds the ideas I desire to implant in them. (*Doctrine* 5–6)

As this passage shows, the physical transmission of sound waves from speaker to listener can be seen as a kind of forced interpersonal sympathy, a way by which a speaker can "implant" a listener's mind with ideas. And this interpersonal sympathy depends very much on the body. Speaking thus could forge a material connection between reader and audience, creating a shared physical experience in which the nerves and organs of different bodies, along with the vibration of air particles between them, are elements of one communication network.

Indeed, reading aloud in the nineteenth century was seen to build community – even to unite the various bodies of the listening audience into one communal entity. Charles Dickens's wildly popular public readings, as such scholars as Ivan Kreilkamp, Philip Collins, and Helen Small have noted, exemplified this ability to create a communal body of listeners. Dickens himself described it as such: "We had an amazing scene of weeping and cheering, at St. Martin's Hall, last night. I read the Life and Death of Little Dombey; and certainly I never saw a crowd so resolved into one creature before, or so stirred by any thing" (*Letters* VIII: 584). Tennyson, who unlike Dickens did not enjoy speaking to crowds and who refused all invitations for public appearances, explained his dislike of public speaking as a concern about his ability (as Dickens put it) to resolve the crowd into one creature:

> I am never the least shy before great men. Each of them has a personality for which he or she is responsible: but before a crowd, which consists of many personalities, of which I know nothing, I am infinitely shy. The great orator cares nothing about all this. . . . *He* takes them all as one man. *He* sways them as one man. (*Memoir* II: 280)

The bodies in the listening audience were of great interest to speakers who wanted to understand the precise ways in which they were able to influence their listeners. In particular, the ability of the speaker to bring other bodies into alignment with his own – to bring them together into one responsive body, to create a communal listening audience – was fundamental to public speaking and reading aloud.[6]

The physiology of listening, then, was important to nineteenth-century theories of affect and sympathetic influence. But if reading aloud invoked interpersonal sympathy as a way of creating a communal listening audience, it also operated on a self-sympathetic level. As the above passage from Carpenter also suggests, listener response was fundamental to physiological examinations of the mechanisms of voice and speech. Moreover, what attracted the most attention in physiological theory was the relationship between voice and hearing *in the same body*. Rather than explore the distance between the speaker and the listener, as Carpenter does in the passage I quoted above, many physiologists were primarily invested in understanding the way in which the ear and the voice work together: listening was seen as a step – the fundamental step, in fact – toward speech.

J. J. Halcombe and W. H. Stone's 1874 text on public speaking illus-trates the way in which voice depends upon the ear: "Speech is, then, an acquirement, not a gift; and its intermediary instrument is the sense of hearing" (143). Indeed, throughout the Victorian period, physiologists insist on what David Tod, in his 1832 *Anatomy and Physiology of the Organ of Hearing*, calls "the intimate connexion which exists between the Ear and the Larynx" (vi).[7] This is an intimacy in which the sense of hearing guides and regulates the production of speech. Carpenter's *Principles of Human Physiology*, written in the 1840s, makes this clear:

> Among other important offices of the power of Hearing, is that of supplying the sensations by which the Voice is regulated. It is well known that those who are born entirely deaf, are also dumb, – that is, destitute of the power of forming articulate sounds; even though not the least defect exist in their organs of voice. Hence it appears that the vocal muscles can only be guided in their action by the sensations received through the Ears, in the same manner as other muscles are guided by the sensations received through themselves. (437–438)

According to Carpenter, the ears and the vocal muscles act together as a kind of united organ; whereas most organs are regulated by their own experiences, he explains, the speaking apparatus requires the guidance of sensations received by the ear.[8]

In a way, this intimate connection between aurality and orality can be understood to be a division of labor: both processes deal in sound waves, one receiving and one producing. At first glance this division seems also like a hierarchy of agency, the voice asserting its dominion over the passive ear. In the nineteenth century, as today, the ear appears as a troublingly helpless orifice.[9] Jonathan Rée's history of deafness and the senses reminds us that, although hearing and listening may be "means of active inquiry, and methods of orienting oneself in the world" (53), hearing is generally passive:

> In several languages, including English, many verbs designating different modes of sensory perception can be turned round and applied to the activity of their objects. You can look at something, to find out how it looks; you smell how it smells, feel how it feels, and taste how it tastes. But the verbs 'listen' and 'hear' cannot be reversed out in the same way: you do not listen to how things listen, or hear how they hear. All you can listen to or hear is how they sound. Hearing, it seems, has nothing active in it: it is mere supine susceptibility. (53)

According to this model, voice is active exactly where hearing is passive: "[y]ou can use your voice to populate your auditory world at will, and nothing remotely comparable applies to the other senses" (55). This same concept of the passive property of the ear can be found in Romantic sense physiology; so can the parallel concept of voice as hearing's active sense. William Gilpin in 1786, taking a cue from Buffon, argued that hearing is a "passive property" which "becomes active through the organ of speech" (qtd. in Rée 55). Volition, in this longstanding model, exists in the mouth but not in the ear. The two are intimately linked, but – as it would seem – the aural is subservient to the active dictation of the oral.

However, as the previous passage from Carpenter illustrates, this simple distinction of hearing as passive and voice as active is not as straightforward as it might first appear. Nineteenth-century physiological theory complicates the relationship between mouth and ear so clearly asserted by Gilpin. The mouth and the ear are intimately linked, to be sure, but the dynamic is not merely one of input and output, of passive hearing and active speech. Instead, in Victorian physiological theory, the ear plays a surprisingly active role. According to sense physiologists like Carpenter, sound needs to enter the body before it can be produced by the body: "the vocal muscles can only be guided in their action by the sensations received through the Ears." Drawing on studies of speech development and the relationship between deafness and muteness, nineteenth-century physiologists insist on a primacy of heard sound over spoken sound: "when the organ of Hearing is imperfect, or becomes the seat of disordered functions, the organ of Speech must sympathize with it, and prove imperfect in its actions also" (Tod 137). You must hear, in other words, in order to speak. Moreover, the quality of the produced sound must be regulated by the ear, for speech depends upon hearing not only to introduce sound into the body but to structure its vocal production. The voice is "guided by the ear" (Bain, *Senses* 434), the body able to correctly produce sound only if it has correctly heard it.

Clearly, then, the nineteenth-century understanding of the relationship between orality and aurality is more complex than we might at first assume; the mouth and the ear exist in what Tod describes as a state of self-sympathy, the vocal organs compelled to "sympathize" with the organs of hearing. This self-sympathetic compulsion relies on an underlying automatism now familiar to us, an automatism that structures the way the body sympathetically responds to itself. Bain's 1859 *Emotions and the Will*, for example, argues that learning to speak is an automatic process in which hearing is transformed into speaking – in which, in other words, aurality is transformed into orality. This process relies on what Bain calls "imitation," a faculty seemingly similar in nature to interpersonal sympathy: "the establishment of a bond of connexion between the appearance presented by a movement as executed by another person, and an impulse to move the same organ in ourselves" (344). But, as in self-sympathy, the original sound ceases to be important; the internal reaction, which reproduces the sound, is prioritized. As listeners learning to speak, we are originally dependent upon actual sound to trigger the imitative response, but eventually we are able to "dispense with the actual hearing of the note or articulation; we can summon up the vocal exertion at the lead of the mere idea or recollection of the sound" (356). Voice, in other words, is inherently *re*productive rather than productive: the ear provides the original sound that the voice then reproduces. If the human voice is an instrument, as Müller claims, it is an instrument that is played by the ear.

As we can see, then, this self-sympathetic model of speech and hearing reverses our easy assumption of the ear's subservience to the active mouth. Tod's *Anatomy* makes this reversal evident: "In discussing the functions of the Ear, we stated that those of the organ of Speech were subservient to them," he writes; as a result of this subservience, all vocal phenomena are "of a passive nature" (137). We may locate volition in the mouth and not in the ear, in other words, but nineteenth-century physiological theory says otherwise. While voice may create sounds, it cannot voluntarily originate them: "[t]he power of the sensorium to display the primary principles of volition in the larynx" simply doesn't exist (Tod 139). Carpenter's *Principles of Human Physiology* makes a similarly complex argument. The "regulation of the voice," Carpenter writes, "can scarcely be termed Voluntary":

> Now it might be supposed that the Will has sufficient power over the vocal muscles, to put them into any state requisite for its purposes, without any further condition: but a little self-experiment will prove that this is not the case. No definite tone can be produced by a voluntary effort, unless that tone be present to the mind, during however momentary an interval, either as immediately conveyed to it by an act of Sensation, recalled by an act of Conception, or anticipated by an effort of the imagination. When thus present, the Will can enable the muscles to assume the condition requisite to produce it; but under no other circumstances does this happen. (464)

What Carpenter implies here is what seems like an act of pure will – the voluntary ability to create vocal expression – is in fact merely an act of imitation of sound, whether that sound is audible, recalled, or imagined. Like the seemingly passive ear, the mouth is an orifice that must be filled with sound that comes originally from an external source.[10]

By emphasizing the involuntary nature of the vocal organs, nineteenth-century physiologists reveal vocal production to be an act of repetition, rather than an origin, of sound. What is more, the imitative action of vocal reproduction – while obviously part of the volitional activity of learning to speak – can also be set into action automatically. According to the physiology of speech and voice, language is so deeply ingrained in the vocal organs that merely thinking of a word can prompt an involuntary vocal expression: in other words, the body can be triggered to speak automatically. As we saw in Hazlitt's definition of poetry, discussed in Chapter Two, the self-sympathetic body produces vocal expression as the result of "involuntary movement" (Hazlitt V: 1); similarly, in Victorian physiology, "whatever excites that part of the brain where the nerves of speech take their origin, or influences the secretions of these nerves themselves, will produce a corresponding effect on the functions of the larynx" (Tod 140). Language, according to these early scientists, resonates simultaneously (and self-sympathetically) in the brain and in the larynx, bringing words to vibrate involuntarily in the vocal organs.

Later Victorian physiologists likewise argued that language participates in a system of involuntary response. Henry Maudsley, in *Body and Mind* (1870), asserts: "Speak the word, and the idea of which it is the expression is aroused, though it was not in the mind previously" (27). Even without conscious thought, the mind is automatically influenced by listening to spoken language. But, as Maudsley goes on to explain, this is a reciprocal relationship:

> Most if not all men, when thinking, repeat internally, whisper to them-
> selves, as it were, what they are thinking about; and persons of dull and
> feeble intelligence cannot comprehend what they read, or what is sometimes
> said to them, without calling the actual movement to their aid, and repeat-
> ing the words in a whisper aloud. (27)

Like Garrett Stewart's theory of "evocalization" (*Reading* 3), Maudsley's physiology of speech suggests that the organs of sound are activated even in silent reading. Even unspoken words vibrate unvoiced in the vocal organs, and written language comes to sound in the mouth, not in the ear: it is there that the automatic activation of sound takes place. And this auto-matic activation operates in listening as well as reading, for even merely hearing "what is sometimes said" can similarly activate the vocal organs. The process of reading – and, what is more, the process of listening – can provoke involuntary vocalization, a kind of repetitive imitation that brings words to life in the mouth.

The most interesting implication of Maudsley's assertion, then, is not merely that language can prompt involuntary thought or even involuntary expression, but rather that heard language can replicate itself in the body to produce vocal language. As we've seen, the mouth and the ear operate in self-sympathy, receiving and (involuntarily) reproducing sound; they appear as a double-acting orifice, a physiological playback system. But at times this model, taken to its extreme incarnation, suggests something even more radical: that the mouth alone is a double-acting orifice, receiving and replicating sounds in a physiological playback system that bypasses the mind and the ear simultaneously: that we listen, as it were, with the mouth. "In acquiring associations of Sounds, we have to encounter the supplanting tendency of the voice," Bain writes; "For while intently listening to a speech, we are liable to follow the speaker with a suppressed articulation of our own, whereby we take the train of words into a vocal embrace, as well as receive it passively on the sense of hearing" (*Senses* 352–353). Bain's "vocal embrace" illustrates the way in which heard language can be seen to fall directly into the mouth, as well as into the ear, in the act of listening; aurality is so intimately linked with orality that the two orifices, mouth and ear, act more or less simultaneously. At times the mouth appears to function as a receiver of speech, like the ear, at the same time that it is an active producer of it.

In the act of reading aloud, this doubled function of the mouth – as both receiver and reproducer – plays a prominent role in mediating the speaker's relationship to the language she speaks. Bain writes: "Cadence, although primarily a spoken effect, is transparent through written composition. In pronouncing the language of Johnson or of Milton, we fall into a distinct strain; this, too, we can acquire and impress upon compositions of our own. We naturally drink in such cadences as are most suitable to the natural march of our own vocal organs" (*Senses* 438). While reading aloud would seem to necessarily depend upon the eyes – the organ through which the reader receives the text – Bain suggests that the sound of language, its "spoken effect," is taken in through the mouth: we naturally drink it in. Like the listener, the reader receives his words in his mouth even as he produces them. If the practice of reading aloud is understood, then, to build a unified listening community out of an assemblage of different listeners, it may also be understood implicitly to create a similarly unified body of speakers who, like the reader, "drink in" spoken language and simultaneously reproduce it.

By presenting the mouth as dependent upon the ear, Victorian physiologists depict voice – and the mouth – as surprisingly complex. It is at once active and passive; sound originates there, and yet at the same time it is the site for involuntary reproduction of sound. As such, spoken sound depends on heard sound, and heard sound can automatically become spoken sound via the self-sympathetic system of the listening body. The physiology of listening suggests that voice is imitative, communal, self-replicating. In dictating to an audience, a reader-aloud does not merely hope to control the way the words fall on their ears: by creating one body of listeners, a reader-aloud may also bring his audience to speak in one voice. If ears dictate mouths, then a reader-aloud possesses an extraordinary power: he possesses the powers of his listeners' speech organs, inhabits their mouths, brings texts alive there.

The "Morte d'Arthur" in 1842: Voice and Resurrection

Bain's "vocal embrace" – the palpability of heard or read language in the mouth – brings us back to the "Morte d'Arthur" and its framing scene of reading aloud. Tennyson's poetry is famously mouthy.[11] Edward FitzGerald, in an 1835 letter to Tennyson, commented on the tangible vocality of his early Arthurian poem: "The 'Morte d'Arthur' has been much in my mouth: audibly: round Warwick" (*Memoir* I: 156). FitzGerald's evocative remark recalls the mnemonic autonomy of the "striking passage" discussed in Chapter One, which turned the bodies of its readers into media for self-replication, "start[ing] up anew in their minds at different times" (Coleridge, *Biographia* II:106). But according to FitzGerald, it's not in the mind that his poetry circulates, unbidden: the autonomous poem bypasses memory and takes up physical, palpable residence in the mouth of its readers. It has presence and location – Warwick, in this case – and it also has sound: it is audible. The wonderful juxtaposition of "mouth" (which we associate with speaking) and "audible" (which, obviously, switches the focus from speaker and source to listener and receiver) suggests that FitzGerald is listening to Tennyson's words in his mouth rather than his ears.

This provocative ambiguity about the site of poetic reception and production is, I think, central to the project of Tennyson's poem. As Herbert Tucker has argued, the subject of the "Morte d'Arthur" itself is "cultural transmission, the handing on or handing over of a communal ideal whose very essence is communication" (*Tennyson* 318): King Arthur and Sir Bedivere engaged in a struggle over the best way to ensure the faithful transmission of Arthur's legend. Tennyson's depiction of reading aloud – the transformation of written language not merely into speech (wherein the focus is on the speaker) but into heard language, which itself can provoke involuntary speech (wherein the focus is on the listener) – is, I believe, central to this question. In the exchange that follows between Arthur and Bedivere, Tennyson prioritizes listening over looking, imagining an ideal audience of listeners – listeners who are then enlisted into the poem's system of reproduction. A now familiar reading of the poem notes that its basic action traces the tension between material and immaterial memory: following the final battle with Modred in Lyonnesse, the wounded Arthur instructs his last remaining knight to dispose of his sword, Excalibur; but Bedivere, hoping to maintain a visible and material relic of his lord, fails to follow the king's orders. Allison Adler Kroll argues that this conflict represents a debate about "whether we must maintain physical contact with the past – to preserve its material traces, in other words – or whether the imaginative realms of poetry, myth, and legend provide a more effective means to conserving cultural memory" (461). Yet this account overlooks the fact that, in Tennyson's scenario, the communication of poetry and legend is not merely imaginative but also material. Everard Hall's rescued paper manuscript, and the poet's performing body, act as the media necessary for the poem's conservation and transmission. Likewise, in the "Morte" itself, the central struggle is not just about the tension between material relic and immaterial memory. Bedivere longs to keep the sword, to be sure, and Arthur wants him to cast it away; but Arthur's commands do not merely promote the immaterial at the expense of the material. Instead, they instruct Bedivere in the materiality of communication – its physical medium – which relies on the body: its eyes, ears, and mouth. One might not think this worth attending to, had not Tennyson himself (as we have seen) made much of it. The tension does not just concern the relation between materiality and immateriality; it concerns the relation between the audience and the legend itself. What, in other words, is the best medium through which to preserve and communicate the memory of Arthur?

The phrasing of Arthur's commands, as well as Bedivere's responses, depicts a struggle between two methods of communication – between two physical senses, in fact. Bedivere insists repeatedly that material proof is necessarily visual and therefore relies on the eyes; Arthur, on the other hand, is interested in promoting a culture of the mouth, of listening and, eventually, speaking. When the dying king first instructs the knight to dispose of his sword, he commands Bedivere to turn vision into language by reporting on what he has seen: "take Excalibur, / And fling him far into the middle mere: / Watch what thou seëst, and lightly bring me word" (34–38). Sight must become speech. For Bedivere, on the other hand, vision is privileged for its own sake, and it is to this sense that he hopes to entrust the legend of Arthur. Distracted by the beauty of Excalibur, he is unable to fling the brand into the mere: "For all the haft twinkled with diamond sparks, / Myriads of topaz-lights, and jacinth-work / Of subtlest jewelry" (55–58). Bedivere stands "dazzled"; the ornate visibility of Excalibur "divides the mind" of the knight, until "at the last it seem'd / Better to leave Excalibur concealed / There in the many-knotted water-flags" (61–63). Bedivere justifies his treason by asserting that he is preserving Arthur's material legacy:

> "And if indeed I cast the brand away,
> Surely such a precious thing, one worthy note,
> Should thus be lost for ever from the earth,
> Which might have pleased the eyes of many men.
>
> . . .
> What record, or what relic of my lord
> Should be to aftertime, but empty breath
> And rumours of a doubt?" (256–268)

Unwilling to trust to descriptive language – "empty breath" – Bedivere is thus unable to fulfill Arthur's command. Instead, he hopes to retain not merely material proof but visual proof, a relic that would please the eyes.[12]

Arthur, on the other hand, insists that breath itself is the proper medium to preserve his legacy: "let thy voice / Rise like a fountain for me night and day" (248–49). Sound and voice, for Arthur, are as communicative as Bedivere hopes his visual relic would be.

But Arthur's promotion of sound over vision privileges aurality as well as orality. Bedivere makes a second attempt to discard Excalibur, which similarly ends in deception; but the erring knight returns to the lake yet again, and on this third and final occasion he succeeds: "Sir King, I closed mine eyelids, lest the gems / Should blind my purpose" (152–153).[13] When Bedivere closes his eyes, he enables himself to dispose of the sword; in doing so he surrenders to Arthur's doctrine of sound. Indeed, by closing his eyes and listening, Bedivere becomes the best medium for the transmission of poetry. Not only does he successfully cast the brand into the lake, but he becomes a conduit for language, a mouth that does not produce but in fact *re*produces speech: for at this point in the poem, there occurs what Tucker calls "a little miracle of narration" (*Tennyson* 334). As Bedivere casts Excalibur into the lake, the narrator tells us:

> But ere he dipt the surface, rose an arm
> Clothed in white samite, mystic, wonderful,
> And caught him by the hilt, and brandish'd him
> Three times, and drew him under in the mere.   (143–146)

When Bedivere describes the event to Arthur, he repeats almost exactly the language of the narrator's previous description:

> "But when I look'd again, behold an arm,
> Clothed in white samite, mystic, wonderful,
> That caught him by the hilt, and brandish'd him
> Three times, and drew him under in the mere."   (158–161)

Once Bedivere closes his eyes, he is no longer the unambiguous source of his own speech. The narrator's words are in Bedivere's mouth, now; in place of the "empty breath" that Bedivere so feared, his breath is filled – filled, in fact, with language that is not his own. Listening, it seems, changes him: in listening he cedes control of his own language to the narrator. Even when he opens his eyes again, returning to the world of vision, his language betrays the fact that his speech is not a first-person account: "behold" is imperative, an instruction to the listener rather than a statement of his own experience. By closing his eyes, he has become a mouthpiece for the narrator of the poem. The effect is one of doubled voice, of repetitive language that expands beyond the individual perspective of the knight. It is as if Bedivere, having learned to listen, can now chime in with the narrator, can speak in chorus with Everard Hall.[14]

Indeed, the poem does not leave us with Bedivere but returns us to the scene of Hall's reading-aloud: with the passing of Arthur, Tennyson pulls us out of the medieval past and deposits us again by the Christmas hearth, where the narrator and his friends have just finished listening to Hall's performance. Back in the frame narrative of "The Epic," though, the logic of vocal repetition continues to resonate throughout the conclusion of the poem. Its final stanzas depict a dream sequence in which voice expands through a community, creating a chorus of repetitive speech. That night, the narrator dreams that he "waited with a crowd" for Arthur's return (292):

> There came a bark that, blowing forward, bore
> King Arthur, like a modern gentleman
> Of stateliest port; and all the people cried,
> "Arthur is come again: he cannot die."
> Then those that stood upon the hills behind
> Repeated—"Come again, and thrice as fair;"
> And, further inland, voices echoed—"Come
> With all good things, and war shall be no more."
> At this a hundred bells began to peal.   (293–301)

Everard Hall's reading has enacted a resurrection, bringing Arthur to life again as a "modern gentleman." He is not lost on the page but resurrected in voice, and – as in the "Morte" itself – this act prompts a series of expanding vocal repetitions. Voices "repeat" from the hills; they "echo" further inland. The echoes and repetitions build on each other, resounding through the masses. Underscoring the communal nature of Tennyson's vision of reading aloud, the people cry with one voice; the same words emerge from many bodies. And the embodied speech that emerges depicts vocal repetition as alive and efficacious.[15] By imagining written poetry as the relic, the almost-forgotten – and heard poetry, in turn, as the living, modern form of poetry – Tennyson imagines a communicative poetics that moves mass audiences to speak together. As FitzGerald's comment suggests, to interact with a poem is not to have it in your ear but in your mouth.

Tennyson was not the only writer, of course, to depict reading aloud as a form of resurrection. A. J. D. D'Orsey, in an essay on "The Art of Reading Aloud" for *Victoria Magazine* in 1871, argues similarly for reading aloud as a form of textual resurrection: "A book contains the thoughts, sentiments and feelings of the author, an author, it may be, who has long passed away, or who is still amongst us, but that book in itself is practically dead. It is the reader who makes it live" (151–152). Tennyson's "Morte" seems to share this hopeful attitude toward the act of reading. In 1842, the comforting mechanisms of the human body, its material susceptibility to and reproduction of heard sounds, allow it to act as a method of communication and even resurrection. Arthur instructs Bedivere to trust to ears and mouths; and Everard Hall demonstrates how voice may spring from the page even in the absence of original sound. Moreover, in Tennyson's Arthurian doctrine of vocal repetition, the ear dictates all: not only does it triumph over the "dazzled" eye, but it commands the mouth, prompting the resurrection of heard speech within the listener's own larynx, bringing forth words that are not his own, words that fall upon his ear and yet resonate again, outward, from his mouth. It is not necessarily speech that resurrects Arthur, but listening.

"The Passing of Arthur" in 1869: Postmortem Voice

In many ways, the "Morte d'Arthur" depicts what Friedrich Kittler described as the discourse network of "alphabetization" that came into play around 1800 – the first tradition that, he writes, "defined writing as composition for the mouth instrument" (33). Kittler analyzes the new phonetic method by which mothers were to teach their children to read – a method that, like the one represented in the "Morte," assumes a somatic experience of language in which the production of voice is tantamount:

> The alphabet is learnable only as 'visual language' translated to 'audible language.' . . . The phonetic method culminated in the description or prescription of a new body. This body has eyes and ears only in order to be a large mouth. The mouth transforms all the letters that assault the eyes and ears into ringing sounds. This was not a new concept as regards the ear, but in relation to the eyes and letters it was a revolution. (33)

Like Tennyson's depiction of reading aloud as an ideal medium for poetry, this method of alphabetization "connected reading and writing by linking both back to a singular kind of listening" (108). But in Kittler's discourse network of 1800, both the speaking body and the originary text are ultimately effaced: "The Mother's Mouth had made speaking so easy that it could be called the representation of a representation, or the hallucination of a fixed idea" rather than a "technique of the body" or an original written or printed source (112); it became "the abyss into which everything written vanished, only to emerge as pure Spirit and Voice" (54). In Tennyson's 1842 poem, conversely, much is made of the materiality of the mouth and the manuscript. While the techniques of the "Morte" resemble Kittler's alphabetization, in that written language is imagined to transform into universal voice, for Tennyson the text and the body are always present.

I mention Kittler here because his theory of alphabetic disembodiment draws attention to one of the key features of Tennyson's earliest version of the death of Arthur: the presence of an embodied voice. When this disappears over the course of the half-century, as Tennyson revises the "Morte" into "The Passing of Arthur," poetry becomes less human, more technological, more phonographic. In 1842, Tennyson depicts orality as secondary (to use Walter Ong's term) – secondary, in fact, not only to written language but also to heard language. And in its status as secondary, it is endowed with resurrectional abilities: it uses the body's reproductive vocality to bring language to life. But as the century progresses, and as the poem itself evolves, Tennyson's depiction of poetic voice loses these abilities. The next time a version of the "Morte" appeared in print, more than a quarter-century later, it was significantly revised. In 1869 it was published for the first time as "The Passing of Arthur" in *The Holy Grail and Other Poems*, along with "The Coming of Arthur," "The Holy Grail," and "Pelleas and Ettarre."[16] In this new position the "Passing" is stripped of its frame narrative – it is no longer read aloud – and as such it would seem to lose its inherent vocality. Its narrator has no body, no mouth. And yet, in the "Passing," voice continues to self-replicate, in increasingly uncanny ways.

In 1869, Tennyson substitutes for the fully embodied, "deep-chested" Everard Hall a ghostly, disembodied Bedivere as the story's oral source. The poem's first stanza serves as a subtitle:

> That story which the bold Sir Bedivere,
> First made and latest left of all the knights,
> Told, when the man was no more than a voice
> In the white winter of his age, to those
> With whom he dwelt, new faces, other minds.   (1–5)

What we have here is not less voice but less body, and less text: Bedivere becomes an Ossianic bard, a lost voice that circulates orally. He does not read aloud; instead, he is a storyteller, a figure whose status as pre-modern, pre-textual voice seems to preclude the negotiations between body and text that structured the "Morte." As a response to print culture in the early

decades of the Victorian era, Kreilkamp writes, "[t]he figure of the storyteller emerged as both a symptom of and an attempt at a solution for this
perception of cultural crisis: ... as a cure for dangerous speech and as
a stable source of good speech" (7). In a way, then, Tennyson's move
toward an Ossianic storyteller seems to signal a retreat from the early-
Victorian modernity that promised the resurrection of Arthur. Yet as
Kreilkamp goes on to argue, by the time the "Passing" was published,
the storyteller was neither a straightforward nor a nostalgically pre-modern
figure. Indeed, Tennyson in 1869 displays an awareness of the complex
situation of his storyteller. He disembodies Bedivere and sends him out as
a strange voice in a cold and modern world, a world that no longer contains
the promising communality of the 1830s and 1840s but that is no less
interested in grappling with the problem of its modernity. In fact,
Tennyson's phrase in 1869 – "no more than a voice" – seems to anticipate
Joseph Conrad's *Heart of Darkness* some thirty years later: there, the
narrator is "very little more than a voice" (48). Conrad's turn toward the
disembodied voice "marks a new stage in the way fiction understood its
relation to speech" (Kreilkamp 184); it establishes what Kreilkamp calls the
"phonographic logic" of turn-of-the-century fiction. But Tennyson's bodiless Bedivere suggests that poetry prefigured this changed logic, already
understood it this way. In 1842, the mechanisms of the human body
allowed poetry to engage with it as a technology of reproduction; but
Tennyson's revisions later in the century reveal his concerns about such
a technology being detached from the body. This is a new kind of
modernity, it seems, and poetry functions differently here.

   Indeed, Tennyson's move to disband the 1842 group of Christmas
listeners reflects an awareness of the changing social status of reading.
While reading aloud surely remained a communal activity, silent reading –
reading to oneself, by oneself – increasingly became a subject of concern as
the century progressed. Kelly Mays reports that, in the second half of the
century alone, periodicals published hundreds of articles debating the
dangers of this new, modern readership (165). Bedivere's isolation in his
newly uncommunal community – they remain merely "those with whom
he dwelt" – could not be further from the setting of the "Morte": compare
Everard Hall's college friends, who prize his poetry because they "loved the
man" (280) with Bedivere, surrounded by "new faces, other minds."
Whereas in mid-Victorian formulations of the storyteller the figure builds
community through orality, Bedivere's storytelling seems somehow sub-
stanceless, solitary. In doing away with reading aloud, Tennyson also does

away with the community that, in the "Morte," helped to resurrect the King.

But Tennyson does not merely disband the communal voice; he also disembodies the speaker. Compare Bedivere's bodilessness with the hyper-mediated body of Everard Hall, "mouthing out his hollow oes and aes, / Deep-chested music." Whereas Hall's voice turns his body into a kind of instrument, played by the speaker, the disembodied Bedivere is stripped of the human agency that the embodied Hall possessed. In 1842, voice was depicted as an instrument of the body – an instrument that *is* the body – with its resonating chest and lungs and its palpable, listening mouth. When Bedivere's mouth repeats the narrator's language, his repetitiveness serves as a model for a kind of vocal efficacy that consolidates a community of listeners through the medium of the body. But the Bedivere of 1869 has no body, and as such, his voice – while it may still be an instrument – is lacking the quality of human agency that made Hall's body at once an instrument and an instrumentalist. Bedivere, in other words, is merely a mouthpiece.

And this disembodied mouthpiece begins to suggest a less organic understanding of vocal production and reproduction than the one Tennyson employed in the 1842 "Morte." Indeed, while the physiological concept of voice as bodily instrument depicts a human vocalizer as the instrumentalist, it also implies that the two can be divided – that voice is somehow mechanical, an organ that can be severed from any sense of human agency. Yopie Prins makes this argument in her reading of Victorian dysprosody ("Historical" 232); similar intimations can be found in theories of vocal physiology. Even Victorian scholars of elocu-tion – the most conscious, most directed form of articulate speech – suggest that their practice relies on an understanding of the body as a mechanical instrument. Scottish elocutionist Alexander Melville Bell, father of Alexander Graham Bell and inventor of a phonographic alphabet known as "Visible Speech," writes in his *Elocutionary Manual*: "The student of Elocution, then, should be made acquainted with the instrument of speech, as an instrument, that all its parts may be under his control, as the stops, the keys, the pedals, and the bellows, are subject to the organist" (7). The elocutionist must master his own organs: but this suggests, of course, the possibility that they may in fact *not* be "under his control." For Bell, the instrument of speech is a "speaking machine" (18). For other writers, the instrument of speech can be divorced even more fully from human agency. Francois Magendie's popular *Elementary Compendium of Physiology* makes clear the ways in which any understanding of voice as an organ relies on a dehumanizing of vocality. In order to prove that the muscles of the larynx must be contracted in order to produce sound, Magendie offers the following experiment as evidence:

> If we take the trachea and larynx of an animal, or of a man, and blow air strongly into the trachea, directing it towards the larynx, there is no sound produced . . . . If, in blowing, we bring together the *arytenoid* cartilages, so that they may touch upon their internal face, a sound will be produced, something like the voice of the animal to which the larynx used in the experiment belongs. (134)

Magendie represents the organs of speech in purely mechanistic terms, a macabre Aeolian harp. The vocal instrument is played – blown into, in this case – by someone other than the owner of the instrument. Voice, here, is truly dehumanized: bodily organs are puppets to be manipulated by outside sources. Magendie goes on, even, to discuss "blowing into the trachea of a dead body" (135). In mechanizing the speech function, physiological theory also suggests that reproduced voice can coexist with death.

It is this understanding of voice as somehow postmortem that begins to take shape in Tennyson's revisions to his Arthurian epic in 1869. While his depiction of vocal reproduction in the "Morte" called into question the agency of the speaker, its version of involuntary speech – speech dictated by the ear and reproduced in the mouth – relied upon a very living human body to negotiate its self-sympathetic interactions, and it trusted that the organic mechanisms of speech and listening could bring the dead back to life. But in 1869, Tennyson's bodiless narrator does away with the body at the same time as he does away with the communal experience of reading aloud. The two go hand in hand, even; and the Bedivere of the "Passing" invokes the more mechanical and decidedly less organic understanding of voice and speech that was steadily rising to the forefront of physiology as the century progressed. Bedivere, as a voice without a body, contains the unsettling implication that his speech is reproduced without his will – that, unlike the resonating speech that resurrected Arthur, his speech may repeat while he remains dead. As in the "Morte," this is not the primary orality of Ossian; now, however, it is a kind of secondary orality divorced entirely from its living origin.

In the "Passing of Arthur," Tennyson introduces a new category of voice in place of the embodied orality of the "Morte": in 1869, voice most frequently comes from outside the body. Following the "last weird battle in the West" (6), Arthur asks Bedivere: "Hearest thou this voice that shakes the world, / And wastes the narrow realm whereon we move, / And beats upon the faces of the dead, / My dead, as tho' they had not died for me?" (115–118). Here, voice is palpable, interacting with the material world and with the human body; and yet the bodies it interacts with are dead, unable to enact the comforting reaction of listening and speaking. Voice is at once ghostly and uncannily material. Dreams, too, have voices: "fainter onward, like wild birds that change / Their season in the night and wail their way / From cloud to cloud, down the long wind the dream / Shrill'd" (15–18). But this voice is equated with the sounds of far-off animals rather than with any human presence. Similarly, Arthur asks whether the dream voice may in fact have come from the empty landscape itself: "doth all that haunts the waste and wild / Mourn, knowing it will go along with me?" (25–26). Sound and voice resonate throughout the "Passing," but they are removed from the realm of the human body.

As voice becomes more external, it also becomes more entwined with death. Voice in the "Passing" operates despite an absence of bodies, an absence of the organic and material processes that produced the resurrectional voice of the "Morte." Here, the dead remain dead, although they continue to speak. In the prelude to the battle, the ghost of Gawain visits Arthur in the form of another disembodied voice:

> There came on Arthur sleeping, Gawain kill'd
> In Lancelot's war, the ghost of Gawain blown
> Along a wandering wind, and past his ear
> Went shrilling, "Hollow, hollow all delight!
> Hail, King! to-morrow thou shalt pass away.
> Farewell! there is an isle of rest for thee.
> And I am blown along a wandering wind,
> And hollow, hollow, hollow, all delight." (7–14)

Just as Bedivere was taught, in the "Morte," to repeat the narrator's exact language in his own mouth, Gawain's ghost repeats the narrated description of his own bodiless passivity: "I am blown along a wandering wind." But this repetition resurrects nothing: poetic language, which in this scenario comes from a narratorial voice without a body, is reproduced in another voice without a body. It comes from death, and it tells of death. It is, in a way, immortal, in that it does not disappear with death; but this form of immortality fails to promise the resurrection we see at the end of the "Morte." Instead, it is stuck forever in the realm of the disembodied: "rolling far along the gloomy shores / The voice of days of old and days to be" (110–111). Where the "Morte" offered vocal repetition as a kind of resurrection – a resurrection of words on the page, of sounds in the ear, even of mythology itself – in the "Passing" vocal repetition occurs without the body, taking on an otherworldly and impalpable immortality.

In the 1869 "Passing," this sense of impalpability proliferates. The other major change Tennyson made in converting the "Morte" to the "Passing" comes at the end of the poem, and it, too, depicts voice as echoing outside of the realm of human agency and corporeality. In 1842, Everard Hall's poem concludes with a simple statement of sound passing away: "And on the mere the wailing died away" (272). In this version of Arthur's death, sound dies alongside the king; but in the narrator's dream that follows in the final stanzas of the frame poem, sound – like Arthur himself – is resurrected by the community of voices that rings in the Christmas Day. In 1869, the after-effects of voice are strikingly different. The sound that carries Arthur to Avilion still passes away – "And on the mere the wailing died away" (416) – but the poem does not end there. In the added stanzas that follow, voice remains in the realm of the ghostly. What is more, it becomes inaudible:

> Then from the dawn it seem'd there came, but faint
> As from beyond the limit of the world,
> Like the last echo born of a great cry,
> Sounds, as if some fair city were one voice
> Around a king returning from his wars.   (428–432)

What in 1842 was a return of Arthur to the present day is displaced to the fairy-realm of Avilion; whereas, in the "Epic," the "fair city" with "one voice" is the narrator's present-day England, in the "Passing" the communal voice remains conditional, inaccessible, disembodied. Even Bedivere cannot actually hear the communal voice: it merely "seem'd" to come to him, modified by so many qualifiers as to rob the experience of any sensate solidity. Moreover, the communal voice – which in fact occurs only "as if" it were a communal voice – is at once otherworldly ("as from beyond the limit of the world") and unoriginal ("like the last echo"). The disembodied voice celebrates the return of Arthur, but it's a return to a world of echoing absence rather than palpable presence.

Bedivere, too, functions oddly like an echo in the final stanzas of the 1869 "Passing." Tennyson follows the final line of the "Morte" – "And on the mere the wailing died away" – with a stanza in which Bedivere continues to bemoan the loss of Arthur:

> At length he groan'd, and turning slowly clomb
> The last hard footstep of that iron crag;
> Thence mark'd the black hull moving yet, and cried,

> "He passes to be King among the dead,
> And after healing of his grievous wound
> He comes again"   (417–422)

The slant rhyme of "groan'd" and "clomb" in the first line signals a kind of internal repetition that in fact structures the entire stanza, which is riddled with repeated language. Bedivere seems to be constructing his own speech, vocalizing his own interpretation of the scene he witnesses; and yet his lines are direct repetitions of earlier phrases in the poem. "He passes to be King among the dead," in line 420, restates Arthur's own assessment of his ghostly regency in line 122: "Behold, I seem but King among the dead." Likewise, Bedivere in line 421 repeats Arthur in line 408, speaking of Avilion: "Where I will heal me of my grievous wound." Bedivere, as a voice without a body, is reproducing the speech of another lost body – the possibly dead Arthur, whose speech lives on, uncannily, in the mouthpiece of his knight. And unlike his repetition of the narrator's description of Excalibur's brandishment – no longer quite a miracle, given that he is now the narrator of the poem – his repetition here is fragmented, a compilation of sound bites.

In his re-envisioning of Arthur's relationship to death, speech, and media, Tennyson moves in 1869 toward an understanding of voice as an unwilled instrument of repetition. The beautifully mysterious yet palpable translation of heard words into spoken words – from the ear (passive yet dictatorial) into the mouth (active yet subservient) – is lost when Bedivere is deprived of his body. At the same time, the removal of this underlying emphasis on the human body provokes in its place a much more mechanistic repetitiveness. In a way, Tennyson is imagining a kind of prephonographic voice – speech that replicates itself via mouth and ear and yet lacks the unifying, resurrectional power of the embodied voice. In many ways this transition toward disembodiment has its roots in the vocal repetition of the "Morte." In written poetry, as Prins argues, there is no original voice: even if the poet imagines a poem read in a certain voice, with certain accents or in a certain tone, the letters on the page do not necessarily retain any trace of that sound. But, in nineteenth-century theories of the body, the reading body (even the silently reading body) may reproduce traces of voice, or even real voice, in the absence of actual sound. In this way, Tennyson imagines the seemingly passive body – the body that receives poetry on its eyes or in its ears – as able to actively reproduce it in its mouth. In doing so he deprivileges the source of sound in favor of its reproduction. And, as I argued above, Tennyson is not alone in this construction of voice as secondary: the physiology of speech and listening similarly depicts voice as reproducing rather than originating sound. This move, however, is also deeply destabilizing, for detaching sound from its original source invites disembodiment. For Prins, this is inherent in the poetry of print culture: "Victorian poems also worked as a mechanism for the disembodiment of voice, and with similar contradictory effects: sometimes invoking and evoking the spoken word, but also revoking it" ("Voice" 44). Without the living mouth, the reproductive technology of poetry renders voice immortal, repetitive, transferable – but no longer entirely human.

"The Passing of Arthur" in 1873: Phonographic Voice

While phonography represented the ability to capture, preserve, and resurrect voice, it simultaneously threatened it with death. A comment in *Scientific American* from 1877 suggests that the phonograph could resurrect voice: "Speech has become, as it were, immortal" (qtd. in Kreilkamp 185). However, once sound was removed from the realm of the body, its immortality began to seem as uncanny, as unwilled, as the echoing voices of Gawain and Bedivere. Consider Horatio Nelson Powers's "The Phonograph," included in the first phonogram Edison sent to London in June of 1888: "I seize the palpitating air. I hoard / Music and Speech. All lips that breathe are mine. / ... / In me are souls embalmed. I am an ear / Flawless as truth, and truth's own tongue am I" (qtd. in Picker 117). Powers's phonograph, like the body, serves at once as receiver and reproducer of sound: an ear and a tongue, it is endowed with possessive force. Yet it also embalms the soul, the very life behind speech. Its reproduced speech is automatic and ghostly, divorced from the source of the living body.

While Edison's phonograph was not invented until 1877, historians and critics such as Kreilkamp, Rée, John Picker, Steven Connor, and Lisa Gitelman have argued for the importance of phonography to the nineteenth century at large. Early attempts at creating a "talking machine" ranged from illusions and magic tricks (like the mid-century "Invisible Girl," which appeared to be a talking balloon) to 1848's "Euphonia," an automaton head with grotesquely visual speech organs, and even to the 1857 "phonoautograph," which recorded sound as visual patterns using a stylus attached to a vibrating membrane (see Connor 350–356). Moreover, the century saw a growing interest in technologies of sound reproduction that relied on writing as a form of both transcription and playback: Isaac Pitman's 1837 shorthand system, "phonography," was the precursor to more elaborate phonetic alphabets such as William Henry Henslow's "Phonarthon" (1840) and Alexander Melville Bell's "Visible Speech" (1868). Indeed, as Gitelman argues, Edison's phonograph was conceived as "an invention that would revolutionize print" – "a better, more immediate means of stenography" that would "objectively and materially realize the author's voice." ("Souvenir" 157, 159). Like stenography, phonography was meant to negotiate the reproduction of sound in print culture.

Moreover, phonography realizes the physiological model of the mouth as a double organ. Like the physiology of speech, phonography relies on an understanding of the intimate relationship between the mouth and the ear, the "vocal embrace" by which the mouth functions at once as receiver and reproducer of sounds. In 1878, as a marketing strategy for the newly released phonograph, Edison's agents and associates put on public exhibitions demonstrating the telephone and the phonograph together; they advertised that "Recitations, Conversational remarks, Songs (with words), Cornet Solos, Animal Mimicry, Laughter, Coughing, etc., etc.," would be "delivered *into the mouth* of the machine, and subsequently reproduced" (qtd. in Gitelman, "Souvenir" 161, emphasis mine).[17] The invention of the telephone, similarly, depended on an automatic interaction between the reception and the production of speech. Connor writes: "For this to happen, voice would need to be thought of both as an input and as an output. The most important part of this process was the adding of some process of automatic hearing to automatic speech" (356). Alexander Graham Bell experimented with such an automatically reversible machine:

> At one end of the process, the diaphragm vibrating in response to the source sound was acting as a kind of ear. At the output end, the diaphragm made to vibrate in an exactly corresponding fashion by the conversion of the electrical fluctuations back into movements, was being made to 'speak.' ... [It was made to] act as both ear and mouth. When you spoke to it, it listened; when you listened to it, it spoke. In the phonograph, the addition of the prosthetic horn, which acted both as the gatherer and the amplifier of sound reinforced this reversibility. (Connor 357)

Phonography can thus be seen as a natural development of the physiological understanding of the human speaking apparatus.

In this way, phonography's system for vocal reproduction is similar to poetry's. Connor notes that stenographic and phonographic "systems for representing sounds moved in two directions at once, out from and back into the body; they removed speech from the actual and particular human body, but tabulated it in ways that allowed its near-automatic imitation and reproduction in other bodies" (348). Connor's description helps us to see how poetry, too, can be seen as an inherently phonographic technology. Poetry – to whatever extent its investment in sound is greater than that of prose – is a way of hearing with the mouth rather than the ear, a way of taking something silent and reproducing it in other mouths. In 1842, Tennyson was invested in exploring the body's ability to reproduce heard sound as spoken sound, and in reading aloud as a medium for transmitting and reproducing poetry; in 1869, and even more in 1873, his interest turns toward phonography's ability to reproduce sound without the body and its implications for poetry as a medium for preserving voice. As the century leans toward the impending invention of Edison's phonograph, in other words, the problem of the disembodied and endlessly reproducible voice comes to figure prominently in Tennyson's revisions to his Arthurian epic.

In 1873, when the complete series of poems were finally published together as *The Idylls of the King* (volumes five and six Tennyson's *Works* of that year, which included for the first time "The Last Tournament"), "The Passing of Arthur" was revised yet again. And here, to my mind, Tennyson makes his most interesting alteration – an alteration that brings the problem of repetition down to the level of the poetic line. At the very end of the poem, he again modifies the stanzas following the line that concluded Everard Hall's poem in 1842: "And on the mere the wailing died away." But now, before continuing to the 1869 addition – the stanza that has Bedivere slowly turning and climbing the "last hard footstep of that iron crag" – Tennyson inserts another passage:

> But when that moan had past for evermore,
> The stillness of the dead world's winter dawn
> Amazed him, and he groan'd, "The King is gone."
> And therewithal came on him the weird rhyme,
> "From the great deep to the great deep he goes."
> Whereat he slowly turn'd and slowly clomb
> The last hard footstep of that iron crag   (441–447)

Left alone in silence, Bedivere is suddenly struck by a striking passage – a line of poetry that arises spontaneously in the mind, unbidden and decontextualized.

"From the great deep to the great deep he goes": Bedivere's "weird rhyme" could not have so arisen in the "Morte," for it is evidence of the poem's new status as the conclusion of a series. To the reader of the complete *Idylls*, Bedivere's striking passage is the third instantiation of the line. It is also the most incomplete, the most isolated. The line occurs for the first time in the first poem of the *Idylls*, "The Coming of Arthur," as part of Queen Bellicent's narration of the mystery surrounding her brother Arthur's birth. Confronted with three conflicting stories of Arthur's origin – born the posthumous son of Duke Gorlois; the result of King Uther's rape of Gorlois's wife, Ygerne; or, most mysteriously, snatched from the ocean by the wizard Merlin – King Leodogran asks Bellicent which story contains the truth. Bellicent responds by reciting the answer given to her by Merlin when, years ago, she asked him the same question. In the "riddling triplets of old time" (401), she says, Merlin sang to her: "Rain, sun, and rain! and the free blossom blows: / Sun, rain, and sun! and where is he who knows? / From the great deep to the great deep he goes" (408–410). Merlin's riddling triplet makes only this one appearance in the first collection of the *Idylls*. But in 1873, when "The Last Tournament" is inserted into the cycle, it appears again, this time broken into a couplet. Guinevere, looking out of a window,

> Watch'd her lord pass, and knew not that she sigh'd.
> Then ran across her memory the strange rhyme
> Of bygone Merlin: "Where is he who knows?
> From the great deep to the great deep he goes." (130–133)

In "The Last Tournament" Merlin's triplet loses one of its lines. It still retains its rhyme – which makes up part of its sense of poetic context – but it has become isolated from its original status as a triplet. And when it finally appears in the 1873 "Passing," it loses even its rhyming phrase ("Where is he who knows?"). The "weird rhyme" that arises in Bedivere's mind as he watches the King's barge depart is only one line, one isolated and decontextualized phrase.

Kreilkamp has traced the development of this kind of detached and replicable unit of language to Conrad's *Heart of Darkness*, wherein the repeated words "the horror! the horror!" announce "the dawning of an awareness that language might function with no clear connection to its human source" by emphasizing its "quotability," its "status as autonomous, detachable phonemes" (179). As I argued in Chapter One, print itself had a similar effect on language, giving the autonomous excerpt free rein to replicate itself mnemonically. The discourses of phonography also worked to reconfigure the physiological theory of memory. Rather than relying on the metaphors of print employed early in the century, later

Victorian models of memory enlist new metaphors of sound reproduction; Carpenter, for example, refers to memory as the "recording process" of the cerebrum (*Principles* 439). What is more, the phonographic logic of the "Passing"'s striking passage insists on a kind of self-excerptability that takes as its point of origin its own detachable sourcelessness. Merlin's riddling triplet highlights its own distance from actual voice. The remembered passage, supposedly the most oral, is in fact hard to put into the mnemonic lilt of scanned verse. Like that oft-memorized, oft-recited Hemans poem "The Boy Stood on the Burning Deck" – which, as Catherine Robson points out, actually resists the sing-song metrics it is most famous for ("Standing" 159) – Bedivere's "weird rhyme" catches on the tongue. The accented feet of the poem's meter fall to pieces here, landing awkwardly on articles: "From *the* great *deep* to *the* great *deep* he *goes*." Or, emphasizing the prepositions to accentuate Arthur's cyclical movement, we end up with this: "*From* the great deep *to* the great deep," with "he *goes*" hanging on the end in an uncomfortable iamb. The best phrasing, perhaps, breaks the line into double iambs, leaving the accents to fall on the line's internal repetition: "From the *great deep* to the *great deep* he goes." This phrasing not only turns the speaker into a stuck record; it also draws attention to the repeated clause's subtle ambiguity about its grammatical subject. "Deep," to be sure, stands for the seas; but another reading of the line is possible, one in which "great" and "deep" are both adjectives, empty without the noun they modify. This nominal emptiness – the great deep what? – hints at Arthur's missing source, and also to the missing source of the line itself. Like Arthur, whose birth and parentage remains a mystery, Merlin's original "riddling triplet" has become detached from any originary source, traveling by repetition from mind to mind and mouth to mouth, in its transit bearing very little relation to original voice.

Despite what might seem to be a retreat from the modern multimedia of the "Morte" – a movement back toward the nostalgic orality of Ossian – Tennyson's final incarnation of the death of Arthur invokes a surprisingly mechanical (and surprisingly modern) understanding of voice and of voice's relationship to poetry. The disembodied detachability of the phonographic striking passage has its own power, although it is not the hopeful humanity of the "Morte"'s vocal resurrection. In "The Passing of Arthur," voice is dead and yet deathless; and poetry, as a technology of vocal reproduction, becomes disembodied and autonomous. Such disembodiment, though, grows out of the very bodily structures that posit voice as a reproducer of sound, rather than a source. The autonomous, detachable repetition of the "Passing"'s striking passages is built upon the self-sympathetic mediacy of the speaking/listening body, which deprivileges the source of sound in favor of its reproduction. Tennyson's evolving depictions of voice in his many deaths of Arthur give us purchase on poetry's own phonographic logic: his striking passages operate not on the logic of print but rather on the logic of embodied sound disconnected from its source. Reading poetry, Tennyson suggests, is always a way of listening with the mouth. But as the century wears on, and as voice comes to be seen increasingly as virtual, what the "Passing" registers is a growing awareness of poetry's own autonomous mediacy. Rather than reproducing speech, the striking passages of the "Passing" reproduce themselves; and they do so in ways that emphasize the self-excerptability of mediated language. In 1842, Tennyson evoked the intimate connection between ear and mouth, the process by which words, heard, find their way into the mouth of the listener. But by 1873, it seems, voice can self-replicate mechanically; poetry, too, can arise out of thin air.

CHAPTER 4

Poetic Afterlives
Automatic Writing and the Mechanics of Quotation

In the discourse of late-nineteenth-century spiritualism, seemingly immaterial long-distance communication technologies often depend upon the
very materials they aspire to transcend, from hands to pens to words
themselves. W. T. Stead, in 1892, offered one of the first inklings of his
impending conversion to spiritualism by musing, "I wonder how many of
the half million readers whose eyes may fall upon this page are aware that if
you let your mind be quite passive, your hand will in a great number of
cases begin to write of itself?" (44). One of the most memorable literary
mediums of the nineteenth century, Robert Browning's Mr. Sludge, poses
the question a different way: "pens, good Lord, / Who knows if you drive
them or they drive you?" ("Mr. Sludge, 'The Medium'" 196–197). Sludge,
sensitive to the fine line between linguistic craft and inspiration, between
mystery and machination, suggests that what Stead sees in automatism
may be inherent in writing itself. As he explains, his sham craft is

> not so very false, as falsehood goes,
> The spinning out and drawing fine, you know,—
> Really mere novel-writing of a sort,
> Acting, or improvising, make-believe,
> Surely not downright cheatery   (425–429)

As he later says, his lies are really no worse than those of poets, who sing of
Greeks that never were in a Troy that never was (1436–1437). Like theirs, his
craft traffics in "helpful lies" (1445), creating rather than channeling spiritual messages. He makes things up, and he gloats about it. Performing as
a medium is, according to Sludge, an act not unlike literary production –
an act in which pretending to be out of your own control is actually a state
of perfect mastery.

But the spontaneous production of poetry is another matter entirely.
There are moments in Browning's poem when this speaker, a master of
blank verse, seems to lose control of his words:

> With Sludge it's too absurd? *Fine, draw the line*
> *Somewhere, but, sir, your somewhere is not mine!*
>
> Bless us, I'm turning poet! It's time to end.   (1182–1184)

And, later in the poem:

> What, sir? You won't shake hands? "Because I cheat!"
> "You've found me out in cheating!" That's enough
> To make an apostle swear! Why, when I cheat,
> *Mean to cheat, do cheat, and am caught in the act,*
> *Are you, or, rather, am I sure o' the fact?*
> (There's verse again, but I'm inspired somehow.)   (1280–1285)

Sludge is startled by his own language, shocked to be speaking in rhyme. (He would be even more shocked to know he was speaking in italics!) Browning's crafty speaker seems to have lost control over his words at the very moment that they draw attention to their own materiality, and we – reading and recognizing his italicized couplets even before he does – gain an interpretive edge. As in the Romantic case of the striking passage, something about the fragmented unit of material poetry disrupts his speech, freeing language to act on him and through him. Sludge, the fraud, has become a true medium.

Sludge's model of autonomous poetry – poetry that operates outside of individual control, poetry that turns bodies into mediums – is central, I've been arguing, to nineteenth-century poetics. And nowhere is this more evident than in the turn-of-the-century spiritualist practice of automatic writing. In fact, this peculiar phenomenon is where a study of poetry and automatism might be expected to begin. But as I hope I've shown, poetry had been entangled with the automatic body for nearly a century by the time the spiritualist movement enlisted the specific practice of automatic writing in its quest to investigate the afterlife. I see this phenomenon as the natural extension of the nineteenth-century tradition of autopoetics. This means I'm reading against a longstanding critical tradition that identifies in automatic writing the defining characteristics of modernism – in particular, a focus on the material nature of communication, especially its fragmentation and dissemination.[1] It should be clear by now that my project here resists such periodization: in tracing the history of autopoetics, I've argued throughout that material language and technologies of transmission are central to nineteenth-century Britain's understanding of the relationship between bodies and media. I am not alone in attempting to reclaim the nineteenth-century roots of automatic writing. Spiritualism's recent critical renaissance has allowed scholars of Victorian Britain to recenter this seemingly marginal and pseudoscientific practice within its contemporary media moment, teasing out its deep ties to Victorian psychology as well as technological innovations such as wireless telegraphy, phonography, and telephony.[2] Much of this work focuses on the remarkable degree to which the development of spiritualist mediumship is bound up in concurrent developments in communication technologies.[3] This chapter, too, examines spiritualist automatic writing practices as a form of communication technology. Yet I have a different target in mind: the status of poetry at the turn of the century, especially in relation to what Leah Price has called "a culture of the excerpt" (5). Rather than consider automatic writing alongside any number of concurrent developments in media, I propose that poetic quotation can be seen as a medium in and of itself – one that, surprisingly, has less to say about turn-of-the-century ideas about composition than it does about turn-of-the-century ideas about reception. In other words, I want to think about what automatic writing tells us about *reading* as a material encounter with other people's words.

In reconsidering spiritualist automatic writing in light of its roots in nineteenth-century autopoetics, my goal is to uncover in this definitive late-Victorian practice a century's worth of investment in the material autonomy of language, and of the fragment of poetry in particular. Poetry has acquired, over the course of century, an uncanny and disruptive autonomy in the literary and medical imagination. At the same time, the body has increasingly come to be seen as an automatic medium for the reproduction of material (and especially poetic) language. Spiritualist automatic writing practices respond to and extend this tradition in complex ways. Indeed, despite the genealogy to which they are indebted, spiritualist automatic writing puts its own turn-of-the-century twist on the history of autopoetics. Where Romantic scientists invoked bodily automaticity to disprove evidence of the existence of ghosts, fin-de-siècle researchers aimed to do the opposite, finding that very evidence in the products of the automatic body. There are other seeming paradoxes as well. In purporting to prove definitively the ultimate survival of the "human," spiritualism turns writing bodies into machines evacuated of agency. Yet I aim to demonstrate that automatic writing practices themselves – and the texts they produce and inspire – fundamentally extend the autopoetics of material and reproducible language by reimagining the uses of fragmented quotation. In order to do so, I want to attend to what the phenomenon of spiritualist automatic writing has to say about poetry itself. Why does poetry do an especially good job of communicating with the dead? What can the phenomenon of automatic writing tell us about the status of poetry at the turn of the century, especially poetry's relationship to materiality and reproduction? And what, ultimately, is the relationship between automatic writing and automatic reading? Spiritualist automatic writing exploits and reconfigures the very terms that structured the Romantic striking passage: it turns bodies into linguistic machines for communicating from beyond the grave – but what these machines actually do, in the end, is quote already-printed poetry.

The Protoplasmic Machine: Spiritualist Automatism and Material Language

The material body plays a complex role in spiritualist automatic writing. In the late nineteenth century, researchers like Frederic W. H. Myers – one of the founding members of the Society for Psychical Research (SPR) and one of the key figures in this chapter's narrative – hoped that this still quite mysterious practice would offer proof of the mind's ability to engage in telepathic and even spiritual communication.[4] Yet automatic writing was just as often used to explore the body's own automaticity, as "a phenomenon liable to be originated in various ways in the human organism," Myers explained (Myers, "On a Telepathic" 223). As the wealth of recent scholarship on spiritualism and media has made clear, automatic writing is in itself a kind of technology, one that makes a machine of the body of the writer: as W. T. Stead explains, an automatist composes language without "any exercise of thought or will on the part of the brain" (44).

> The spiritualist theory is that the hand is taken possession of or controlled by a disembodied spirit . . . . In many cases, especially those in which the person writing is susceptible to these outside influences, the handwriting bears a curious resemblance to that of the alleged control when it was on this world, and frequently the writing will contain information not known to the writer or to any person present. (Stead 44)

Even in Stead's idealized depiction, automatic writing reveals its ties to materiality, to the physicality of mediation. That the spirit must move someone's hand – that it, in fact, has something as mundane and recognizable as handwriting – suggests that the body is an essential tool.[5] Famed medium Hester Travers Smith – who channeled (among other things) an entire play written by the departed spirit of Oscar Wilde – explained in her autobiography the extent to which a controlling spirit was made to work with the very material particulars of the automatist: "external influences of some nature work through us, using our senses, eyes, ears, brains, etc., their messages, however, being highly colored by the personalities of their mediums" (*Voices* 5). Travers Smith's scripts contain many messages from spirits commenting on the varying degrees of sensitivity of their medium's brain and body. Wilde himself (or, rather, his spirit) compares Travers Smith to that favorite image of Romantic passivity, the Æolian harp: "I found you less sensitive to my ideas than before, but even when you are tired you are a perfect Æolian lyre that can record me as I think" (*Psychic* 640). But much more common is a less Romantic image of the automatist not as inspired lyre but as bodily tool. One psychic researcher went so far as to refer to one of the celebrated automatists of the SPR's experiments, Leonora Piper, as a "delicate protoplasmic machine" (Hodgson 357).[6]

Despite much of its own rhetoric, then, the Victorian automatist was hardly an example of spiritual transcendence of the body. Automatic writing relied entirely on the body of the writer, and even on the bodily specificities of each particular automatist. The pages of the *Proceedings of the Society for Psychical Research* are filled with excerpts of automatic scripts, produced by amateur mediums under experimental conditions, in which the chief subject is the relationship between automatic writing and the body of the automatist. The scripts of Alice Fleming, for example – who went by the pseudonym "Mrs. Holland" – contain frequent admonitions from the controlling spirit. "Your hand gets tired soon because it is not passive enough. Make it limp," one spirit complains; another remarks, "The pain in your shoulder is new to you, isn't it? . . . Let your hand be more flexible and the shoulder will not suffer" (Johnson, "On the Automatic" 183). Fleming's hand, writing furiously, directs itself to be limp, to be passive. When Stead wrote, then, that "if you let your mind be quite passive, your hand will in a great number of cases begin to write of itself," he is perhaps more accurate than even he knew. These hands write not merely by themselves but also *of* themselves, about themselves. And as they do so they insist, somewhat paradoxically, on their own bodily passivity.

Bodily automatism is a fraught topic within the discourse of psychical research, illustrating a deep tension between the material and the spiritual that scholars such as Pamela Thurschwell, Jill Galvan, and John Durham Peters have rightfully identified as central to the problem of spiritualist mediumship. Yet the same tension can be found in the problem of language, which is similarly cast as simultaneously material and immaterial, of the body and of the spirit. We can see this in the relationship between the spiritual medium and her external media. The most common method of automatic writing involved a medium, a pen or pencil, and paper; frequently it also employed a planchette, a small triangular plank supported by two casters, which held a pencil vertically and allowed the automatist to write with very little bodily effort. Yet increasing the medium's bodily passivity was not the only effect of the planchette: it also shielded the automatist's writing from her own eyes. This was crucial to the success of automatic writing, Myers argued: the writer's conscious self needed to be removed from her produced text. If written words fell under the writer's eye, they tended to "arrest his attention" ("On a Telepathic Explanation" 224). The writer's mind, it seems, is dangerously susceptible to what Myers depicts as the arresting visibility of words. As in the automatic writing we encountered in the Romantic physiology of hallucination – now, nearly a century later, understood to spring from the workings of the unconscious, which was a relatively new psychological term at the fin de siècle – written language has a kind of power even over its writer.

For this reason, the practice of automatic writing frequently required the automatist herself to be reading. Keeping the automatist's own brain engaged with language was, psychical researchers insisted, one way of proving that the automatic writing they produced was not born of her own consciousness. Myers describes a common scenario in *Human Personality and Its Survival of Bodily Death*: an entranced subject is read aloud to; when he awakes, he writes out the words he heard while entranced, while at the same time he reads aloud, "with waking intelligence, from a book of stories," and remains "quite unconscious of what his hand (placed on a planchette behind a screen) [is] at the same time writing" (*Human* II: 89).[7] Reciting memorized language could work as well, as in the case of renowned spiritualist Moses Stainton, who states that he received clear spirit messages while "carefully occupying [his] mind by reciting some passages of Virgil while the message was being given" (58). As a writing machine, Stainton needs to guarantee that his input differs from his output, and Virgil provides the screen. He explains: "This, I may here say, is a precaution that I habitually took in order to eliminate the disturbing element of my own mental action. The automatic writing, which has brought to me the greatest weight of evidence, has been, in very many cases, executed while I was occupied in reading a book" (58–59). Reading and reciting serves to evacuate the self in a way that recalls Garrett Stewart's model of gothic reading.[8] Indeed, this particular form of literary possession seems to be a necessary prerequisite for spiritual possession. The act of engaging with someone else's language – of participating in the mentally absorptive act of reading or reciting – helps to build a better medium.

The ideal automatist, then, is often required to keep her brain engaged with words in order to verify that the words she produces do not come from that same brain. But from whose brain do they come? This question, central to debates about spiritualism and telepathy, is more complicated than it may at first seem. Jill Galvan, in her important study of the feminization of mediation in the latter half of the nineteenth century, argues that the rise of the female medium depended upon "subtracting her intellectually from the path of communication" (12). Indeed, medium after medium attests to her lack of control over her language. However, it is important to note that the medium's own language – the words in her own brain – are not fully removed from the path of communication, even if her agency over them is indeed subtracted. In Geraldine Cummins's autobiography, for example, the noted medium describes the composition of *The Scripts of Cleophas*, her automatic work purportedly dictated to her by a first-century Christian: "for this work, I suggest that only the memory-centre for words in my brain was employed. It might be conjectured that I had borrowed someone else's imagination, or at least an E.S.P. strata of my mind played the primary part in its composition" (82). Cummins's own store of words is used to supply the language of the composing spirit. She is not merely its typewriter: she is its entire vocabulary.

Indeed, the materiality of language comes to be crucial in determining the division between intellectual or creative agent (mind) and bodily machine (brain). As Myers explains in *Human Personality*, automatic writing is not a transcendent communication of minds but rather "a communication between a mind and a body, – an external mind, in place of the mind which is accustomed to rule that particular body" (II: 191):

> There is in such a case no apparent communication between the discarnate mind and the *mind* of the automatist. Rather there is a kind of contact between the discarnate mind and the *brain* of the automatist, in so far that the discarnate mind, pursuing its own ends, is helped up to a certain point by the accumulated capacities of the automatist's brain;—and similarly hindered by its incapacities. (II: 191)

The alien mind acts upon the embodied brain, and language often appears to be firmly located in the latter. While there is ample evidence of automatists writing in languages that they claim not to know, many psychical researchers insisted that the possessing spirit was limited by the language center of its medium's brain. Myers was among the most adamant of this school, arguing that spirits use their mediums as linguistic machines: "the spirit selects what parts of the brain-machinery he will use, but he cannot get out of that machinery more than it is constructed to perform" (II: 190–191). What is interesting here is that in automatic writing, language appears to be embodied and even, at times, explicitly material. Myers writes of the "Modes in which Messages are given," one of which is via images that appear in a crystal ball: "Sentences sometimes appear; which, oddly enough, look to [the medium] just like scraps of coarse printing;—as though a piece of newspaper were held beneath the ball. There have even seemed to be ragged edges, as though the paper had been torn" ("On the Trance-Phenomena" 70). If the medium's own store of words provides the material media of the spiritual communication, this store of words is composed of material fragments of extant, published language, sometimes (as in this case) still entangled in their original media. The vocabulary of the spirit depends upon the vocabulary of the medium, which depends, in turn, upon what she has read. As one of the SPR's automatists once reported, in the words of a controlling spirit, "I got the WORD by choosing a quotation in which it occurs and which was known to the normal intelligence of my machine" (G. Balfour 124).

For the spirit who must scour the automatist's brain for quotations, who must pick whole words from her memory of quotations, the medium is a whole-word typewriter, a language-generating system much like the magnetic poetry kits that adorned many a late-twentieth-century refrigerator. And much like magnetic poetry, the words from which a spirit must choose are somehow startlingly material. Travers Smith's *Psychic Messages from Oscar Wilde* makes this clear:

> Pity Oscar Wilde. To think of what is going on in the world is terrible for me. Soon the chestnuts will light their white candles and the foxgloves flaunt their dappled, drooping bells. Soon the full moon will swim up over the edge of the world and hang like a great golden cheese—Stop! Stop! Stop! Stop! This image is insufferable. You write like a successful grocer, who from selling pork has taken to writing poetry. (Mrs. T.S.—Who said that?)[9] Oscar. I find the words in my medium's mind. Try again—like a great golden pumpkin hanging in the blue night. That is better, but it is a little rustic. (634)

Pity Oscar Wilde indeed: his expressions are limited by the words he can find in his medium's mind. Travers Smith's script suggests that composition itself is dependent upon both mind and brain, upon the spiritual impulse to communicate and the material fact of language itself.

Poetry's Telepathic Effects: Frederic Myers and the Poetics of Plagiarism

If language is material – and if engaging with it, especially while in acts of reading or recitation, helps to turn those readers and reciters into mediums – then poetry, we should not be surprised to learn, has a prominent role to play in discourses of spiritualist and psychical communication. Poetry's status as an especially material and reproducible form of language made it a key tool for researchers who wanted to trace the paths of communication that seemed to be illuminated by automatic writing. As we've seen, automatic writing has a doubled propensity for manipulating its own medium: it manipulates the automatist's body, turning it into a writing technology, but it also manipulates the medium of her communications, drawing attention to their own status as language. To this end, automatic scripts are often full of word games and puzzles. Myers, in his own experiments with automatic writing, was wont to produce baffling anagrams, which he then spent days trying to decode: "Wvfs yoitet," he determined, meant "testify, vow"; "Tefi Hasl Esble Lies," unscrambled, became "Every life yes is" ("On a Telepathic Explanation" 231, 228). And when "Mrs. Holland"'s automatic script – supposedly dictated to her by the spirit of the departed Myers himself – was found to contain the puzzling phrase "A gurnet among the sedge which grew in the mires," it was decoded by a psychical researcher to be "somewhat crude punning on the names Gurney, Sidgwick, and Myers," all three former (and deceased) founders of the SPR (Johnson, "On the Automatic" 247).[10] Given automatic writing's own hypermediacy, then, it is no surprise that these scripts also exhibit a propensity for poetry. In fact, as Helen Sword remarks, turn-of-the-century mediums were inundated with messages dictated by versifying spirits. Oscar Wilde may have regretted his postmortem inability to compose effective prose, but W. T. Stead, drowned on the *Titanic*, returned to séances to express his yearning for poetry, and T. E. Lawrence demonstrated his newfound capacity to write in verse, which (he explained) he could not do while he was alive (Sword 15). Poetry – possibly the highest form of wordplay – appeared to be an obsession of turn-of-the-century automatism.

While famous writers like Stead and Lawrence discovered new poetic talents in the afterlife, Myers had the advantage in that he was a poet – and, to a degree, a celebrated one at that – while he was still alive. While at Trinity College, Cambridge, he won prizes for his compositions in Latin and Greek, and he claimed to have learned all of Virgil's works by heart (see Beer, *Providence* 120); as an adult he authored many volumes of poetry, including *St. Paul* (1867) and *The Renewal of Youth* (1882).[11] A former protégé of George Eliot (Luckhurst 54), Myers was also a noted essayist (expert, in fact, on Wordsworth), and frequently drew upon his favorite poets to provide evidence for the kind of spiritual and telepathic philosophies he developed with the SPR. Beyond providing corroborating evidence for telepathy and spiritualism, however, the figure of the poet played an important role in Myers's theories of language and communication more generally. In his 1889 collection, *Science and a Future Life*, he argues that poets are in fact prophets, serving as great Arnoldian disseminators of high culture: "In Tennyson and Browning we have veritable fountainheads of the spiritual energy of our time. 'Ranging and ringing thro' the minds of men,' their words are linked in many a memory with what life has held of best" ("Tennyson as Prophet" 163). For Myers, poets like Tennyson and Browning act as transmitters between minds: poetry, here, is peculiarly mobile. Indeed, in quoting a line from Tennyson's "The Coming of Arthur" – "Ranging and ringing thro' the minds of men" (415) – Myers seems to recognize that epic poem's fascination with the autopoetics of quotation. If Tennyson's *Idylls of the King* (as I argued in Chapter Three) was interested in exploring the ghostly traces of endlessly reproducible voice, Myers uses a passage from that very text as evidence of the ability of poetic quotation to haunt the memories of its readers. Later, in his spiritualist opus *Human Personality and Its Survival of Bodily Death*, Myers argues that a poet is, in essence, a telepathic communicator: "He has transformed the sheet of paper into a spiritual agency; – nay, the mere memory of him persists as a source of energy in other minds" (I: 30). In Myers's formulation, it is not merely the poet's language that transcends its medium, but also the poet himself, who – via the telepathic effects of language – lives on in the memories of others. Myers's ghostly, bodiless poets render explicit the haunted pleasure of critical recognition that structures poetic quotation, a pleasure that attempts to transcend the material sheet of paper but which, ultimately, must always refer back to it.

It is worth noting that Myers's theory of poetry here is strikingly similar to his theory of "telepathy" – a term which he coined in 1882, defined as "the communication of impressions of any kind from one mind to another, independently of the recognised channels of sense" (*Human* I: xxii). To the twenty-first-century reader, telepathy is remembered as one of the many pseudo-scientific ideas of the Victorian era, often placed alongside mesmerism, phrenology, and spiritualism. For the psychical researchers of the SPR, however, telepathy – or "thought-transference," as it was also called – was considered to be the scientific answer to the problems posed by spiritualism. Yet as Roger Luckhurst has shown, the telepathic explanation is not any less richly complex than the spiritualist one.[12] Myers's 1886 *Phantasms of the Living*, a key text in the study of telepathy, purported to prove that ghosts are not visions of the dead but actually telepathic projections of people who are still living (albeit often in the process of dying). Where Sir David Brewster and the other Romantic scientists whom I discussed in Chapter One interpreted spectral illusions as an imprinting of the body's visual system, Myers and his colleagues gathered evidence for a new theory of hallucination as a form of telepathy. Human beings, they argued, have the ability to project their thoughts – often delivered by way of a ghostly image of their own body – to distant people at the moment of their death. Telepathy, then, explains away the ghost in a manner far different from that of Romantic science: it claims it as an intimate mental encounter between living beings. And although Myers himself came to believe in the ability for such messages to be transmitted postmortem by more traditional spirits, his spiritualism was informed by this understanding of telepathic communication as an extreme form of intimacy, one that challenged contemporary notions of the human mind.[13]

Myers's theory of poetry as telepathy suggests something inherently immaterial about poetic affect. However, Myers also contributed (less publicly, perhaps) to a body of discourse that, while similarly tracing the peculiar mobility of poetic quotation, locates such quotation firmly in material textuality. In 1863, while still at Cambridge, Myers wrote a prizewinning poem on the theme of "India pacificata"; the prize, however, was revoked after another candidate traced some of the lines of Myers's composition to a number of poems previously published in a collection of Oxford Prize Poems. Once Myers's verses were examined in detail, it was found that some of the plagiarized passages were several lines long; nearly one quarter of the poem, in fact, was composed of other people's work (see J. Beer, *Providence* 129). While it looked for a while as if Myers would be severely penalized, the episode was eventually forgotten and Myers escaped with merely a reprimand. But what makes this episode most interesting is that Myers himself refused to acknowledge that this kind of plagiarism could be construed as academic misconduct. For Myers, the act of poetic composition is inherently plagiaristic. While composing his own poem, he explains, he was inspired to "preserve" lines of poetry written by students at his rival university, Oxford:

> I saw in my bookshelves a collection of Oxford prize poems, which I had picked up somewhere in order to gloat over their inferiority to my own. I laid this out on my table, and forced into my own new poem such Oxford lines as I deemed worthy of preservation. When my friends came in, I would point to this book and say, 'Aurum colligo e stercore Ennii' – 'I am collecting gold from Ennius' dung heap,' – a remark which Virgil used to make with more valid pretensions. (qtd. in J. Beer, *Providence* 123)

Myers recollects an act of collection and preservation, not plagiarism; by incorporating lines from poems that he deemed "inferior," at large, to his own, he "preserves" them in the superior context of his own composition. And, he claims, he was merely drawing on an established theory of poetry – that of Virgil, who played a key role in the development of Myers's own poetic theory.

William Whewell, master of Myers's college and his mother's brother-in-law, called Myers's theory of poetic composition a "theory of literary annexation," and with good reason (qtd. in J. Beer, *Providence* 125). In a letter to Whewell immediately after his prize was revoked, Myers writes:

> I fancied that I discerned traces of a similar view in several of the poets whom I most admired; most of all in Virgil of whom after Mr Conington's editions it is surely hardly too much to say that almost every line in his works is a translation an adaptation or an actual theft. At any rate the number of such thefts in him is enormous, but it seemed to me that this did not in the least detract from the merit or real originality of the work, which I considered to be in the masterly rhythmical and poetical judgment which enabled him to select and arrange his booty. (qtd. in J. Beer, *Providence* 125)

In this passage Myers extends the concept of the writer as a whole-word typewriter; here the writer, the communicative medium of language, composes poetry by drawing upon a store of extant phrases and passages. Another excerpt from Myers's letter explains:

> I had thought a good deal on the theory of poetry, & had come to the conclusion ... that the essence and value of a poem consists entirely in the impression which it makes as a whole, and that the special parts have no separate function, as it were, but are only valuable as building up & subserving the symmetry of the whole. For example any criticism which

was content to compare two poems by comparing the beauties of their
special portions ... appeared to me unsatisfactory. (124)

Beauties, extracts, quotations – these, Myers insists, are useless on their
own. Yet real poetry can be made from a kind of editorial recollection of
such quotations.

While Myers's own plagiarisms were particularly egregious, he was not
the only late-Victorian thinker to equate poetic composition with critical
collection. As Paul Saint-Amour and Robert MacFarlane have demonstrated, defenses of plagiarism like the one offered here by Myers were
becoming surprisingly common in the later decades of the nineteenth
century. For Saint-Amour, this trend of celebrating literary borrowing is
linked to a "shift in value theory" that began to privilege the scene of
consumption over the scene of production (24); writing, he argues, came to
be seen as "a record of reading, and the new literary product nothing more
than an agglomeration of prior consumptions" (40). John Churton
Collins, for example, wrote an entire treatise elaborating upon
Tennyson's reworkings of previously published texts: for Collins,
Tennyson and Virgil are strikingly alike in "the use ... which they have
made of the work of their predecessors" (23). For Collins, Tennyson's skill
lies not in his originality but in his ability to draw upon "types which have
long been commonplaces in fiction," deriving his material "not from the
world of Nature, but from the world of Art" (6). More radical defenses of
plagiarism insisted that critical acts of selection and recontextualization
were in fact acts of creative skill. Charles Reade's 1871 *Trade Malice* lauds
"the inventive scholar who has the skill to select, and interweave another
writer's valuable facts into his own figment" (16); similarly, Edward
Wright's 1904 essay on "The Art of Plagiarism" defends it as "an art in
which the finest critical power is exhibited by means of creation" (515) and
asserts that the best writer is one "whose genius is as much critical as
creative" (517).[14] But Myers's particular contribution here – both in the
plagiarisms he enacted while alive and in the culture of spirit-quotation
that was his legacy – is one that has interesting things to say about the place
of poetry in relation to the culture of plagiarism and recontextualization
that Saint-Amour identifies. In fact, Myers's ideas about composition and
reception can be seen to underwrite the entire project of spiritualist
automatic writing. The questions he asks about the mobility of the poetic
quotation – does it exemplify immateriality or materiality? does it come
from another mind or from another book? – are the same questions that
come to motivate decades' worth of experiments in spirit communication.

Fragmenting the Lyric: Textual Identity in the Cross-Correspondences

Myers's theory of composition as collected quotation had a long afterlife – as did, in a way, Myers himself. The psychic researcher was keen to use his own death as an opportunity to test his theories of the survival of human personality, and the preferred medium of his intended test was, perhaps unsurprisingly, poetry. He left a sealed envelope to be opened after his death in 1901; in the event that any medium received a posthumous communication from Myers, the validity of the message could be tested against the contents of the envelope. When it was opened in 1909, it was revealed to be a quotation from Wordsworth's "Laodamia": "The invisible world with thee hath sympathized; / Be thy affections raised and solemnized" (J. Balfour 223n).[15] Myers's postmortem message established a dynamic that came to define the SPR's approach toward automatism throughout the early decades of the twentieth century, a dynamic that placed poetic quotation and recognition at the heart of automatic writing. Excerpts of poetry were used to identify both the automatist and the spirit communicator; likewise, they constructed a network of quotations that required a specific kind of reader capable of locating, collecting, and analyzing their often mysterious messages.

Myers's own posthumous communications – or so they were said to be – were a driving force in the SPR's most ambitious study of automatic writing. This was the decades-long case of the "Palm Sunday" cross-correspondences, which engaged multiple automatists over the course of almost 30 years, beginning shortly after Myers's death. The concept of cross-correspondence (or concordant automatism, as it was also known) involved tracing pieces of fragmentary messages delivered via different mediums in different parts of the world – messages that seemed to make no sense on their own, but that formed some complete message when compiled. Alice Johnson, a research officer in the SPR who (among other things) helped to prepare Myers's *Human Personality* for posthumous publication, was the first to attempt an in-depth concordance of fragmentary messages collected from different automatists. Johnson's work on the cross-correspondences began in earnest in 1903, when Alice Kipling Fleming (sister of Rudyard) wrote to the SPR an unsolicited letter including ten lines of verse, which, Fleming explained, "my pencil wrote this morning" (qtd. in Johnson, "On the Automatic" 171). Fleming, who lived in India at the time, began her own experiments with automatism after reading *Human Personality* shortly after Myers's death. From the very beginning the messages claimed to come from the spirit of Myers. Eventually Fleming's scripts indicated that they should be compared to those of another medium, and soon Johnson and the SPR were involved in compiling and analyzing the scripts of five different automatists: Leonora Piper, the famous American medium; Margaret Verrall, a close friend of Myers's; her daughter Helen Verrall Salter, wife of another psychic researcher; and eventually Winifred Margaret Coombe-Tennant, a society lady and League of Nations delegate, who worked with the SPR under the name "Mrs. Willett."[16] Fleming herself adopted the pseudonym "Mrs. Holland." The messages delivered via these mediums were rarely straightforward; nor were they often, strictly speaking, original speech. This is important to note. As explained in the *Proceedings of the SPR*, "the essence of a cross-correspondence is that fragmentary messages, such as quotations, or allusions to literary subjects, written independently by several automatists, which are meaningless if taken singly, are found to be intelligible *when they are combined together*" (J. Balfour 84, emphasis original). Rather than speaking in his own voice, as it were, the spirit of Myers speaks in other people's language.

The fact that the messages were primarily composed of quotations and allusions is evidence of the peculiar relationship between immaterial spirit and material language that I outlined in the first section of this chapter. More than that, though, the nature of quotation was essential to the ultimate goal of the cross-correspondences. The SPR's theory was that evidence of concordant automatism would prove definitively that spirit messages were not merely the product of the automatist's own brain. This relied upon proving that these fragmentary messages would necessarily be meaningless to each individual automatist, which Johnson and her collea-gues did by painstakingly tracking down each snippet of often erudite and obscure literary quotations and allusions that appeared in the automatic scripts.[17] If the communicating spirit quoted from texts that the automatist did not know, it was taken as proof that the knowledge came from an external mind. What is more, the body of literature from which the automatic script drew was also used to identify the communicating spirit. At times the spirits referenced their own published writings: J. D. Piddington, another SPR researcher, called this "literary personation" (16). At other times, the scripts seem to appeal to a body of literature that the spirit had read and committed to memory. These references establish an important precedent in which automatic script references and even replicates extant publications. Like Myers's crystal-gazing medium who receives spiritual messages in the form of newsprint, and like Myers's own plagiarisms, the automatic writing of the cross-correspondences constructs a method of identification that relies on the quotation and replication of very material language. The search for "literary personation," moreover, resulted not only in the identification of Myers's personality but also in its fragmentation. The SPR believed that Myers was dictating these cryptic messages to all five automatists. But in order to analyze the complete set of cross-correspondences, researchers devised a notation system that served to divide Myers's postmortem personality, notating his communications delivered via each medium with its own subinitial: $Myers_H$, $Myers_P$, and $Myers_V$ indicated, for example, Myers via Holland, Myers via Piper, and Myers via Verrall, a division that was necessary due to "contamination of the communicator" by his automatist medium (Luckhurst 265). Each "protoplasmic machine" – each medium herself – infected the spirit of Myers to the point that his personality was divided and reassembled in combination with theirs. It was his "literary personality" that remained somewhat intact; his literary knowledge, that is, differentiated him from his multiplying media.

Automatic writing thus maintained a vexed relationship to the literary. Spiritualist scripts were rarely considered to be part of a valid artistic tradition; nor, for the most part, did they claim to be.[18] Many of the most famous mediums produced works ostensibly composed by well-known (deceased) writers – including Wilde, Shakespeare, Shelley, and Scott – but automatists were keen to insist, as evidence of the spiritual source of their texts, that they had no literary gifts themselves. Such disavowals were particularly popular whenever the automatic script was in verse. On many occasions, any faculty for poetic production was cited as evidence of true spirit possession; mediums like Travers Smith insisted that, on their own, they were never "guilty either openly or secretly of writing poetry!" (*Voices* 30), and therefore that any display of poetic skill must come from some external mind. That such disavowal was *de rigueur* only makes all the more noteworthy the crucial role that quotation and literary allusion came to play in automatic writing, particularly in the cross-correspondences. In the automatic script I discussed at the beginning of this chapter – "I got the WORD by choosing a quotation in which it occurs and which was known to the normal intelligence of my machine" – the spirit accesses the vocabulary of the automatist by accessing her store of memorized quotations. Indeed, as the cross-correspondences' focus on "literary personation" indicates, this particular form of communication relies very much on literature and, particularly, on poetry.[19] The automatist may deny any poetic ability of her own, but her knowledge of other people's poetry (or lack of knowledge) was a central, indeed crucial, concern.[20] Analysts often found it necessary to construct tables that identified "'sources' and 'correspondences,' showing in each case whether the corresponding passage was within [the medium's] normal knowledge and whether its context supplied a reason for associating it" (Verrall 190). The "normal knowledge" – the conscious or unconscious stockpile of memorized poetry – enables the communicating spirit to speak in allusive quotations at the same time as it calls into question that spirit's very existence. Striking passages, in other words, are no longer aberrations of the mnemonic imprint; here they underwrite identity.

There are, of course, many spiritualist tomes produced via automatic writing that purport to add new texts to an established canon – see, for example, the works communicated posthumously by Oscar Wilde.[21] But in the cross-correspondences, the impulse is the opposite: what is most striking about the scripts is the way they privilege re-expression over self-expression, quotation over original speech. In other words, they are extraordinarily aware of their own mediation. The hypermediacy of the automatic scripts suggests the uncanny notion that, as Jill Galvan writes, "the other world was a textual phenomenon" – that ghosts "amounted to words on a page" ("Tennyson's Ghosts"). Take, for example, Fleming's script from 11 July 1905:

> January 2nd. 1886—ALICE'S DAY.
> "To fashion the birth robes for those
> Who are just born—being dead." (1)
> "A lady the flower of her kind
> Whose form was upborne by her lovely mind." (2)
> "And on her grave with shining eyes
> The Syrian stars look down." (3)
> In accord—in perfect accord.
> "Only one youth—and the bright light was clouded." (4)
> But Alice has no regrets.
> "Like tombs of pilgrims that have died—
> About the Holy Sepulchre." (5)
>
> (qtd. in Johnson, "On the Automatic" 267)

The parenthetical numbers are Johnson's, and what they indicate is a remarkable degree of quotation from other published poems – as if, in composing it, she condensed an entire anthology or book of "Beauties" into one short verse. The first couplet, Johnson notes, is a modified borrowing from Dante Gabriel Rossetti's "The Blessed Damozel";[22] the second couplet, also a modification, is from Shelley's "The Sensitive-

Plant";[23] the third is taken from Matthew Arnold's "Obermann Once More";[24] the fourth quotation compounds a couplet from Alice Meynell's "A Letter from a Girl to Her Own Old Age";[25] and the final couplet is taken directly from Rossetti's "The Portrait" (107–108). In the course of this short poem, then, five different texts are excerpted and recollected; only two lines cannot be traced back to pre-existing poems, and these lines serve as connective tissue, offering a modicum of structure. "In accord—in perfect accord," Fleming writes, insisting that this strange compilation of fragments works together as a unified whole. In a way, then, Fleming's automatic poetry operates on the same theory that Myers claimed when he plagiarized his prize poem at Cambridge.

Fleming is not alone in her tendency toward poetic quotation in automatic writing. It would not be too much to say that, in fact, such a tendency is *the* defining feature of the cross-correspondences. By the time we get to the scripts of "Mrs. Willett" – the last automatist to join the cross-correspondences – such allusions and quotations are incessant. The following excerpt, written in 1912, was supposedly communicated from the spirit of psychic researcher Edmund Gurney:

> the plighted troth—roses for a maiden dead[26] —say that try again Gurney—let the pencil move freely—Help—there is one who asks your help—try again.
>   this is he was great by land as thou by sea—that has a meaning[27]
>   She is trying to speak—will anyone hear—will anybody hear—not distant—not set in other spheres—but near—nearer than hands and feet—speak for she hears, and spirit with spirit meet[28].
>   The long silence that yet has meant no sundering—the sharpness of the pang has been overlaid with many many other things, rolled round with rocks[29] —My love involves the love before—I shall not lose thee though I die—say that[30] (J. Balfour 112–113)

In this one excerpt "Mrs. Willett" quotes from or alludes to five separate poems, all canonical nineteenth-century texts (Shelley and Wordsworth make appearances, but Tennyson is the most popular: three different poems of his are cited here, as I've noted below).[31] Moreover, the script contains not only fragments of quotations, recollected, but also instructions for both their communication and their interpretation. "Try again Gurney," the composing spirit insists, repeating "say that." The automatist herself receives instruction – "let the pencil move freely" – and so does the interpreter, who is alerted to the quotation from Tennyson's "Ode on the Death of the Duke of Wellington" by the phrase "that has a meaning." Another "Willett" script makes this dynamic even more readily apparent:

Sing no sad songs for me[32]—there the body of Helen Adair and there the Heart of—I shall love no more, no more till Helen Adair comes back to me[33] You have it not right—The maidens who praise the companions of Mary[34] Ave—say that—there is a Sonnet I want to allude to—I said, is it Death and the answer was nay it is love—now reverse that—reverse it, I say[35] (J. Balfour 116)

Here, the automatist alludes to five different poems, and these allusions make clear the degree to which the communicating spirit seems to be struggling with the linguistic machine that is its medium's brain. What is less obvious is that the communicating spirit must rely on the poetic vocabulary of both automatist and interpreter, one in order to access language and the other in order to establish its meaning. The same auto- matist's script reveals its dependence on the psychic researcher to whom these messages were intended to be delivered: "what is that poem where Rossetti speaks of the death of his sister – Is it Xmas Eve?" (J. Balfour 112). If there is a hero in this psychic research-drama, it is neither the spirit who dictates nor the automatist who writes but rather the analyst who interprets.

And it matters, I think, that the quotations deployed in these texts are fragments of poetry. While much attention has been paid to the problem of authorship and technology in the cross-correspondences, few critics have questioned why the automatic scripts are so consistent in their borrowing from one particular genre.[36] Yet I would argue that there is a specific autopoetics at work in the cross-correspondences. This is a poetics that encourages a certain kind of reading, one that takes poetry as decontextua- lizable and allusive and that seeks, through a system of recollection and interpretation of allusions, to recontextualize it. Quotations are a uniquely useful unit of language in this system. As Coleridge insisted a century earlier, poetic quotations operate as isolated fragments that insist on their own portability and reproducibility; at the same time, they retain a residue of connection to the longer poems from which they came, alluding to meanings and contexts that may be larger than they themselves contain. Here at the other end of the century we find ourselves back in the realm of the ghost, of memory haunted by text. We're back in the realm of the striking passage as well, but again with a twist: in spiritualist automatic writing, fragments of poetry arise spontaneously, but they point toward the ghost rather than away from it. More importantly, they are ubiquitous, and that very ubiquity suggests a changed understanding of the relationship of poetry to the automatic body, one that privileges reception over composi- tion and imagines expression as indistinguishable from quotation.

I mentioned already the defenses of plagiarism whose popularity at the fin de siècle has led critics to identify a particularly complex attitude toward originality and expression in the late Victorian period. We can also recognize this drive to trouble the boundaries between composition and reception in Victorian poetics – especially, perhaps, in the late-Victorian vogue for the "cento," a poem explicitly composed of lines and couplets taken from other published poems. The cento (also called collage poem or mosaic poem) exhibits a formal peculiarity: each composite poem identifies its own source poems in a column that runs alongside the verse, drawing explicit attention to its status as compiled quotation.[37] Many of the automatic scripts generated by the cross-correspondences engage directly with this popular tradition. Yet they can be read as the uncanny version, as it were, of the particular genre of the cento: these composite poems render explicit the haunted pleasure of critical recognition that structures quotation and allusion.[38] What had been lyric poetry is dismantled and reassembled to function as dramatic: it points explicitly away from self-expression. Instead, each automatic script becomes a puzzle of a dramatic monologue in which the reader is made all too aware of the distance between the writer and the expression. And it is the role of the reader – or, in this case, the psychic researcher – to correctly interpret these expressions and use them to identify and understand the speaker. As in the dramatic monologue, the speaker's identity is a textually constructed one; but here, the texts used to construct identity are all re-expressions – quotations from and allusions to already published poems. Rather than identifying the character of Mr. Sludge, the medium, these texts identify "Mr Sludge," the poem itself.

Authorizing the Reader: The Haunted Pleasures of Critical Recognition

In the broadest sense, what I see here is a shift in the way the seemingly random reproduction of other people's language is interpreted. In Coleridge's oft-cited anecdote about the involuntarily mimetic German servant, the girl's automatized speech is used as evidence of the individual memory's imprintedness and mediacy; here it is used to cohere a collective body of knowledge, a spirit, a canon. Spiritualist autopoetics requires the psychic researcher – as well as the automatist – to possess a vast mental stockpile of poetic quotations, out of which is constructed its necessary network of allusions and recognitions. This model relies in complex ways upon embodiment: in addition to their more visible physical automatism, the enlisted mediums are transformed into searchable data-bases of often quite material language, used as protoplasmic machines by the controlling spirits. The mediums dramatize a way of being with poetry that imagines reading as a means of constituting identity, which can then be recreated and performed for a critical analyst by quoting from and alluding to a particular body of literature. While the bodies of the mediums are automatized in complex ways, it would seem thus far that the bodies of the critical analysts remain nonparticipants in the autopoetics of spiritual-ist automatic writing. But this is not necessarily the case. For if mediums can be turned into quotation machines because they have read and mem-orized poetry, what does this say about the people who recognize the quotation? In this concluding section, I want to turn our attention to the potential for automatism inherent in the critical stance. I have two goals in mind here. One is that attending to this problem – to the role of the observer or analyst in the case of poetry that performs someone else's expression – affords a new perspective on one of the period's most famous literary depictions of automatic writing: Rudyard Kipling's 1902 short story, "'Wireless,'" which explores precisely the uncanny telepathic effects of spiritualist autopoetics. Moreover, the reading of "'Wireless'" I offer here makes visible the ways in which spiritualism's model of the automatic body implicates the critic in involuntary, even mechanized interactions with other people's language. In the autopoetics of the cross-correspondences, poetry comes (as we might expect) from beyond – but even in this earnest attempt to locate that beyond in the realm of the immaterial, the printed page is revealed to be the space from which the soul speaks. Human identity appears as a collage, a cento rather than a lyric, a collection of imprints that suggests, ultimately, the uncanny notion that we are what we read. Kipling's tale interrogates this model by shifting this haunted sense of textual identity away from the automatist and onto the critic.

"'Wireless'"'s obvious concern with technology and communication has made it a particularly productive text for recent scholarship on new media.[39] In Kipling's story, a consumptive young druggist, John Shaynor, unknowingly replicates the poetry of another consumptive young druggist, John Keats. This pseudo-mediumship is placed in dialo-gue with a contemporary communication technology, the newly invented wireless telegraph: the narrator of "'Wireless,'" who has come to the druggist's shop ostensibly to witness a display of Marconi's new technol-ogy, is distracted by a parallel display of seemingly otherworldly commu-nication when Shaynor falls into a trance in the next room and begins writing a garbled version of "The Eve of St. Agnes." Criticism of "'Wireless'" tends to read this as a failed transmission, emphasizing the tale's depiction of spiritualism and wireless telegraphy as equivalent, and equivalently suspect, communication technologies. But in the tradition of spiritualist autopoetics, successful communication depends less on straightforward self-expression than on circuitous critical recognition. As we've seen, spiritualist evidence of what Myers termed "human personality and its survival of bodily death" seems to depend in large part upon the transmission of lines of poetry – garbled, often, like Shaynor's, and delivered through the automatic writing of a medium who claims to be unaware of its source. The "induced Keats" of Kipling's tale (194), in light of this, can be read as not merely a manifestation of cultural anxieties surrounding new technology but an exploration of the uncanny relationship between automatism and poetry in particular. And, like the SPR's experiments, Kipling's story investigates the fine line between conscious and unconscious transmission, between quotation and plagiarism. That Kipling put the name of his story in quotes – "'Wireless'" rather than simply "Wireless" – suggests not only that he intends to query the new technology in question but also that quotation may in fact be a part of that technology. Building on the work of media scholars who have used Shaynor to productively interrogate turn-of-the-century concerns about authorship and communication, I want to turn our attention to the figure of the receiver – the unnamed narrator of Kipling's tale who is enlisted to recognize these fragmented quotations. "'Wireless'" renders explicit the hauntedness of poetry by allowing it to assume the function of the ghost – and by querying the stakes of a mechanics of transmission that privileges critical recognition over authorial inspiration.

The wireless telegraphy that features so prominently in Kipling's tale was a very new technology in 1902, one that would officially be dubbed "radio" a few years later.[40] Like telepathy and spirit communication, wireless telegraphy materialized language out of the ether. Kipling's "'Wireless'" explores an attendant question: how is language transmitted through time and space, and how is it mediated? The tale is attuned to the relationship between thought and automatism, conscious and unconscious actions.[41] When the narrator first strikes up a conversation with the druggist, Shaynor describes his uncanny ability to serve customers "without stopping [his] own thinking":

> I've been reading Christy's New Commercial Plants all this autumn, and that needs keeping your mind on it, I can tell you. So long as it isn't

a prescription, of course, I can carry as much as half a page of Christy in my
head, and at the same time I could sell out all that window twice over, and
not a penny wrong at the end. As to prescriptions, I think I could almost
make up the general run of 'em in my sleep, almost. (183)

As Richard Menke notes, Shaynor's early description of his automatized
behavior "hints at the connections [Kipling] will draw between information transfer, intellection, and automatism" (223–224). It's worth noting as
well that these connections have been drawn before: they echo the
mechanics of imprinted memory that underwrote Romantic studies of
spectral phenomena. In a move that is by now unsurprising, Shaynor's
ability to "carry" printed texts in his head is deliberately tied to his
hauntedness, his ripeness for inhabitation by ghosts. Memorization divides
the memorizer, allowing room for the inhabitation of language that
arrives – like the transmitted poetry we find in telepathic and spiritualist
automatic writing – from external texts and minds.[42]

Kipling's tale reproduces spiritualist autopoetics in another important
way as well: as in the system of allusion and quotation established by the
SPR's experiments, the critical observer in "'Wireless'" is enlisted to
participate as the medium loses control over the production of textual
meaning. Shaynor's poetry, like that of Browning's Mr. Sludge, allows the
observer-reader to gain an advantage over the author-medium. Like
Browning's reader (who recognizes italicized poetry before Sludge does),
Kipling's narrator (who recognizes quoted poetry before Shaynor does)
draws upon his own knowledge of poetry in order to identify the fragmented, allusive phrases that he sees produced before him. The narrator
experiences jolt of recognition when he learns that Shaynor's love interest is
named Fanny Brand: "the name struck an obscurely familiar chord in my
brain – something connected with a stained handkerchief, and the word
'arterial'" (190). Like Alice Johnson teasing out the allusions embedded in
Alice Fleming's automatic poetry, Kipling's narrator is prompted to recall
a series of fragmented associations, associations that include both images
and single words.[43] Much depends, then, on the narrator's ability to
interpret Shaynor's relationship to Keats – and most importantly, to
determine whether the young druggist could possibly have memorized
the poem. "It had never occurred to me, though we had many times
discussed reading and prize-competitions as a diversion, that Mr Shaynor
ever read Keats, or could quote him at all appositely," the narrator observes;
"Night, my drink, and solitude were evidently turning Mr Shaynor into
a poet" (191). But as the evening goes on the narrator becomes obsessed
with explaining the phenomenon: "If he has read Keats it's the chloric-

ether. If he hasn't, it's the identical bacillus, or Hertzian wave of tuberculosis, plus Fanny Brand and the professional status which, in conjunction with the main-stream of subconscious thought common to all mankind, has thrown up temporarily an induced Keats" (194).[44] The revelation at the end of the story that Shaynor has never read Keats – "'Oh! I haven't much time to read poetry, and I can't say that I remember the name exactly. Is he a popular writer?'" (198) – comes as no surprise; rather, it merely underscores the necessity of the narrator's interpretive presence for the recognition of the poem.

As in Myers's poetics of plagiarism, the role of aesthetic judgment is shifted here to the reader, not the writer, of poetry. Shaynor, like many of the SPR's mediums, goes out of his way to disavow any taste for or knowledge of poetry. But the narrator is continually drawing attention to his own aesthetic taste. When Shaynor finally commits the first of his transmissions to paper – "And threw warm gules on Madeleine's young breast" – the narrator responds with critical approval: "As I remembered the original it is 'fair'—a trite word—instead of 'young,' and I found myself nodding approval" (194). By the time the druggist has moved on to an attempt at the seventh stanza of "Ode to a Nightingale," the narrator's critique becomes nearly histrionic:

> My throat dried, but I dare not moisten it lest I should break the spell that was drawing him nearer and nearer to the high-water mark but two sons of Adam have reached. Remember that in all the millions permitted there are no more than five—five little lines—of which one can say: "These are the pure Magic. These are the pure Vision. The rest is only poetry." And Mr Shaynor was playing hot and cold with two of them! (196)[45]

This scene amplifies the dynamics of the spiritualist trance by heightening the disparity between the automatic writer's knowledge of poetry and that of the critical receiver: here the narrator can claim, with confidence, that he knows the "five little lines" that transcend all other written poetry. It is as if Shaynor's true mediation is not the transmission of poetry from a departed brain but rather the triggering of poetry that exists already in the narrator's brain – the activation of these striking passages not in their original context but in the new context of the critical mind. As Shaynor becomes increasingly non-agential, the narrator's aesthetic judgment becomes increasingly authoritative. In other words, Kipling assumes the model of spiritualist automatic writing – a model in which the observer, not the writer, is the agent of poetry – and amplifies it into a drama of critical ecstasy. And in an ultimate expression of self-sympathy, the cause of the narrator's ecstasy is not any new, original experience but rather a return to a text he already knows.

"'Wireless'" isn't the only place where Kipling articulates a theory of literary reception that emphasizes the importance of critical recognition. In his lecture on "The Uses of Reading," given at Wellington College in May of 1912, Kipling describes "the position of the man who has no knowledge of Literature" as "ignorant, that is, of all previous plans. Such a man is more likely that not to waste his own time and the patience of his friends—perhaps even to endanger the safety of his community—by inventing schemes for the conduct of his own, or his neighbours' affairs, which have been tried, and found wanting, and laid aside any time these thousand years" (57). Kipling argues for an informed readership, one that prioritizes communal knowledge over individual ignorance. More than this, however, he depicts the informed reader as akin to the definitively modern poet we find in T. S. Eliot's seminal "Tradition and the Individual Talent."[46] Eliot famously suggests that "the most individual parts" of a poet's work "may be those in which the dead poets, his ancestors, assert their immortality most vigorously" (22). If Eliot suggests a theory of poetic composition that looks peculiarly like spiritualism,[47] Kipling goes one step further and extends this haunted genealogy to include readers: "If a man brings a good mind to what he reads he may become, as it were, the spiritual descendant to some extent of great men, and this link, this spiritual hereditary tie, may just help to kick the beam in the right direction at a vital crisis" (60). He offers as an example an incident after the battle of Sanna's Post, during the Second Boer War, in which as many as five hundred men were reported lost: he encounters one of the returning soldiers, who quotes to him: "Thank Heaven we have within the land five hundred as good as they." Kipling notes that this "steadying quotation from the ancient, but quite modern, ballad of 'Chevy Chase'" allows the soldier to go "on with his job" (61–62). For Kipling, the "spiritual hereditary tie" that links dead writers to the present operated not just through writers but also through readers (and memorizers), who are as much "spiritual descendent[s]" of dead writers as are Eliot's modern poets.

If "'Wireless'" represents a fantasy of critical empowerment, however, it simultaneously complicates such a fantasy by slyly equating the narrator's stance of critical recognition with that of the automatized medium. This is Kipling's most telling twist, and the place where my reading of "'Wireless'" departs most significantly from the body of criticism I cited above: Shaynor is not the only source of mediumistic poetic repetition in the story. Instead, if we trace the instances of bodily automatism in "'Wireless,'" we can see that the phenomenon of mechanized, involuntary action originally identified with the consumptive druggist ultimately proliferates beyond him. From the opening of the story, Kipling's paralleling of telepathy and telegraphy draws attention to Shaynor's increasingly mechanical movements as the unwitting medium loses control of his conscious brain. When he first takes medicine for his cough, for instance, the narrator notes the mechanized actions that immediately follow: "He put his letter into an envelope, stamped it with stiff mechanical movements, and dropped it in the drawer" (188). In the midst of his poetic trance, Shaynor's mechanization becomes even more explicit: "The head, moving machine-like, turned right" (192). Shaynor's automatization is in keeping with his status as an automatist, of course. Yet in Kipling's tale of transmission this "machine-like"-ness is not restricted to the medium. It spreads as well to the narrator – a contagion of mechanization, as it were. In other words, Kipling's tale insists that the dispersed, collective process of interpretation requires bodily engagement on the part of the observer as well as the medium. And as the story goes on, the narrator seems to become embroiled in another aspect of this uncanny poetic transmission: its material (and even mechanical) mediation.

The narrator's own mechanization begins with a kind of trance, a self-fragmentation: "I was whispering encouragement, evidently to my other self, sounding sentences, such as other men pronounce in dreams" (193). Menke describes the scene as one of modern mediation: "Reaching for a reasonable explanation, the narrator feels a sense of self-division before the spectacle of Shaynor's 'machine-like' poetic production or reproduction – just the sort of 'fractured subjectivity' associated today with modern media" (231). However, as Shaynor's transmission becomes more and more accurate – more and more closely aligned with the textual original – the narrator increasingly draws attention to the traditional media of writing: "That's it," I murmured. "That's how it's blocked out. Go on! Ink it in, man. Ink it in!" (195). And the ultimate achievement, according to the narrator, is when the lines of poetry "[come] away under his hand as it is written in the book – as it is written in the book" (195). In this tale of newfangled media technology, the medium and the observer alike find themselves unexpectedly entranced by the hypermediated act of materializing someone else's book by hand. Indeed, the narrator's moments of obsession with the material media of poetry – the ink, the hand, the book – coincide interestingly (and not, I think, accidentally) with moments where the narrator himself falls into the kind of automatism that aligns him most strongly with the unconscious druggist. These are moments, of course, of repetition: moments where the narrator finds himself as prone as Shaynor to the reproduction of language. "Ink it in" comes twice; so does "as it is written in the book." And soon the narrator finds himself also repeating poetry: "I vowed no unconscious thought of mine should influence the blindfold soul, and pinned myself desperately to the other three, repeating and re-repeating" the final lines of "Kubla Khan" (196). Here the narrator himself uses poetic quotation as a kind of mental planchette, just as the SPR's automatists did. And like the SPR's automatists, his repetition and re-repetition of poetry stems from his desire not to "influence" Shaynor – stems, in other words, from a belief in the possible power of telepathy to implant language in another human's brain. Yet while he takes great pains to distinguish himself – and his knowledge of poetry – from the "blind-fold" druggist, the narrator's attempts to command his own unconscious thoughts only implicate him further in the system of poetic-transmission-as-*re*production that Kipling depicts. When Shaynor's trance finally concludes in a wrenching shudder, it is the narrator, not the druggist, who moves mechanically: "From head to heel he [Shaynor] shook—shook from the marrow of his bones outward—then leaped to his feet with raised arms, and slid the chair screeching across the tiled floor where it struck the drawers behind and fell with a jar. Mechanically, I stooped to recover it" (197). Here, finally, the narrator himself is the machine; the emphasis on Shaynor's embodiment serves to contrast only more sharply with the narrator's mechanization.

Galvan notes that attention to the role of embodiment in occult communication technologies can help to make visible "the desire for authentic interconnection—the transfer, precisely, of thought or inwardness, intention or understanding—through bodily relays of various kinds" (*Sympathetic Medium* 16). But it seems that what we have here is also an intimate transfer of something inauthentic, unintended, unthought: automatism itself, that is. One claim I have been making throughout this book is that writerly intuition and readerly absorption alike are revealed to be embodied and automatic: they both demonstrate the body's automatic mediation of language. In this case, "'Wireless'" implicates in the pleasures of critical recognition a kind of involuntary bodily automatism that reproduces other people's language.[48] "*You* ought to be grateful that you know 'St Agnes' Eve' without the book" (193), the narrator reminds himself. But should he be grateful? Shaynor carries Christy in his head – knows it without the book – and this, in the nineteenth-century tradition of autopoetics, renders him susceptible to Keats's textual haunting. Yet the narrator, too, carries a book in his head – or, rather, has done away with the book by reprinting its words into his memory. This is what it looks like to memorize language; and, as in the SPR's cross-correspondences, it is eerily close to the kind of mental possession that leads to the automatic reproduction of language. In Kipling's model of mediated language, automatism seems to spread throughout the transmission system. But Kipling's tale also illustrates the cumulative effects of a century's worth of autopoetics: poetry exists here in a state of transmission, turning the minds and bodies of its readers and writers into material media for its replication. The observer, like the automatist, is embroiled in the mechanics of repetition.

The central question in Kipling's tale is not, then, merely the question of whether the bowdlerized "Eve of St. Agnes" is produced by Shaynor or by Keats. What "'Wireless'" also implicitly asks is this: is any of it produced by the witnessing narrator? Indeed, Kipling leaves open the tantalizing possibility that the narrator's own role in the uncanny production may be greater than even he realizes: "But though I believed my brain thus occupied [in reciting "Kubla Khan"]" the narrator admits, "my every sense hung upon the writing under the dry, bony hand, all brown-fingered with chemicals and cigarette smoke" (197). Despite his best attempt to keep his contaminating thoughts away from the obviously susceptible medium, the narrator remains a possible telepathic transmitter, his own knowledge of Keats being one possible source for the mysterious communication he witnesses. Like Shaynor, who knows Christy by heart, the narrator is implicated in this strange cycle of poetic possession and collective language production because he knows Keats "without with book." As in the spiritualist depictions of mediums reading and reciting, it seems as if focusing your thoughts on other people's language can turn you into a medium. Knowledge by heart of someone else's poetry, Kipling seems to be implying, is much like being possessed. What is more, the reader of Kipling's tale is implicated in the project of poetic recognition as much as the narrator. While the narrator may not experience that striking of an "obscurely familiar chord in [his] brain" until the mention of Fanny Brand on page 190, Kipling drops hints for the reader long before this: Shaynor walks his as-yet-unnamed girlfriend to a church named St. Agnes, for instance – an allusion never commented upon by the narrator (184).[49] Kipling's story depicts varying levels of textual recognition while leaving the final level to be enacted by the reader.

Criticism of "'Wireless'" tends to assume that any less-than-literal transcription of "St. Agnes" means that the Keatsian transmission is a failure, a parallel of the fragmented messages received by the wireless telegraph. Pamela Thurschwell, for example, argues that Kipling depicts both spiritualism and wireless telegraphy as "untrustworthy methods of information transmission" (30); for Jeffrey Sconce, both communications are "less messages than lonely soliloquies offered to the very ocean that defeats and absorbs all attempts at interpersonal interchange" (70). In the broader context of turn-of-the-century media theory, too, the system of fragmentation that dismantles the coherent writing subject is seen as merely a precursor to what we recognize as traditionally modernist angst about mechanization.[50] But considering the tale in the context of nineteenth-century autopoetics allows us to see the problem of mechanization in a more complex light. Rather than longing nostalgically for an authentic, Romantic moment of individual composition, "'Wireless'" suggests that the real "magic," as it were, of the literary experience comes in the moment of critical recognition – in reading.

I've been arguing throughout this chapter that spiritualist autopoetics can be seen as a natural extension of the century's interest in the interaction between automatic bodies and autonomous poetry. As the body comes increasingly to be understood as an important medium for transmitting and recording poetry, theories of bodily automatism develop a sense of a physical memory that at once stores its own experiences and reproduces them. For Myers and the automatists of the SPR, knowledge of poetry functions as a kind of telepathy: it allows other people's language to circulate in the ether, recollected in new minds and, then, re-collected in the plagiaristic poetics of spiritualist communication. Poetry's transmission technology relies on its existence in memories and bodies, where it acts with self-reproductive autonomy. What we see here at the turn of the century is an extreme example of this material mnemonics, one in which access to the intertextual medium of memorized language seems to be collectively enabled by readers and writers alike. What we also see is a new privileging of critical extraction and recognition as components of or even alternatives to traditional models of creativity – even when such acts of critical recognition are somehow involuntary. It is not merely that the critic ascends as the traditional construct of the autonomous poet is dismantled; it is that even this new model of the critic is embroiled in the automatic reproduction of language that has been so surprisingly central to materialist theories of poetic agency throughout the century.

The Autonomous Poem
New Criticism and the Stock Response

I posed a question at the beginning of this study – "Why did it become productive for nineteenth-century writers to think of the human body as one of the material media of poetry?" – which, I suggested, cannot be answered without also considering an unexpectedly related question: Why did it become productive for nineteenth-century writers to conceive of poetry as possessing autonomy? As I have been arguing throughout this book, both concerns reveal the ways in which ideas about poetry are deeply implicated in the media moment of the nineteenth century – a period in which theories of poetic agency become invested in questions of material mediation. In the spiritualist autopoetics of the turn of the century, we see material mediation depicted (and enacted) as a process that relies on critical engagement with decontextualized, collectively interpreted poetry. So it is perhaps unsurprising, albeit counterintuitive, that the narrative of poetic autonomy I have been tracing here finds its apotheosis in another early-twentieth-century experiment with decontextualized, collectively inter-preted poetry: I. A. Richards's monumental study of close reading, *Practical Criticism* (1929). Both sets of experiments – the SPR's work with telepathically transmitted poetry and Richards's investigation of poetic interpretation – allow for poetry to have a certain kind of autonomy. The SPR's experiments, for all the work they do to identify some conscious source for these transmitted fragments of poetry, are fundamentally invested in the phenomenon of poetry that seems to come into the mind (and body) unbidden, of autonomous poetry that acts on the body. But Richards's *Practical Criticism* does something new: it canonizes the auton-omous poem as the foundation upon which literary criticism must operate. In introducing the founding practices of close reading, in other words, Richards renders the autonomy of poetry – an autonomy, as I've been arguing throughout, born of the media ecology of the nineteenth century – sacrosanct to New Criticism. But rather than implicating it in the hypermediated system of the automatic body, Richards works to defend the autonomous poem against the "critical trap" of automatism (14).

The development of New Criticism is, of course, bound up in the development of English studies as a discipline.[1] Richards in particular has begun to receive attention from twenty-first century scholars interested in historicizing close reading. Indeed, while New Criticism appears to mark a significant break with the nineteenth-century tradition of literary studies – a tradition deeply informed by physiological aesthetics – scholars such as Nicholas Dames and Benjamin Morgan have worked to reposition Richards as a more transitional figure, one whose relationship to physiological aesthetics is more complex. Dames, who discusses Richards's early training in physiology and neurology in *The Physiology of the Novel*, reads Richards's 1924 *Principles of Literary Criticism* as part of a "final, brief moment of efflorescence and withering" of physiological aesthetics (247).[2] Morgan's *The Outward Mind*, too, works to excavate a more complex picture of Richards's early criticism as remaining open to "the nineteenth-century possibility that aesthetic experience can be understood in terms of a stimulus and response relationship" (245). For Morgan, reconsidering Richards alongside the physiological aesthetics of Vernon Lee makes visible the ways in which New Criticism "opt[s] out" of a model of criticism that saw the quantitative and the somatic as compatible (252). To an extent, my argument contributes to a similar project. Viewed through the lens of nineteenth-century autopoetics, Richards's critical practices mark a crucial but not uncomplicated turning point. In this narrative close reading appears less as rupture than as development – the ultimate expression of a model of poetic affect that relies upon autonomy. What New Criticism comes to reject, however, is also important, and my goal here is to provide a more complete picture of what was gained and lost with the codification of close reading practices. In considering Richards not alongside Lee but rather alongside the SPR's experimental autopoetics, I want to shift our attention to *Practical Criticism* and, in particular, to Richards's discussion of what he calls the "stock response." For Morgan, the "stock response" is one example of the larger general category of "unruly personal interpretations of poetry" (243). By refocusing attention on the language of automatism in Richards's criticism, I suggest something different: the stock response is a phenomenon of *im*personality, one that is rooted in the intertextuality of the autopoetic tradition. Historicizing close reading, in this case, reveals the ways in which its methodologies forcibly exclude not only the somatic but also the random and the intertextual.

To do this, I want to look more deeply into Richards's depiction of poetic autonomy. In *Practical Criticism*, Richards – like the SPR – employs poetry toward purportedly empirical ends: stripping thirteen poems of their authorial and contextual information, he records the interpretive responses of student readers in order to determine what he calls the "chief difficulties of criticism" (12).[3] His project seeks to identify and classify possible errors of interpretation. Each category of error (which for Richards includes everything from the simple and practical difficulty of "making out the plain sense" of the poem to more slippery categories like "sensuous apprehension," "mnemonic irrelevance," and "sentimentality") appears as an obstacle to the reader's ability to be correctly moved by the poem. Indeed, *Practical Criticism* imagines a poet-reader relationship that can (and should) be dictated entirely by the poet: the problem of "imagery," he writes, is a "special danger" because the "vivid and precise images which arise before us, owe much of their character and detail to sources which are quite outside the poet's control" (224). That the poet should control the interpretation of his or her own poem is perhaps not surprising. But what is striking is Richards's insistence on the agency of the poem itself. We "must respect the liberty and autonomy of the poem," he writes (227). Stripping the sample poems of their authorial and contextual information, then, extends beyond the confines of Richards's experiment: it becomes, as every beginning student of literature very well knows, the foundational act of literary analysis. The autonomous poem becomes a critical necessity.

What, then, poses the biggest obstacle to the liberty and autonomy of the poem? For Richards, the most puzzling of all the "critical traps" he outlines are "stock responses": in these instances, the "ordinary meaning, the automatic, habitual interpretation, steps in too quickly for the context of the rest of the poem to make its peculiarities effective" (229).[4] This particular critical trap signals a lapse in vigilant individualism, a distasteful slipping into "ordinary" response at the expense of attention to peculiarity. More importantly, however, stock responses allow readerly agency to encroach upon the autonomy of the poem: "These have their opportunity whenever a poem seems to, or does, involve views and emotions already fully prepared in the reader's mind, so that what happens appears to be more of the reader's doing than the poet's" (14). Richards's description of these stock responses partakes wholeheartedly of the discourse of automatism. When a stock response is activated, Richards writes, "The button is pressed, and then the author's work is done, for immediately the record starts playing in quasi- (or total) independence of the poem which is supposed to be its origin or instrument" (14). Buttons, records, instruments: readerly automatism is dangerously mechanical, it seems. Whereas nineteenth-century constructions of poetic automatism worked to destabilize the boundary between the reader and the poet, implicating passivity and involuntary response as part of the creative process, Richards seeks instead to reinforce the agency of the author. "Whenever this lamentable redistribution of the poet's and reader's share in the labour of poetry occurs, or is in danger of occurring," he writes, "we require to be especially on our guard" (14). Readerly automatism is problematic not only because it is mechanized but also because it threatens the hierarchical dynamic between poet and reader. As we have seen throughout this study, readerly automatism contributes to a kind of counterintuitive creativity – a creativity that, for Richards, is dangerous. Indeed, despite Richards's attempt to purge readerly automatism from the act of interpretation, his model of the autonomous poem still draws upon the dynamics established by the autopoetics of the nineteenth century. For Richards, any "ideas" conjured up by a poem (even the dangerous ideas that make up stock responses) are active agents:

> An "idea," as we are using the term here, is not merely a passive form of consciousness, dragged up by the pull of blind forces at the mercy of routine laws of association. It is rather an active system of feelings and tendencies which may be pictured as always straining to appear and ready to seize any opportunity of disporting itself. We shall not understand the phenomena of stock responses unless we regard them as energy systems which have the right of entry, unless some other system of greater energy can bar them out of perhaps drain their energy away from them. (229)

Richards depicts the phenomenon of the stock response as one that utilizes both the body's own automatic responsiveness and the threatening agency of the "idea," which operates precisely outside of the routine and predictable laws of association.[5]

Moreover, Richards is quick to note that some poems (read: bad poems) contain these very agents. "Here – instead of distorting the poem or of setting up an irrelevant external standard – the stock response actually is in the poem," he writes (231). In poems like these, the dangerous quality that promotes and enables such automatic responsiveness is, in fact, "familiarity": "every item and every strand of meaning, every cadence and every least movement of the form is fatally and irrevocably familiar to anyone with any acquaintance with English poetry" (231).[6] This stock response, then, is audience-specific: it depends on what readers have read, how acquainted they are with the British canon. But Richards specifies that this problematic familiarity is "not of the kind which passages of great poetry ever acquire, however often we may read them or however much we have them by heart" (231). Instead, Richards outlines an almost paradoxical kind of familiarity, one that occurs instantaneously: "The familiarity of these poems belongs to them as we first read them, it is not an acquired familiarity but native" (231). This is because "the mental movements out of which they are composed have long been parts of our intellectual and emotional repertory . . . . In other words their familiarity is a sign of their facility as stock responses" (231). Here, counterintuitively, the sense of the canon Richards describes is one built not of texts themselves but rather of critical responses to texts. This is a kind of intertextual allusiveness that invents its own intertextuality: these texts seem familiar, and thus they are.

For Richards, in fact, intertextuality itself is dangerous. "A special case which well illustrates the general situation occurs when what is thought of is some other poem," he writes; "If it another poem by the same author, the association is likely to be relevant; but if the title, the subject, or some similarity of a single phrase is responsible, the dangers of aberration are obvious" (226). The threat of intertextuality here lies in its ability to construct the very kind of mental database of context that the SPR's autopoetics relied upon. A "single phrase" – an allusive striking passage – can move the reader out of the realm of the decontextualized poem. In this way, Richards's depiction of intertextuality draws upon (at the same time as it departs from) nineteenth-century discourse on poetic autonomy and readerly automatism. For Coleridge, the autonomous movement of the striking passage was a powerful function of poetry in print. For Hallam, it was a movement to be celebrated: it constructed the inner libraries that gave richness and depth to readers' interactions with poetry. In fact, it was this ability of the poetic fragment to move through readerly memory that first contributed to the concept of poetry as autonomous. As I have been arguing throughout this book, the development of this idea of a poem's – not a poet's – autonomy is born of the nineteenth century's innovations in thinking about media, which come to emphasize poetry's ability to reproduce itself and to act out of context. But Richards, who demands that we respect the autonomy of the individual poem, seeks to purge poetry of the very qualities that gave it such autonomy to begin with – its allusiveness, its random movements, its ability to operate in decontextualized and recontextualizable fragments.

New Criticism is, of course, also deeply suspicious of any readerly reaction that can be seen to depend upon the individual vagaries of subjective somatic response. To some degree this move is a rejection of emotion in favor of thought. In *Principles of Literary Criticism* (1924) – which famously begins, "A book is a machine to think with" (1) – Richards complains: "Mixed modes of writing which enlist the reader's feeling as well as his thinking are becoming dangerous to the modern consciousness with its increasing awareness of the distinction" (3). However, one of Richards's primary goals in *Principles of Literary Criticism* is to differentiate his new model of criticism from that of physiological aesthetics. Singling out Vernon Lee in particular, he argues that proponents of physiological aesthetics have misled us into an overestimation of the chaos created by individual sensual response: "Even so unambiguous an object as a plain colour, it has been found, can arouse in different persons and in the same person at different times extremely different states of mind" (*Principles* 9). If a simple color can provoke such a wide variety of reactions, according to this doctrine, a complex object such as a poem must therefore always fail to produce any consistent response in its critics. But for Richards, practical criticism suggests instead that *more* complexity, rather than less, will actually standardize the potential critical response – primarily because more complexity provides more context and thus prevents the free play of association: "The range of variety with a single word is very little restricted. But put it into a sentence and the variation is narrowed; put it into the context of a whole passage, and it is still further fixed; and let it occur in such an intricate whole as a poem and the responses of competent readers may have a similarity which only its occurrence in a whole can secure" (10). Richards anchors his principles of close reading in a rejection of the fragment at the same time as he rejects individual sense-based response. In his disavowal of the mediacy of the body in critical response, then, Richards similarly disavows the mediacy of decontextualized language – the free play of smaller linguistic units (such as words and sentences) outside of the context of the poem.

What might Richards's rejection of the stock response mean for those of us looking to historicize the practices of close reading we've inherited from the New Critics? Benjamin Morgan has described Richards's denunciation of the "chaos" of physiological aesthetics as a strategic move that "rejects the body as a site of linguistic meaning, turning instead to the brain" (244); the goal of the New Critics, he writes, was "not to cultivate individual sensibilities but to establish a set of principles that would prevent as far as possible the confusion of personal feeling and poetic meaning" (243–244). For Morgan, the relationship between Richards's criticism and Lee's allows us to reevaluate the many recent challenges to New Critical close reading methods offered by twenty-first century scholars, from Franco Moretti's "distant reading" to Stephen Best and Sharon Marcus's "surface reading"

(51). Of these challenges, Peter Schwenger's "obbligato effect" perhaps most directly contests the insistence on orderly and uniform response we find in Richards's rejection of the stock response. Tracing the potential range of associations and allusions that arise while reading a paragraph from *Tess of the d'Urbervilles*, Schwenger offers a playful but productive account of the pleasures of readerly "indirection" (122). He notes that readers, while "following the story line as (tacitly) instructed, will freely embroider that line with associations that are nothing if not ad lib"; and yet, at the same time, these associations "arise in the mind unbidden, so that it is almost never possible to read at the denotative level alone" (121). In a somewhat similar vein, Best and Marcus assert that "even if we cannot exhaustively explain what causes our responses, we can strive to describe them accurately, and that there is nothing inherently truthful or misleading about them. Sometimes our subjectivity will help us see a text more clearly, and sometimes it will not" (18). These contemporary commentaries offer, in their critiques of close reading, a glimpse of a scholarly tradition of analysis that comes closer to embracing (or at least acknowledging) the presence of random responsiveness in a way that recalls the nineteenth-century tradition of autopoetics I have been outlining in this book. The problem, of course, is that allowing too much free play in the act of close reading ultimately threatens to undo the authority of the critic entirely; neither Schwenger nor Best and Marcus fully endorse the random or mechanical response as an act of critical agency. Yet in attending to Richards's hostility to stock responses, it becomes increasingly remarkable – increasingly worth remarking upon – the degree to which New Criticism has reified a fantasy of poetic autonomy in alignment with critical agency. This is a fantasy in which texts can be taken from their original context and, if read closely and with a disciplined eye, more or less the same meaning can be extracted over and over again.

I have been arguing for the importance of media theory to nineteenth-century poetics and critical theory; I wonder to what extent our current critical anxieties are similarly informed by our media moment, one in which texts and bodies are potentially virtual in ways the Romantics and Victorians could never have conceived. Our recent reconsiderations of close reading – our drive to compile critical alternatives, from "distant" to "surface" to "obbligato" reading – may be underwritten by a new recognition of the pleasures of intertextuality, of stock responses, of proliferation rather than isolation. We are at a moment when any given reader's "inner library" may be wildly different than another's, and yet this difference matters far less – a moment in which such inner libraries are outsourced, as it were, to the digital. We are, perhaps, grappling with our own version of the concerns about mass literacy and canonization that the Romantics were confronting during the second printing revolution. In the newly immaterial media of the twenty-first century, the striking passage may be (if you'll allow me the pun) striking back. It seems all the more important, then, to historicize and contextualize New Criticism's emphasis on decontextualization and autonomy. My goal here is not to add yet another adjective to the potential challenges to close reading. But if we understand the degree to which nineteenth-century autopoetics inter-twines the somatic with the reproductive, we can see a new connection between Richards's treatment of the chaos of physiological aesthetics and his abhorrence of the stock response. The stock response – while it need not utilize the body directly – introduces a similar species of chaos into the act of interpretation. The stock response blurs the boundaries of the discrete text by acknowledging that texts live not only on the page but also in the deeply embodied memories (the inner libraries, as it were) of their readers. The fact that such memories can be automatically activated, as Richards is the first to admit, makes the intertextuality of the stock response all the more threatening. What New Criticism finds distasteful is not merely that the body might mediate critical response but that the body might, in so doing, serve as a site for the reproduction of poetry outside the bounds of the discrete text.

My study has worked to uncover a tradition in nineteenth-century poetics that locates a surprising amount of authority and efficacy in unoriginal thought, in re-expression instead of self-expression. It has also worked to uncover a theory of poetic affect that is far more comfortable with random and mechanical responses to poetry than our critical narra-tives of the nineteenth century usually allow – and one which, perhaps, affords a new perspective on our own critical moment. For while Richards insists on the one hand that authorial agency must be respected, the real protagonist of his interpretive drama is, of course, the critic. In *Practical Criticism*, the act of close reading is called upon to restore order to the dangerously messy mediacy that defined nineteenth-century interactions between readers and texts. If the autopoetics of the nineteenth century destabilize the agency of the poet in favor of the poem, in other words, it is a natural extension of this agential instability that allows New Criticism to step in and assert critical authority over the poem. But it does so by disavowing the productive instability of our interactions with poetry. By restoring attention to the nineteenth century's investment in involun-tary response as a valid form of engagement with poetry, I wonder whether we as critics might reevaluate the degree to which "stock responses" can function as important avenues of poetic mediation. What might it mean to reconceive of the stock response not as a critical error, a lapse in vigilant individualism, but rather as an inherent element in poetic mediation? One way nineteenth-century thinkers conceived of criticism was as an activation of a shared body of text, as it were – a communal response that is important for its very repetition rather than for its individuality, one that draws deeply upon the ability of language to provoke involuntary response. Indeed, considering Richards's use of the word "autonomy" helps us to recognize the degree to which we have naturalized this idea that poetry can operate on its own terms and that we as critics are simultaneously disciplined and liberated by its autonomy. Our own critical drive to divest the author of authority – a drive that finds its most famous expression in Barthes, perhaps – is one that has its roots in the autopoetics of the nineteenth century.

Notes

Introduction

1. As Cohn especially does, I attend to the problem of agency in order to reconsider traditional narratives about form in the reading experience. Cohn's compelling study offers a new perspective on the ideology of the novel form: lyrical passages in Victorian novels – passages that "rediscover nonreflective pleasure" by dwelling on states of diminished agency and consciousness – work to suspend the novel's traditional drive toward self-reflection and *Bildung* (3). My focus is instead on poetry; another, more subtle, difference in approach lies in my attention to automaticity, distinguished from reverie in its reliance on often overtly mechanical processes. Such mechanistic imagery, I argue, underwrites the autopoetic tradition's challenge to our historical idealization of poetic immateriality.

2. Other important recent works that situate poetry (and especially poetic meter) firmly in material culture include Noel Jackson's *Science and Sensation in Romantic Poetry* (2008), Meredith Martin's *The Rise and Fall of Meter: Poetry and English National Culture, 1860–1930* (2012), and Catherine Robson's *Heart Beats: Everyday Life and the Memorized Poem* (2012).

3. Thomas Laycock was one of the first mental physiologists in Britain to engage in this debate; he argued in 1845 that the brain was subject to the laws of reflex action, as was the entire nervous system ("On the Reflex Functions"). William Benjamin Carpenter's expanded 1852 edition of his *Principles of Human Physiology* introduced the term "ideomotor action" to describe the ways in which ideas can produce automatic actions, labeling hallucinations and automatic compositions as "unconscious cerebrations." His 1874 *Principles of Mental Physiology* takes this argument further, stating that "a large part of our Intellectual activity – whether it consist in Reasoning processes, or in the exercise of the Imagination – is essentially automatic" (515).

4. In *The Spirit of the Age*, Hazlitt describes Coleridge as one who "delights in nothing but episodes and digressions, neglects whatever he undertakes to perform, and can act only on spontaneous impulses without object or method" (XI: 36).

5. Coleridge himself seems to have cultivated this perception, especially with regard to his addiction; see, for example, Richard Holmes 354–422.

6. For Wordsworth, meter should be used to guard against the "infinite caprices" of poetic diction, which can lead the reader astray ("Preface" 404). I address this more fully in Chapter One.

7. For more on the history of meter and memorization, see Catherine Robson's *Heart Beats,* which offers a compelling study of the complexities of "learning by heart" in the context of nineteenth- and twentieth-century school curricula (in both Great Britain and America), which required students to memorize and recite a standardized set of poems.

8. As Gillian Beer notes, rhyme "creates memory within the poem, raising again words that might die out in the mind and straining them across lines as echoes, deformations, recurrences" (191); and Carpenter himself complains that the rhythms of poetry increase the dangers of "what we call 'learning by heart,' – which should be rather called learning by Sense, instead of by Mind" (*Mental* 450).

9. My brief reading of Wordsworth here is indebted to Kevis Goodman's work on nostalgia and volition, where she offers a compelling reading of Wordsworth's emphasis on automatism in the "Note" to "The Thorn" in *Lyrical Ballads* ("Nostalgia").

10. Celeste Langan and Maureen McLane point out that this trope is carried forward into much canonical Romantic criticism, evident even in the titles of such works as Harold Bloom's *The Visionary Company* and Geoffrey H. Hartman's *The Unmediated Vision.* See "The Medium of Romantic Poetry."

11. See Benjamin Morgan's discussion of Dallas's *The Gay Science* and the critical response to it (79–81). I build here on Morgan's striking supposition that, ultimately, Dallas identifies poetry as *the* medium of the aesthetic unconscious (79); as Dallas explains, "Art is poetical in proportion as it has this power of appealing to what I may call the absent mind" (I: 316).

12. Dallas's example is of the Countess of Laval, who spoke "gibberish" in her sleep until it was determined that she was actually speaking Breton; for Dallas this is evidence of the mind's retentive ability, for of course it is revealed that the Countess was in fact born in Brittany, though she had not spoken her native tongue since she was an infant (I: 211). (He also repeats Coleridge's oft-quoted tale of the German servant girl that I discuss above.) Dallas's criticism is deeply rooted in physiology: he credits automaticity with being the source of the same physiological phenomena that Romantic and early-Victorian scientists classify as self-sympathetic: "fear fills the bladder, rage dries the mouth, shame reddens the cheek, the mere thought of her child fills the mother's breast with milk" (I: 244). I discuss these physiological phenomena at length in Chapter Two.

13. Essays by Jenny Taylor and Winifred Hughes were among the first to restore attention to Dallas's rather neglected role in the history of literary criticism. Since then, scholars including Nicholas Dames (*The Physiology of the Novel* 58–70, 185–187), Elisha Cohn (*Still Life* 22–24), and Benjamin Morgan (*The Outward Mind* 75–81) have compellingly argued for the importance of his criticism to the rise of physiological aesthetics. As Morgan writes, the nineteenth-century fascination with embodied subjectivity and materialist aesthetics has remained "largely absent from the stories that humanities disciplines tell about their origins" (10).

14. Marshall McLuhan's influential argument that media can be understood as "extensions" of the human set the stage, in 1964, for the development of media studies as a discipline.

15. See, for example, Lisa Gitelman's *Scripts, Grooves, and Writing Machines: Representing Technology in the Edison Era* (1999), John Picker's *Victorian Soundscapes* (2003), Ivan Kreilkamp's *Voice and the Victorian Storyteller* (2005), Richard Menke's *Telegraphic Realism: Victorian Fiction and Other Information Systems* (2008), and Jill Galvan's *The Sympathetic Medium: Feminine Channeling, the Occult, and Communication Technologies, 1859–1919* (2010).

16. Following Kittler, the problem of voice in print has proved an especially fruitful topic for scholars of Victorian poetry. Eric Griffiths's *The Printed Voice in Victorian Poetry* helped to establish the terms of the debate: is poetic voice a production of orality, of textuality, or of something in between? Yopie Prins and Margaret Linley have provocatively argued for the primacy of the text in constructions of "voice" in Victorian poetry.

17. See Paul Hamilton's chapter on "Romanticism and Poetic Autonomy" in *The Cambridge History of English Romantic Literature*, wherein he discusses Romantic poetry's bid for "emancipation" from "the rule of other forms" (435).

18. I want to add complexity to the narrative that reads the century as progressing steadily from a regime of original creativity to one of intertextual borrowing – what Robert MacFarlane has identified as a trajectory from "*creatio*" to "*inventio*" (6). Instead, I trace the interplay of these concepts throughout the century, suggesting that even the Romantic "*creatio*" relied in complex ways on intertextuality.

19. Like such scholars as John Durham Peters, Roger Luckhurst, Sam Halliday, and Steven Connor, I am interested in thinking discursively about technological innovation. Halliday and Luckhurst demonstrate that the spiritualist discourse of telepathy circulated important ideas of ethereal long-distance communication before the actual invention of wireless telegraphy. Connor's history of ventriloquism details the "cultural invention" of radio

and telephony in advance of their actualization (*Dumbstruck* 295). Peters explores the history of "the idea of communication" in a variety of techno-cultural contexts; he argues of the telegraph, for example, that it "both stimulated and drew on older discourses about immaterial action at a distance" (94).

Striking Passages

1. See, for example, Maureen McLane's useful discussion of the cultural politics of the ballad revival: "Poets in this period turned to the sophisticated resources of print culture to satiate the nostalgia for a poetry and an epoch that preceded print" ("Ballads and Bards" 425).

2. Jerome Christensen likens this "feverish glossolalia" (111) to Coleridge's own "marginal method" in the *Biographia* (96).

3. Barbara Benedict's and David Allan's important work on commonplace books provides a useful background for the rise of the poetic excerpt, as I discuss in the Introduction.

4. Elfenbein's *Romanticism and the Rise of English* also draws attention to Romanticism's propensity for excerpting, noting that the "Elegant Extracts and Beauties" genre "treated poetry as an early form of clip art, often reproduced without reference to author or title of the original work" (170).

5. One of nineteenth-century Britain's leading scientists in the field of optics, Brewster was friends with Walter Scott, to whom the *Letters* were addressed. This was not his only tie to the world of poetry: he also happened to be married to Juliet Macpherson, the daughter of celebrated Ossian poet James Macpherson.

6. Brewster's language echoes Wordsworth's familiar formulation, from "Tintern Abbey," of visual imagery as half perceived and half created by the eye (106–107).

7. Studies of hallucination play an under-recognized role in the development of Romantic materialist science: as Hibbert himself claimed, "a theory of apparitions is inseparably connected with the pathology of the human mind" (14). Edward S. Reed has argued that the deconstruction of Cartesian dualism in the late eighteenth century allowed for early physiologists such as Erasmus Darwin and Dugald Stewart to bridge the gap between the previously isolated categories of mind and body, sensation and reflection, matter and spirit. The problem of hallucination, existing as it does at the interstices of these dualisms, provided uniquely fertile ground for a physiological exploration of sensory perception.

8. Nicolai took meticulous notes during these hallucinations and presented his case before the Royal Society of Berlin in 1799; his testimony was later printed

(in English) in the *Journal of Natural Philosophy, Chemistry, and the Arts* in 1803 and soon became the most celebrated case study of hallucination in the Romantic period.

9. The physicality of hallucination is made evident, moreover, in Nicolai's description of the hallucinated phantasms themselves: when he recommences his semi-annual blood-letting, the phantoms disappear in an odd fashion, as if they are being drained of blood: "I then observed that the figures began to move more slowly; soon afterwards the colours became gradually paler . . . . At half past six o'clock all the figures were entirely white, and moved very little" (170). This suggests that these ocular spectra – physiologically explained as memory gone awry – are intimately linked not only with Nicolai's mind but also with his body. Through the medium of his material senses, these phantasms are embodied, and as such they can be drained of life.

10. Ferriar insists that understanding the nature of hallucination renders ghosts inoffensive, even enjoyable: "Now I freely offer, to the manufacturers of ghosts, the privilege of raising them, in as great numbers, and in as horrible a guise as they may think fit, without offending against true philosophy" (vii). And yet his conclusions are far from reassuring. Ghosts are explained away by insisting that they exist not in the external world but in the malfunctions of the body's sensory apparatus, which is literally imprinted with audiovisual experiences.

11. Muri challenges the longstanding narrative of eighteenth-century physiology (exemplified by Theodore M. Brown's "From Mechanism to Vitalism in Eighteenth-Century English Physiology") as a clear movement away from the language of mechanism and toward instead the language of vitalism: "the human-machine was never displaced by vitalism, animism, or sensibility. What we see, instead, is a gradual convergence of the scientific language used to describe the invisible and active structures and processes of nature, human, and machine" (77). For Muri, the early capaciousness of the term *mechanical* is in part what enables the shift toward a more secular understanding of human physiology.

12. See, for example, La Mettrie's infamous claim in *L'homme machine* (1747) that "man is a machine and that there is in the whole universe only one diversely modified substance" (39).

13. In a response to Nicolai's article published in the *Journal of Natural Philosophy* in 1806, a correspondent known only as "L. M." similarly maintains that Hartley's theory is "manifestly unfounded" – proof of which is the fact that the author, while suffering from hallucinations, is unable to direct the appearance of the apparitions (292).

14. Hamilton sums it up nicely: "Sometimes we observe in mad people an unexpected resuscitation of knowledge; hence we hear them describe past

events, and speak in ancient or modern languages, or repeat long and interesting passages from books, none of which, we are sure, they were capable of recollecting in the natural and healthy state of their mind" (237).

15. It's important to note that Darwin's phrase refers to the anthologies of English poetry that were so popular in the late eighteenth century; the girl has memorized a book of poems removed from their original context and relocated into this new collection.

16. This is, in a way, similar to the guiding words that appear at the bottom of print pages in early-nineteenth-century texts, words that serve to guarantee a continuous reading experience despite the necessary material fact of turning the page. Thanks go to Nick Williams for drawing this to my attention.

17. Kittler argues that the development of primers (intended for mothers in order to teach their children how to read aloud) in turn-of-the-century Germany constructs an ideal of Nature (and natural language) as "Woman," whose "function consists in getting people – that is, men – to speak." See Kittler 25.

18. Coleridge, too, recounts a similar experience. Writing to Thomas Poole on October 9, 1797, he notes that as a child he read the Arabian Nights stories, one of which – a love story, not a ghost story – "made so deep an impression upon me . . . that I was haunted by specters, whenever I was in the dark – and I distinctly remember the anxious & fearful eagerness, with which I used to watch the window, in which the books lay – & whenever the Sun lay upon them, I would seize it, carry it by the wall, & bask, & read" (*Collected* I: 347).

19. Abercrombie, for example, recounts the tale of a "gentleman at one of the English universities [who] had been very intent during the day in the composition of some verse which he had not been able to complete: during the following night he rose in his sleep and finished the composition; then expressed great exultation, and returned to bed" (219).

20. These early studies of hallucination often uncover instances of unconscious repetition that a twentieth-century psychoanalyst would be quick to diagnose as repetition-compulsion. Indeed, Freud's language in *Beyond the Pleasure Principle* (1920) emphasizes the same contrast between repetition and recollection that I've been highlighting in Coleridge: the repetition-compulsion sufferer is "obliged to *repeat* as a current experience what is repressed, . . . rather than *recollecting* it as a fragment of the past" (18). Romantic theories of mind predate, of course, the concept of the "unconscious," which for Freud becomes the source of the repetition-compulsion (19).

21. One strain of this criticism views Coleridge as involuntarily susceptible to fragmentation. D. F. Rauber, for example, calls Coleridge the "master of the fragment," but then goes on to ask – "or did the fragment master him?" (216).

22. I am reminded of Elfenbein's comment that, in much late-eighteenth- and early-nineteenth-century writing, we find "the fantasy that ambiguity will disappear if typography were insistent enough" (*Romanticism* 125).

23. Brewster, in fact, cites "Kubla Khan" in an essay for the *Edinburgh Review*, using it as evidence that the delusions of the brain are much too complex to be simply the result of gastric distress (as was argued by many of his contemporaries, such as Ferriar and Hibbert). As Jennifer Ford notes, Coleridge's interest in a physiological understanding of the imagination has been "more readily recognized by nineteenth-century physiologists than by twentieth-century literary critics" (204). Ford's argument is that Coleridge adopted a "fundamentally physiological doctrine of the source and production of dreams" in order to investigate the medical nature of the imagination (3).

24. Rei Terada reminds us that Coleridge collected his own experiences with "spectra" – optical illusions and sensory oddities – in his notebooks, contrasting them with the "specters" of obsessive memories and dreams (1).

25. Poems will be cited parenthetically by line number.

26. Some of Coleridge's critics felt that his own poetry operated with a similarly disruptive autonomy within his own publications. The *Annual Review* complained that his juvenilia – which had been published previously but were reprinted in his most recent volume – "now boldly thrust themselves into the body of the volume, without apology and without abbreviation" (12).

27. When Coleridge revised the poem for the 1800 edition, he removed many of the archaic spellings ("Ancyent Marinere" became "Ancient Mariner," for example), and in 1817 he added pseudo-antiquarian notes in the margins summarizing the more obscure passages.

28. Like Russett's reading of "Christabel," my argument is informed by recent scholarship that builds on a Derridean understanding of orality as an effect of print in print culture. Susan Stewart, for example, argues that "the literary tradition was able to create an idealization of itself through a separation of speech and writing" by appropriating folklore genres such as the ballad (8), but that the "literary 'voicing' of folklore forms emphasizes their new textuality all the more" (11); and Eric Griffiths writes of the "double nature in printed poetry, making it both itself and something other – a text of hints at voicing, whose centre in utterance lies outside itself, and also an achieved pattern on the page, salvaged from the evanescence of the voice in air" (60). I discuss the problem of orality in print culture, along with the critical discourse surrounding it, in greater depth in Chapter Three.

29. Much, of course, has been made of Coleridge's plagiarisms. As De Quincey noted, he "reproduced in a new form ... that maniacal propensity which is sometimes well known to attack enormous proprietors and millionaires for

acts of petty larceny" (qtd. in Russett 70); even his plagiarism, in other words, is a reproduction "in a new form." For critical discussions of Coleridge's plagiarisms, see Wolfson 67; Russett 70–90; Tilar Mazzeo's *Plagiarism and Literary Property in the Romantic Period* (17–48); Susan Eilenberg's *Strange Power of Speech: Wordsworth, Coleridge, and Literary Possession*; and Rachel Crawford's "Thieves of Language."

30. Dorothy Wordsworth notes in an earlier letter, also to Lady Beaumont, that while she is pleased with Scott's *Lay*, it does not compare to "Christabel": it lacks "beautiful passages to remember, and to turn to again" (590).

31. It is not a coincidence, I suspect, that one of the most notable repetitions is itself about vision: in line 569 Geraldine "looked askance at Christabel"; this repeats in line 575: "At Christabel she looked askance!"; and finally, in 596, we are told that Christabel is "[s]till picturing that look askance."

32. The lines describing Sir Leoline's reaction to the mention of his estranged friend Roland de Vaux ("Alas, they had been friends in youth, / But whispering tongues had poisoned truth") were also widely circulated, but for the opposite reason: they were appreciated as a (rare) moment of "fine poetry" by those who generally despised the poem as a whole (396–414). Unlike the poem's opening lines, this passage was frequently excerpted and reprinted in those very collections of "Elegant Extracts" that Coleridge so disparaged.

33. Langan likens this built-in "rereading" ("Pathologies" 146) to Coleridge's description of the "retrogressive movement" of the reader, who "at every step . . . pauses and half recedes" (*Biographia* II: 14).

34. See Reiman 890.

Internal Impressions

1. See Rae Greiner's *Sympathetic Realism* for a detailed examination of these eighteenth-century models of sympathy and their impact (especially Smith's) on nineteenth-century literature.

2. Wordsworth fears that readers can be involuntarily carried away – "that the excitement may be carried beyond its proper bounds" – and cites as an example the overpowering emotion produced by reading the "distressful" parts of *Clarissa* (406). For Wordsworth, of course, regular meter helps to prevent the reader from being "utterly at the mercy" of the writer (404). But for scholars of sympathy, meter may in fact induce such sympathetic manipulation: see Blair.

3. This Wordsworthian critical legacy also shows signs of what Greiner has identified as a tendency for critics to view readerly sympathy in terms of Humean principles: she writes that the "key distinction between Smith and

Hume – that Smith's sympathizer abstracts feeling, routing it through cognition, while Hume allows for sensation to be transmitted both directly and unconsciously from one person to the next – has elicited a kind of continental drift in a criticism understandably enamored with Humean tropes of vibration, cognition, and 'force'" (5).

4. I don't mean to suggest that the theory of self-sympathy supplanted associationism immediately or entirely. Bostock notes, "We must be careful not to confound the effects of sympathy with those of association" – yet he insists that, "in most cases, [it is] not difficult to discriminate between them" (760n1).

5. Although noted proponents of mesmerism like Elliotson were among those who contributed to the body of medical literature on self-sympathy, the doctrine itself (as I discuss at greater length later) offered an explanation of mesmeric phenomena that rejected the theory of animal magnetism by relocating seemingly external stimuli internally.

6. Another example from Parry demonstrates the distinction these scientists draw between nervous and sympathetic action – namely, that sympathy serves to explain seemingly random relationships. Noting that "[s]ome physiologists have attributed these effects to the communications of the branches of different nerves," Parry rebuts: "That the communication by nerves is unnecessary to motion connected with sensation, is evident in the case of the iris; which does not move by any known stimulus applied to its own fibres, but suffers elongation by the influence of light, and I believe light only, on the retina, with which it has no nervous communication" (210).

7. I do not mean "unconscious" in the Freudian sense, of course; these theories of self-sympathy predate the development of this term in British psychology.

8. Jonathan Crary argues that attention did not become central to theories of mind – did not become "a fundamentally new object within the modernization of subjectivity" (17) – until the 1860s, but we can see in these studies that it played a central role in understanding the relationship of mind to body as far back as the late Romantic period.

9. Fox locates the secret of modern poetry's success in its close relationship with the advancing science of mind: "The poetry of the last forty years already shews symptoms of life in exact proportion as it is imbued with this science" (213). Fox's metaphor depicts poetry as a body, Frankenstein-like, being animated by a force outside itself.

10. See, for example, Coleridge's lecture on *Hamlet*: "one of Shakspere's modes of creating characters is, to conceive any one intellectual or moral faculty in morbid excess, and then to place himself, Shakspere, thus mutilated or diseased, under given circumstances" (*Lectures* 345).

11. For more on Fox's metaphor of the nervous system, see Rudy 46–58.

12. Gregory Tate notes that this reference to the pineal gland – according to Descartes, the point of contact between body and soul, and by 1830 a somewhat anachronistic reference – provides a useful metaphor of "a physical organ which grants access to a poetic 'landscape' of the mind" that advances Fox's argument that "mental states are rooted in bodily sensations" (28) Elisha Cohn reads it differently: as an "image of absurdist vitality," it "reinstates the authority of privileged discourses that value mind over matter" (21, 22). In my argument, as will become clear, Fox's recasting of Tennyson as a cranial conquistador indeed injects the act of poetic creation with volition, but it makes this volition dependent upon material physiology.

13. Wordsworth's individual "truth" defeats the masses, but ultimately Hallam rejects Wordsworth as well: "the right of private judgment was stronger than the will of Luther; and even the genius of Wordsworth cannot expand itself to the full periphery of poetic art" (616). According to Chandler, this disavowal of Wordsworth-worship stems from Hallam's rejection of public opinion in general: even a "victory for the opinion that great poetry can exist outside" of the sphere of public opinion remains, at its core, "a victory in the sphere of public opinion" ("Hallam" 532).

14. Again, this diverges from early Romantic theories of how poetry affects readers: for Wordsworth of the 1802 *Lyrical Ballads*, if his internal process has worked correctly, his reader will be enlightened (as long as he is in a "healthful state of association" [394]) – but by 1815, he has given up this credo and expresses a much less confident idea of how readers can be made to think and feel: "without the exertion of a co-operating power in the mind of the reader, there can be no adequate sympathy with either of these emotions: without this auxiliary impulse, elevated or profound passion cannot exist" ("Essay, Supplementary to the Preface"). See Chandler 533 for more on Hallam's relationship to Wordsworth.

15. Psomiades contends that representations of femininity allow an increasingly commercialized aestheticism to see itself as essentially separate from the market by endowing it with a paradoxical doubleness of tangible surface and inaccessible depth: femininity functions as "a system of representation through which ideological incoherence may be simultaneously recognized and disavowed" (33).

16. Likewise, in his essay "On Reading Old Books," Hazlitt similarly emphasizes the role of self-sympathy in reading: "In reading a book which is an old favourite with me (say the first novel I ever read) I not only have the pleasure of imagination and of a critical relish of the work, but the pleasures of memory added to it. It recalls the same feelings and associations which I had in first reading it, and which I can never have again in any other way. Standard productions of this kind are links in the chain of our conscious

being. They bind together the different scattered divisions of our personal identity" (XII.221).

17. Hallam's depiction of reading draws attention to the frequent presence of intertextual themes in Tennyson – poems that make of reference to preexisting texts. "Recollections of the Arabian Nights" is one, of course; other notably intertextual poems include "Mariana," "The Lotos-Eaters," and the *Idylls of the King*.

Listening with the Mouth

1. It's useful here to remember Herbert Tucker's insight that the "Morte" is a departure from Mill's theory that "poetry is overheard" ("Dramatic" 227). Instead of being self-expressive only, a spoken statement not intended for an audience, it is explicitly written and explicitly performed.

2. Robson's *Heart Beats: Everyday Life and the Memorized Poem* charts the rise and fall of recitation in British and American schools. As recitation assumed a vital role in the classroom, Robson notes, the memorization of poetry was credited with a wide variety of educational benefits, including underscoring religious and moral teachings, developing taste, and promoting patriotism (7).

3. For more on reading aloud in Victorian culture, see Philip Collins, who charted oral reading practices in his 1972 study *Reading Aloud: A Victorian Métier*; John Picker; Ivan Kreilkamp.

4. By late-century, reading had lost most of its supposed health benefits. Soon-to-be Poet Laureate Alfred Austin, for example, in an 1874 essay for the *Temple Bar* titled "The Vice of Reading," launched a tirade against the "flabby, flaccid, aqueous, unstable" bodies of people who neglect their health and exercise in favor of reading silently to themselves (257). This shift is due in no small part to the growth of silent reading in place of the physically stimulating practices of reading aloud.

5. For more on these recommendations of reading-as-exercise to female readers, see Flint.

6. Roger Chartier, in his study of reading practices in early modern Europe, notes that this communal, interpersonal element has always been inherent in the act of reading aloud. Before the rise of silent reading, he writes, "[r]eading was considered not some privileged solitary retreat, but rather as the very articulation of one person's rapport with others, with all the complexity such relations imply" (117). By the nineteenth century, though, silent reading was very much an established practice; reading aloud stands out even more markedly as a communal version of a potentially private experience. In fact, Dickens's public readings were so popular in part because his stories were already familiar in print. The dominant textuality that

underlies Victorian reading aloud differs from both the non-textuality of pre-modern storytelling and the limited textuality of early modern reading.

7. This depiction of the ear departs from Romantic notions of aurality, in which the relationship of sound and self is perhaps a less alienated one. See, for example, Hazlitt's formulation in "The Letter-Bell" – sound "strikes upon the ear, it vibrates to the brain," and eventually, as Hazlitt writes, brings him "as it were to myself" (XVII: 377) – or Wordsworth's *Excursion*, which describes "the passages / Through which the ear converses with the heart" (4: 1154–1155). Kevis Goodman remarks on this seemingly immediate relationship between sound and self: "the trope of sound and auricular perception, that pathway that leads into the ears, renders uncomfortable proximity" (138). In these Victorian studies, as we shall see, the ear's relationship with the mouth seems to bypass such central seats of self as "brain" and "heart."

8. Carpenter was neither the first nor the last to make this assertion: the idea that the ear guides the voice appears in numerous other studies from the period. "We acquire our ideas of the tone of the voice entirely by the ear," John Bostock writes in the 1830s; "in the case of speech, we derive our knowledge principally from the same sense" (760). Alexander Bain similarly promoted the ear as "the regulator of the effects produced by the spontaneity of the Voice" in his mid-century treatise *Senses and the Intellect*; even in "Articulate Speech, we have likewise a case of vocal execution guided by the ear" (434).

9. Derrida famously comments on the passivity of the ear, its permanent vulnerability to sensual assault: "the ear is the most tendered and most open organ, the one that, as Freud reminds us, the infant cannot close" (33). Picker quotes a mid-Victorian *Times* leader that expresses virtually the same thought: the ear as the "most helpless faculty we have" – "the most ethereal and most persecuted of our senses" (66).

10. Derrida reminds us too that the ear and mouth share the quality of being orifices: the "invaginated folds and the involuted orificiality" that are sensitive to sound waves "whether or not they come from the outside, whether they are emitted or received" (36).

11. Ezra Pound, for example, preferred Robert Browning to Tennyson because he did not "gum up the sound" of his poetry (qtd. in Tucker, *Tennyson* 73).

12. Arthur, when he learns of Bedivere's failure, acknowledges his knight's overdependence on the visual: he angrily sends him back again, accusing him of "[v]aluing the giddy pleasure of the eyes" (128).

13. Arthur's interrogation, too, changes at this point: "Speak out: what is it thou hast heard, or seen?" (150). Whereas in his earlier inquiries the King sought the visual narrative first and the aural narrative second ("Watch what thou seëst, and lightly bring me word" [34–38]; "What is it thou hast seen? or what hast

heard?" [67–68]), this third command reverses the order and calls immediately for the aural – and its first injunction, of course, is to "speak."

14. This is not to ignore the fact that Bedivere and Everard Hall do not exist at the same level of fiction within the poem; Bedivere cannot be said to "hear" the narrator exactly, but as a storyteller (first only to Arthur and then, in 1869, to the readers of the *Idylls*) his narration is an echo of the narrator's narration. And vice-versa. Tucker sums up the nuances of this "miracle of narration": "The coincidence between lines 159–161 and 144–146 is so close that we must wonder whose words they are. Historical common sense . . . tells us that the words are Bedivere's and that his speech to Arthur initiates a faithful communication passing through Malory, whom Tennyson follows here quite closely, culminating in the present text. But such common sense then makes nonsense of Excalibur's aerial transit, which Bedivere has just disclaimed seeing" (334).

15. A similar vocal community appears, in later versions of the complete *Idylls*, as the very formation of the Round Table: "Arthur sat / Crowned on the dais, and his warriors cried, / 'Be thou the king, and we will work thy will / Who love thee.' Then the King in low deep tones / And simple words on great authority, / Bound them by so strait vows to his own self" ("The Coming of Arthur" 256–261).

16. A series of Arthurian idylls had appeared in 1859, made up of "Enid," "Vivien," "Elaine," and "Guinevere"; in 1870 revised versions of these poems were printed in a full collection of the extant *Idylls of the King* (minus "The Last Tournament," "Gareth and Lynette," and "Balin and Balan"). Although *The Holy Grail*'s title page is dated 1870, the book was actually printed in late 1869, just in time for the Christmas season; thus its publication actually predates the collected edition. For a detailed account of the changes between the various editions of "The Passing of Arthur," see Jones and Pfordresher.

17. An interesting side note: Edison's hearing deficit forced him to hear through his mouth, as it were, gripping the legs of pianos with his teeth in order to feel the vibrations (see Picker 133).

Poetic Afterlives

1. Tim Armstrong's *Modernism, Technology, and the Body*, for example, suggests a discontinuity between Victorian and modernist automatic writing practices, the latter being defined by their new interest in modes of production and reception (187). Helen Sword's *Ghostwriting Modernism*, likewise, argues that supernatural tales from the early twentieth century "betray a characteristically modernist obsession with all things textual:

reading, writing, literature, authorship, publication, libraries, and even the discourses and methodologies of literary criticism" (11). Roger Luckhurst describes the SPR's cross-correspondences, which I will address at length in this chapter, as an "audacious posthumous experiment" that anticipates many of the precepts of modernist collage (264).

2. As John Durham Peters writes, "Spiritualism was one of the chief sites at which the cultural and metaphysical implications of new forms of communication were worked out" (100). Peters's *Speaking into the Air* and Pamela Thurschwell's *Literature, Technology, and Magical Thinking* position spiritualism in the context of technology and media. Lawrence Rainey's "Taking Dictation" does the same for automatic writing in particular; Steven Connor's "The Machine in the Ghost" investigates acoustic technologies; Roger Luckhurst focuses on telepathy. Jill Galvan's *The Sympathetic Medium* explores the problem of gender in particular in spiritualist communication technologies.

3. The very event that birthed the modern spiritualist movement engendered its fascination with language: the mysterious rappings heard by the Fox sisters in upstate New York in 1848, rappings that laboriously spelled out, letter by letter, tidings from the other world. In the decades that followed, spiritualist technologies of writing evolved dramatically. Table-rapping – already a species of letter-based writing – grew to incorporate more literal writing, as séance participants would attach pencils to the legs of levitating tables and let them write upon sheets of paper (see Rainey 127). These crude writing devices were supplanted by a variety of machines for inscription, from the spiritualist "telegraph" to the Ouija board. Psychical research, which explored such purportedly paranormal phenomena as telepathy, hypnosis, and the afterlife, was necessarily a system of research into problems of material and immaterial communication.

4. In its earliest days, automatic writing appeared as a tool with more potential than precise application. "Automatic writing is not a key to all the recesses of our being," Myers wrote in 1886, summarizing the topic for the newly founded Society for Psychical Research; "But it is a key to *something*, and it is a key that will actually turn in the lock" ("Automatic Writing III" 261).

5. Such materialism is at odds with late-twentieth-century readings of the spiritualist movement, which understood it as a response to the Victorian era's movement toward agnosticism. According to this critical tradition, spiritualism seemed to refocus the cultural spotlight on immaterial properties of the mind and soul. See, for example, Janet Oppenheim and Jeffrey Sconce. Much of the work on spiritualism and media technology that I reference in this chapter's introductory paragraphs works to rewrite this critical narrative.

6. At times language itself is depicted as protoplasmic: "Students of *language* are, as might be expected, particularly liable to this trick [of writing unconsciously]; and many an odd Greek word, oozing its way, so to speak, from some recess of memory, has been unconsciously scribbled on the edge of composition papers in the nervousness of examination" (Myers 222–223). In this formulation, words achieve the pseudo-material status of ectoplasm, the most famous physical manifestation of spiritualist mediums: Greek words "ooze" out of the recesses of the mind, just mysterious substances were produced from the recesses of mediums' bodies.

7. As in Romantic studies of hallucination, reading and reciting poetry seems to be a common trigger of automatic trance. Another report begins with the writer strolling through the garden, "repeating aloud to myself the verses of a poem," when they enter an automatic trance state (II: 105).

8. In fin-de-siècle fiction, Stewart writes, the "phenomenology of reading is renarrativized as gothic melodrama," emphasizing the close relationship of "textual contact to hypnotic co-optation" (345–346).

9. In automatic scripts, questions posed by sitters (or by the automatist herself) are included in parentheses.

10. Such wordplay was indeed often crude, and at times it even tended toward obscenity: "Planchette," Myers testifies, "is sadly given to *swear*" ("Automatic Writing II" 44).

11. His widow published a volume of his collected writings after his death, fittingly titled *Fragments of Prose and Poetry* (1904). Overall, Myers's literary work has not attracted much attention from scholars. See John Beer's *Post-Romantic Consciousness* and *Providence and Love*, which situate Myers's poetry alongside more canonical poets of the late nineteenth century; and Helen Groth's "Subliminal Histories: Psychological Experimentation in the Poetry and Poetics of Frederic W. H. Myers."

12. In *The Invention of Telepathy*, Luckhurst argues for the necessity of resisting categorizing telepathy as a pseudo-science.

13. For Myers, automatic writing played a key role in the investigation of both telepathy and spirit communication. While telepathy and spiritualism claimed to provide valid explanations for automatic writing as the interaction of an external mind on a passive body, they also allowed for the fact that that body's automatism could in itself be the source of the automatic script. In his introductory investigation of automatic writing – "On a Telepathic Explanation of Some So-called Spiritualistic Phenomena," published in the second volume of the *Proceedings of the SPR* – Myers argues that "automatic writing is a phenomenon liable to be originated in various ways in the human organism" (223).

14. MacFarlane writes that plagiarism comes to be thought of as "an extreme form of empathy; an identification so acute that it required a near-total abolition of the writer's being" (210). In Myers's case, however, we see the opposite move: a way of establishing critical superiority via practices of plagiarism and extraction.

15. As it turned out, no medium was able to correctly predict the message it contained. Myers's selected excerpt, of course, is apt: if the automatist had indeed received this very message, it would enact the sentiment contained in Wordsworth's poem.

16. For a more detailed history of the cross-correspondences, see Galvan's *BRANCH* essay "Tennyson's Ghosts: The Psychical Research Case of the Cross-Correspondences" and Leigh Wilson's chapter on "The Cross-Correspondences, the Nature of Evidence, and the Matter of Writing."

17. For example, Fleming acknowledged that she owned the *Oxford Book of English Verse*, so when she automatically reproduces lines from Roden Noel's "Tintagel," Johnson must track down whether that particular poem is in that collection (see Johnson, "On the Automatic" 326).

18. While French surrealist experiments recognized automatic writing as part of a specific literary movement, no analogous movement existed in Britain (see London 155).

19. Fleming readily admitted to reading Myers's published poetry; as she indicates, she was inspired to experiment with automatic writing after reading about the practice in *Human Personality*. But the extent to which Myers's language finds its way into her automatic writing exceeds even the SPR's standards of "literary personation." As Johnson notes, much of Fleming's later script is derived directly from quotations of Myers's *Fragments of Prose and Poetry* ("On the Automatic" 267).

20. Fleming, for instance, was known for her remarkable ability to memorize. A family friend describes her as possessing "a rare literary memory. I believe there is not a single line of Shakespeare's which she cannot quote." A cousin similarly notes, "Her memory was extraordinary, and everything she read was retained, pigeonholed and produced at will. One family amusement was to give a quotation from Shakespeare, and she would immediately continue it till the scene or play was finished." And another friend complains: "She had but one flaw; a tendency to interminable poetic quotation. At times, it really was Half Hours with the Best Authors!" (qtd. in Lee 18, 121, 99).

21. Jason Rudy examines the spiritualist poetics of composition – the "paradoxical notion of touching a material yet spiritual poetic instrument" – in order to investigate Elizabeth Barrett Browning's depiction of Aurora Leigh as "a fully realized and corporeal electric poetess" (176, 183).

22. "To fashion the birth robes for them / Who are just born—being dead" (113–114).

23. "A Lady, the wonder of her kind, / Whose form was upborne by a lovely mind" (II.5–6).
24. "And on his grave with shining eyes / The Syrian stars look down" (175076).
25. "Only one youth, and the bright life was shrouded; / Only one morning, and the day was clouded" (46–47).
26. Percy Bysshe Shelley, "Remembrance": "Roses for a matron's head— / Violets for a maiden dead" (18–19).
27. Alfred Tennyson, "Ode on the Death of the Duke of Wellington": "this is he / Was great by land as thou by sea" (83–84).
28. Tennyson, "The Higher Pantheism": "Speak to Him thou for He hears, and Spirit with Spirit can meet— / Closer He is than breathing, and nearer than hands and feet" (11–12).
29. William Wordsworth, "A slumber did my spirit seal": "Roll'd round in earth's diurnal course / With rocks, and stones, and trees!" (7–8).
30. Tennyson, *In Memoriam* II: "My love involves the love before" (21); "I shall not lose thee tho' I die" (28).
31. Galvan argues that Tennyson was a particularly important poet for the cross-correspondences because of the way his work engaged with problems of modernity and cultural change, and particularly with the complex nature of faith and materialism ("Tennyson's Ghosts").
32. Christina Rossetti, "Song: When I Am Dead": "When I am dead, my dearest, / Sing no sad songs for me" (1–2).
33. Tennyson, "Edward Gray": "But I will love no more, no more, / Till Ellen Adair come back to me. / . . . / There lies the body of Ellen Adair! / And there the heart of Edward Gray!" (31–36).
34. Dante Gabriel Rossetti, "The Blessed Damozel": "Where the lady Mary is, / With her five handmaidens" (104–105).
35. Elizabeth Barrett Browning, "I thought once how Theocritus had sung" (*Sonnets from the Portuguese* I): "'Death,' I said, But, there, / The silver answer rang,—'Not Death, but Love'" (13–14).
36. Of the critical studies of the cross-correspondences, Jill Galvan gives the most sustained attention to genre in her essay "Tennyson's Ghosts"; which argues that Tennyson's poetry played its particularly prominent role in the scripts because of the poet's own complex relationship to cultural change. For Galvan, Tennyson's presence here is notable particularly because it "points up the place of modernity in the Victorian past," resisting models of periodization that posit a clean divide between nineteenth-century thought and twentieth-century modernism ("Tennyson's Ghosts").
37. As Saint-Amour contends, the later Victorians' increased interest in the cento poem suggests that "the literary object is the sum of its maker's readerly acts

of consumption"; the column identifying the cento's source poems acts as a "miscellaneous poetic mini-canon" (42).

38. As Neil Hertz has argued, underwriting many assumptions of literary scholarship is a self-sustaining cycle in which the reader's own knowledge shapes the limits of allusion (158). He equates this desire to arrive at the limits of allusion with the process of uncovering an act of plagiarism: "What is sought in each case is an end to an ongoing interpretive process" (158).

39. My interpretation of "'Wireless'" builds especially on the work of Richard Menke, Jill Galvan, Sam Halliday, Roger Luckhurst, Pamela Thurschwell, and Jeffrey Sconce, each of whom raise important questions about Kipling's depiction of technology. Where my reading departs most drastically from theirs, however, is in my attention to the role of the critical observer, which leads me to reevaluate assumptions about the success of the transmission.

40. Wireless was the invention of Guglielmo Marconi, a young Italian who moved to England in the 1890s, founding his wireless company there in 1897. As Roger Luckhurst establishes in *The Invention of Telepathy*, this effectively placed Britain at the forefront of research in wireless communication, and it trained the public eye upon the promise of ethereal communication and the potential relationship between telepathy and wireless technology. And, like telepathy and spirit communication, it carried with it the suggestion of ethereal communication as a strangely embodied experience. As we've seen in the previous sections, spiritualist automatic writing established the body as a kind of shared technology. The wireless telegraph provoked similar speculation: Jeffrey Sconce's history of technology recounts that press coverage of the new wireless medium portrayed it as "an omnipresent and inescapable force that could bathe and even occupy the body," noting that "[s]ome believed the human body itself could function as an aerial or even a transmitter for these strange signals" (67). The human aerial, like the human "protoplasmic machine" of spiritualist automatic writing, emphasizes the mediacy of the body in seemingly immaterial long-distance communication technologies.

41. When Kipling met Marconi in 1899, he depicted his own information-gathering as possibly unconscious, much like his consumptive druggist who unconsciously channels the language of Keats: "During the talk I consciously or unconsciously was gathering much material for my story, 'Wireless,' in which I carried the idea of etheric vibrations into the possibility of thought transference" (qtd. in McGivering 33).

42. The very first signs of Shaynor's mediumship act to disavow his conscious mind and focus on his body. When the ailing druggist first drinks the concoction that provokes his trancelike state, the narrator notes that he "beheld all meaning and consciousness die out of the swiftly dilating

pupils" (188). When Shaynor begins to speak, his body is at the mercy of the language that travels through him:

> His lips moved without cessation. I stepped nearer to listen. 'And threw—and threw—and threw,' he repeated, his face all sharp with some inexplicable agony.
> I moved forward astonished. But it was then he found words—delivered roundly and clearly. These:
> And threw warm gules on Madeleine's young breast. (191)

When this compulsive speech turns to compulsive script, the narrator watches over his shoulder, reading "half-formed words, sentences, and wild scratches" (192):

> Under the blue-veined hand—the dry hand of the consumptive—came away clear, without erasure:
> And my weak spirit fails
> To think how the dead must freeze" (192)

Shaynor's pupils, his lips, his contorted face and blue-veined hand – these fragmented body parts echo the fragmented nature of the poetry he (not quite accurately) replicates.

43. Like the SPR's automatists, too, Shaynor produces poetry that provokes these associations despite the fact that it is incorrectly quoted: for example, Keats's "The owl, for all his feathers, was a-cold; / The hare limp'd trembling through the frozen grass" (2–3) is transmitted, via Shaynor, as "The hare, in spite of fur, was very cold" (192).

44. As this quote makes clear, the text never fully resolves the question of the source of Shaynor's poetry. While it could be argued that the scene is one of composition alone, most critics read it as a scene of garbled transmission or pseudo-mediumship; the explicit parallel Kipling draws between poetic production and the transmission of wireless signals substantiates this reading.

45. It is worth noting that both these instances of aesthetic judgment are accompanied by a focus on the narrator's bodily state. In the first, he "finds himself" nodding in agreement with the editorial intervention – an involuntary bodily response. In the second, his state of anxiety registers physically, parching his throat.

46. Galvan and Sword both argue that Eliot's 1919 essay draws upon the discourse of spiritualism (Galvan 182–184; Sword 94).

47. "Someone said: 'The dead writers are remote from us because we know so much more than they did,'" Eliot writes; "Precisely, and they are that which we know" (25). The dead poets, then, make up more than the body of language from which modern poetry draws. In fact, they make up the

body of knowledge of the modern person, the "we" who encounters poetry, both old and new.

48. As Menke argues, Kipling's tale "hints at something mechanical within the human, something machinelike in the human 'brain'" (220). I want to extend this insight, though, and note that this mechanization of the human is tied deliberately to the memorization and transmission of language.

49. Menke details these hints: "a frosty night, a consecrated portrait, light through colored glass, the smell of incense; a druggist, a lover named Fanny, a journey in the cold, a cough and a drop of blood. The tale's elaborate descriptions were really Keats's pre-scriptions all along. ... [E]xamined closely, each realistic detail reveals itself as a micro-quotation from that collection" (232).

50. Friedrich Kittler claims that writing in 1900 is "disconnected from all discursive technologies, is no longer based on an individual capable of imbuing it with coherence through connecting curves and the pressure of the pen; it swells in an apparatus that cuts up individuals into test materials" (*Discourse Networks* 223).

The Autonomous Poem

1. Catherine Gallagher's "The History of Literary Criticism" traces the movement and its impact on the profession, particularly in America. Jane Gallop's "The Historicization of Literary Studies and the Fate of Close Reading" argues for the centrality of New Critical reading practices to the future of the profession. For a discussion of the cognitive strategies demanded by Richards's New Criticism, see Andrew Elfenbein's "Cognitive Science and the History of Reading."

2. Dames also makes the important point that *Principles* moves explicitly toward poetry and away from the study of fiction, despite Richards's initial interest in publishing a physiological theory of the novel (247–255).

3. In the process, Richards raises the concern that his research may provide for commercially minded writers a catalog of easy-to-exploit readerly weaknesses: "I am not without fears that my efforts may prove of assistance to young poets (and others) desiring to increase their sales. A set of formulae for 'nation-wide appeal' seems to be a just possible outcome" (8n3).

4. Richards emphasizes the importance of this particular critical trap for both the study of literature and the study of human culture: "So much that passes for poetry is written, and so much reading of even the most original poetry is governed, by these fixed conventionalized reactions that their natural history will repay investigation. Their intervention, moreover, in all forms of human activity – in business, in personal relationships, in public affairs, in Courts of

Justice – will be recognized, and any light which the study of poetry may throw upon their causes, their services, their disadvantages, and on the ways in which they may be overcome, should be generally welcome" (228).

5. Richards also describes the practical (if lamentable) utility of the stock response in terms of such "energy systems." "[A]n extensive repertory of stock responses is a necessity," he acknowledges; "Few minds could prosper if they had to work out an original, 'made-to-measure' response to meet every situation that arose—their supplies of mental energy would be too soon exhausted and the wear and tear on the nervous system would be too great" (228).

6. Richards's depiction of this kind of fatal familiarity echoes at times Eliot's "Tradition at the Individual Talent": "The only touches of character that anyone can point to are the echoes of other poets. Each of them might well have been written by a committee" (231). Where Eliot celebrates the ability of dead poets to speak through live ones, Richards views this kind of ventriloquism as corporate.

Bibliography

Abercrombie, John. *Inquiries Concerning the Intellectual Powers, and the Investigation of Truth.* 1830. Rev. ed., New York: Robert B. Collins, 1853.

Ablow, Rachel. *The Marriage of Minds: Reading Sympathy in the Victorian Marriage Plot.* Stanford University Press, 2007.

Alderson, John. *An Essay on Apparitions: In Which Their Appearance Is Accounted for by Causes Wholly Independent of Preternatural Agency.* Rev. ed., London: Longman, Hurst, Rees, Orme, Brown, and Green, 1823.

Alison, William Pulteney. "Observations on the Physiological Principle of Sympathy." *Transactions of the Medico-Chirurgical Society of Edinburgh*, vol. 2, 1826, pp. 165–228.

Allan, David. *Commonplace Books and Reading in Georgian England.* Cambridge University Press, 2010.

Armstrong, Tim. *Modernism, Technology and the Body: A Cultural Study.* Cambridge University Press, 1998.

Arnold, Matthew. "Obermann Once More." *The Poems of Matthew Arnold.* Edited by Kenneth Alcott, Longman, 1979, pp. 559–576.

Austin, Alfred. "The Vice of Reading." *Temple Bar Magazine*, 42, September 1874, pp. 251–257.

Austin, Linda M. *Nostalgia in Transition, 1780–1917.* University of Virginia Press, 2007.

Bain, Alexander. *The Emotions and the Will.* 1859. 3rd American ed., New York: D. Appleton and Company, 1886.

The Senses and the Intellect. 1855. 3rd ed., London: Longmans, Green, and Co., 1868.

Balfour, Gerald. "A Study of the Psychological Aspects of Mrs. Willett's Mediumship." *Proceedings of the Society for Psychical Research*, vol. 43, 1935, pp. 43–318.

Balfour, Jean. "The 'Palm Sunday' Case: New Light on an Old Love Story." *Proceedings of the Society for Psychical Research*, vol. 52, 1960, pp. 79–267.

Banfield, Ann. *Unspeakable Sentences: Narration and Representation in the Language of Fiction.* Routledge & Kegan Paul, 1982.

[Barnett, E. S., and William Gifford.] Review of *Lectures on the English Poets*, by William Hazlitt. *Quarterly Review*, vol. xix, July 1818, pp. 424–434.

Barrett Browning, Elizabeth. "I Thought Once How Theocritus Had Sung." *Selected Writings*. Edited by Josie Billington and Philip Davis, Oxford University Press, 2014, p. 117.

Beer, Gillian. "Rhyming as Resurrection." *Memory and Memorials, 1789–1914: Literary and Cultural Perspectives*. Edited by Matthew Campbell, Jacqueline M. Labbe, and Sally Shuttleworth, Routledge, 2000, pp. 189–207.

Beer, John. *Post-Romantic Consciousness: Dickens to Plath*. Palgrave, 2003.

    Providence and Love: Studies in Wordsworth, Channing, Myers, George Eliot, and Ruskin. Clarendon Press, 1998.

Bell, Alexander Melville. *Elocutionary Manual: The Principles of Elocution*. 7th ed., Washington, DC: Volta Bureau, 1887.

Benedict, Barbara. "The 'Beauties' of Literature, 1750–1820: Tasteful Prose and Fine Rhyme for Private Consumption." *1650–1850: Ideas, Aesthetics, and Inquiries in the Early Modern Era*, vol. 1, 1994, pp. 317–346.

    "The Paradox of the Anthology: Collecting and Différence in Eighteenth-Century Britain." *New Literary History*, vol. 34, no. 2, 2003, pp. 231–256.

Best, Stephen, and Sharon Marcus. "Surface Reading: An Introduction." *Representations*, vol. 108, no. 1, 2009, pp. 1–21.

Blair, Kirstie. *Victorian Poetry and the Culture of the Heart*. Oxford University Press, 2006.

Bostock, John. *An Elementary System of Physiology*. 4th ed., London: Henry G. Bohn, 1844.

Brewer, John. "Sentiment and Sensibility." *Cambridge History*, pp. 21–44.

Brewster, David. *Letters on Natural Magic: Addressed to Sir Walter Scott, Bart*. 6th ed., London: John Murray, 1851.

The Broadview Anthology of Victorian Poetry and Poetic Theory. Edited by Thomas J. Collins and Vivienne J. Rundle, Broadview, 1999.

Brown, Theodore M. "From Mechanism to Vitalism in Eighteenth-Century English Physiology." *Journal of the History of Biology*, vol. 7, no. 2, 1974, pp. 179–216.

Browning, Robert. "Mr. Sludge, 'The Medium.'" *Dramatis Personae*. London: Chapman and Hall, 1864. pp. 171–236.

The Cambridge History of English Romantic Literature. Edited by James Chandler, Cambridge University Press, 2009.

Carpenter, William B. *The Doctrine of Human Automatism*. London: Sunday Leisure Society, 1875.

    Principles of Human Physiology. 3rd American ed., Philadelphia: Lea and Blanchard, 1847.

    Principles of Mental Physiology. New York: D. Appleton & Company, 1874.

Castle, Terry. "Phantasmagoria: Spectral Technology and the Metaphysics of Modern Reverie." *Critical Inquiry*, vol. 15, Autumn 1988, pp. 26–61.

Chambers, William, and Robert Chambers, editors. *Chambers's Information for the People*. London: Orr and Smith, 1835.

Chandler, James. "Hallam, Tennyson, and the Poetry of Sensation: Aestheticist Allegories of a Counter-Public Sphere." *Studies in Romanticism*, vol. 33, no. 4, 1994, pp. 527–537.

"The Languages of Sentiment." *Textual Practice*, vol. 22, no. 1, 2008, pp. 21–39.

Chartier, Roger. "Leisure and Sociability: Reading Aloud in Early Modern Europe." *Urban Life in the Renaissance*. Edited by Susan Zimmerman and Ronald F. E. Weissman, University of Delaware Press, 1989, pp. 103–120.

Christensen, Jerome. *Coleridge's Blessed Machine of Language*. Cornell University Press, 1981.

Clarke, Edwin and L. S. Jacyna. *Nineteenth-Century Origins of Neuroscientific Concepts*. University of California Press, 1987.

Cohn, Elisha. *Still Life: Suspended Development in the Victorian Novel*. Oxford University Press, 2016.

Coleridge, Samuel Taylor. *Biographia Literaria*. The Collected Works of Samuel Taylor Coleridge. Edited by James Engell and W. Jackson Bate, vol. 7, Princeton University Press, 1983.

"Christabel." *Romanticism: An Anthology*. 2nd ed. Edited by Duncan Wu, Blackwell, 2004, pp. 475–490.

The Collected Letters of Samuel Taylor Coleridge. Edited by Earl Leslie Griggs, Clarendon Press, 1959. 6 vols.

The Complete Poetical Works of Samuel Taylor Coleridge. Edited by Ernest Hartley Coleridge, vol. I: *Poems*, Clarendon Press, 1912.

"The Eolian Harp." *The Complete Poetical Works of Samuel Taylor Coleridge*. Vol. I. Edited by Ernest Hartley Coleridge, Clarendon Press, 1912, pp. 100–102.

"Kubla Khan: A Vision in a Dream." *Romanticism: An Anthology*. 2nd ed., Edited by Duncan Wu, Blackwell, 2004, pp. 522–524.

Lectures and Notes on Shakspere and Other English Poets. George Bell and Sons, 1904.

Letter to Thomas Boosey, Jr., May 20, 1817. *Collected Letters of Samuel Taylor Coleridge*, vol. IV. Edited by Earl Leslie Griggs, Clarendon Press, 2002, pp. 730–731.

"The Rime of the Ancyent Marinere." In *Lyrical Ballads and Related Writings*. Edited by William Richey and Daniel Robinson, Houghton Mifflin, 2002, pp. 23–43.

Collins, John Churton. *Illustrations of Tennyson*. London: Chatto & Windus, 1891.

Collins, Philip. *Reading Aloud: A Victorian Métier*. Tennyson Research Centre, 1972.

Conder, Josiah. Review of "Christabel," by Samuel Taylor Coleridge. *Eclectic Review* 2nd series, V, June 1816, pp. 565–572. Reprinted in Reiman, vol. I, pp. 373–376.

Connor, Steven. *Dumbstruck: A Cultural History of Ventriloquism*. Oxford University Press, 2000.

"The Machine in the Ghost: Spiritualism, Technology and the 'Direct Voice'." *Ghosts: Deconstruction, Psychoanalysis, History.* Edited by Peter Buse and Andrew Stott, Macmillan, 1999, pp. 203–225.

Conrad, Joseph. *Heart of Darkness.* Edited by Robert Kimbrough, Norton, 1988.

Crary, Jonathan. *Suspensions of Perception.* MIT Press, 2000.

Crawford, Rachel. "Thieves of Language: Coleridge, Wordsworth, Scott, and the Contexts of 'Alice du Clos'." *European Romantic Review,* vol. 7, no. 1, 1996, pp. 1–25.

Cummins, Geraldine. *Unseen Adventures: An Autobiography Covering Thirty-Four Years of Work in Psychical Research.* Rider and Company, 1951.

Dallas, E[neas] S[weetland]. *The Gay Science.* London: Chapman and Hall, 1866. 2 vols.

Dames, Nicholas. *The Physiology of the Novel: Reading, Neural Science, and the Form of Victorian Fiction.* Oxford University Press, 2007.

Darwin, Erasmus. *Zoönomia; or, The Laws of Organic Life.* 1796. 2nd American ed., Boston: Thomas and Andrews, 1803.

De Quincey, Thomas. *Recollections of the Lakes and the Lake Poets.* Edited by David Wright, Penguin, 1985.

Derrida, Jacques. *The Ear of the Other: Otobiography, Transference, Translation.* Translated by Peggy Kamuf, edited by Christie V. McDonald, Schocken Books, 1985.

D'Orsey, A. J. D. "The Art of Reading Aloud." *Victoria Magazine,* vol. 18, 1871, pp. 146–160.

Eilenberg, Susan. *Strange Power of Speech: Wordsworth, Coleridge, and Literary Possession.* Oxford University Press, 1992.

Elfenbein, Andrew. *Byron and the Victorians.* Cambridge University Press, 1995.

"Cognitive Science and the History of Reading." *PMLA,* vol. 121, no. 2, 2006, pp. 484–502.

Romanticism and the Rise of English. Stanford University Press, 2009.

Eliot, T. S. "Tradition and the Individual Talent." 1919. *Selected Prose.* Edited by John Hayward, Penguin, 1953, pp. 21–31.

Elliotson, John. *Human Physiology.* London: Longman, Rees, Orme, Brown, Green, and Longman, 1835.

Ferriar, John. *An Essay Towards a Theory of Apparitions.* London: Cadell and Davies, 1819.

Fleming, Alice Macdonald (Kipling). *A Pinchbeck Goddess.* New York: D. Appleton and Company, 1897.

Flesch, William. "Quoting Poetry." *Critical Inquiry,* vol. 18, no. 1, 1991, pp. 42–63.

Flint, Kate. *The Woman Reader, 1837–1914.* Clarendon Press, 1993.

Ford, Jennifer. *Coleridge on Dreaming: Romanticism, Dreams and the Medical Imagination.* Cambridge University Press, 1998.

Fox, William Johnson. Review of *Poems, Chiefly Lyrical,* by Alfred Tennyson. *Westminster Review,* vol. xiv, Jan. 1831, pp. 210–224.

Freud, Sigmund. *Beyond the Pleasure Principle.* Translated from 2nd German ed. by C. J. M. Hubback, Hogarth Press, 1948.

Gallagher, Catherine. "The History of Literary Criticism." *American Academic Culture in Transformation: Fifty Years, Four Disciplines.* Edited by Thomas Bender and Carl E. Schorske, Princeton University Press, 1998, pp. 151–171.

Gallop, Jane. "The Historicization of Literary Studies and the Fate of Close Reading." *Profession*, 2007, pp. 181–186.

Galvan, Jill. *The Sympathetic Medium: Feminine Channeling, the Occult, and Communication Technologies, 1859–1919.* Cornell University Press, 2010.

"Tennyson's Ghosts: The Psychical Research Case of the Cross-Correspondences, 1901–c.1936." *BRANCH: Britain, Representation and Nineteenth-Century History.* Edited by Dino Franco Felluga, Extension of *Romanticism and Victorianism on the Net.* www.branchcollective.org. Accessed March 31, 2014.

"The Victorian Post-Human: Transmission, Information and the Séance." *The Ashgate Research Companion to Nineteenth-Century Spiritualism and the Occult.* Edited by Tatiana Kontou and Sarah Willburn, Ashgate, 2012, pp. 55–78.

Gigante, Denise. *Taste: A Literary History.* Yale University Press, 2005.

Gitelman, Lisa. *Scripts, Grooves, and Writing Machines: Representing Technology in the Edison Era.* Stanford University Press, 1999.

"Souvenir Foils: On the Status of Print at the Origin of Recorded Sound." *New Media, 1740–1914.* Edited by Lisa Gitelman and Geoffrey B. Pingree, MIT Press, 2003, pp. 157–174.

Goodman, Kevis. *Georgic Modernity and British Romanticism: Poetry and the Mediation of History.* Cambridge University Press, 2004.

"'Uncertain Disease': Nostalgia, Pathologies of Motion, Practices of Reading." *Studies in Romanticism*, vol. 49, Summer 2010, pp. 197–227.

Greiner, Rae. *Sympathetic Realism in Nineteenth-Century British Fiction.* Johns Hopkins University Press, 2012.

"Sympathy Time: Adam Smith, George Eliot, and the Realist Novel." *Narrative*, vol. 17, no. 3, Oct. 2009, pp. 291–311.

Griffiths, Eric. *The Printed Voice of Victorian Poetry.* Clarendon Press, 1989.

Groth, Helen. "Subliminal Histories: Psychological Experimentation in the Poetry and Poetics of Frederic W. H. Myers." *19: Interdisciplinary Studies in the Long Nineteenth Century*, vol. 12, 2011, www.19bbk.ac.uk. Accessed September 28, 2011.

Halcombe, J. J., and W. H. Stone. *The Speaker at Home: Chapters on Public Speaking and Reading Aloud.* 3rd ed., London: George Bell & Sons, 1874.

Hallam, Arthur Henry. "On Some of the Characteristics of Modern Poetry, and on the Lyrical Poems of Alfred Tennyson." *Englishman's Magazine*, vol. 1, no. 5, Aug. 1831, pp. 616–628.

"On Sympathy." *The Writings of Arthur Hallam.* Edited by T. H. Vail Motter, MLA, 1943, pp. 133–142.

Halliday, Sam. *Science and Technology in the Age of Hawthorne, Melville, Twain, and James: Thinking and Writing Electricity.* Palgrave Macmillan, 2007.

Hamilton, Paul. "Romanticism and Poetic Autonomy." *The Cambridge History of English Romantic Literature.* Edited by James Chandler, Cambridge University Press, 2009, pp. 427–450.

Hamilton, William. *Lectures on Metaphysics.* Given at University of Edinburgh, 1836–1837. New York: Sheldon and Company, 1860. 2 vols.

Hartley, David. *Observations on Man, His Frame, His Duty, and His Expectations.* 6th ed., London: Thomas Tegg and Son, 1834.

Hazlitt, William. *The Complete Works of William Hazlitt.* Edited by P. P. Howe, J. M. Dent and Sons, 1930. 21 vols.

Review of "Kubla Khan," by Samuel Taylor Coleridge. *Examiner,* 2 Jun. 1816, pp. 348–349. Reprinted in Reiman, vol. II, pp. 530–531.

Hertz, Neil. "Two Extravagant Teachings." *The End of the Line: Essays on Psychoanalysis and the Sublime.* Columbia University Press, 1985, pp. 144–159.

Hibbert, Samuel. *Sketches of the Philosophy of Apparitions; or, an Attempt to Trace such Illusions to Their Physical Causes.* 2nd ed., Edinburgh, 1825.

Hodgson, Richard. "A Further Record of Observations of Certain Phenomena of Trance." *Proceedings of the Society for Psychical Research,* vol. 13, 1897–1898.

Holland, Henry. *Medical Notes and Reflections.* London: Longman, Orme, Brown, Green, and Longmans, 1839.

Holmes, Richard. *Coleridge: Darker Reflections, 1804–1834.* Pantheon, 1999.

Hood, Thomas. "The Death-bed." *Selected Poems of Thomas Hood.* Edited by John Clubbe, Harvard University Press, 1970, p. 64.

Hughes, Winifred. "E. S. Dallas: Victorian Poetics in Transition." *Victorian Poetry,* vol. 23, no. 1, 1985, pp. 1–21.

Hutton, R. H. "Tennyson." *Literary Essays.* 3rd ed., rev. and enlarged. London: Macmillan and Co, 1888, pp. 361–468.

Jackson, Noel. *Science and Sensation in Romantic Poetry.* Cambridge University Press, 2008.

Jaffe, Audrey. *Scenes of Sympathy: Identity and Representation in Victorian Fiction.* Cornell University Press, 2000.

Johns, Adrian. "Changes in the World of Publishing." *Cambridge History,* pp. 377–402.

Johnson, Alice. "On the Automatic Writing of Mrs. Holland." *Proceedings of the Society for Psychical Research,* vol. 21, 1908, pp. 166–391.

"Third Report on Mrs. Holland's Script." *Proceedings of the Society for Psychical Research,* vol. 25, 1911, pp. 218–303.

Jones, Richard. *The Growth of the Idylls of the King.* Philadelphia: J. B. Lippincott Company, 1895.

Keats, John. "The Eve of St Agnes." *Romanticism: An Anthology.* 2nd ed. Edited by Duncan Wu, Blackwell, 2004, pp. 1043–1053.

Letter to Richard Woodhouse. October 27, 1818. *Romanticism: An Anthology.* 2nd ed., Edited by Duncan Wu, Blackwell, 2004, p. 1042.

Kipling, Rudyard. "The Uses of Reading." *Writings on Writing.* Edited by Sandra Kemp and Lisa Lewis, Cambridge University Press, 1996, pp. 56–67.

"'Wireless.'" *Traffics and Discoveries.* 1904. Penguin, 1987, pp. 180–199.

Kittler, Friedrich. *Discourse Networks 1800/1900.* Translated by Michael Metteer with Chris Cullens, Stanford University Press, 1990.

    Gramophone, Film, Typewriter. Translated by Geoffrey Winthrop-Young and Michael Wutz, Stanford University Press, 1999.

Kreilkamp, Ivan. *Voice and the Victorian Storyteller.* Cambridge University Press, 2005.

Kroll, Alison Adler. "Tennyson and the Metaphysics of Material Culture: The Early Poetry." *Victorian Poetry,* vol. 47, no. 3, 2009, pp. 461–480.

"L. M." "On the Phantasms produced by Disordered Sensation. In a Letter from a Correspondent." *Journal of Natural Philosophy, Chemistry, and the Arts,* vol. 15, Sept./Dec. 1806, pp. 288–296.

La Mettrie, Julian Offray de. *Machine Man and Other Writings.* Translated and edited by Ann Thomson, Cambridge University Press, 1996.

Langan, Celeste. "Pathologies of Communication from Coleridge to Schreber." *South Atlantic Quarterly,* vol. 102, no. 1, 2003, pp. 118–152.

    "Understanding Media in 1805: Audiovisual Hallucination in *The Lay of the Last Minstrel.*" *Studies in Romanticism,* vol. 40, Spring 2001, pp. 49–70.

Langan, Celeste, and Maureen N. McLane. "The Medium of Romantic Poetry." *The Cambridge Companion to British Romantic Poetry.* Edited by James Chandler, Cambridge University Press, 2008, pp. 239–262.

Laqueur, Thomas. "Bodies, Details, and the Humanitarian Narrative." *The New Cultural History.* Edited by Lynn Hunt, University of California Press, 1989.

Laycock, Thomas. "On the Reflex Functions of the Brain." *British and Foreign Medical Review,* no. 19, 1845, pp. 298–311.

Lee, Lorna. *Trix, Kipling's Forgotten Sister: Unpublished Writings of Trix Kipling.* Oxford: Hawthorns, 2003.

Levinson, Marjorie. *The Romantic Fragment Poem: A Critique of a Form.* University of North Carolina Press, 1986.

Linley, Margaret. "Conjuring the Spirit: Victorian Poetry, Culture, and Technology." *Victorian Poetry,* vol. 41, no. 4, 2003, pp. 536–544.

London, Bette. *Writing Double: Women's Literary Partnerships.* Cornell University Press, 1999.

Luckhurst, Roger. *The Invention of Telepathy, 1870–1901.* Oxford University Press, 2002.

MacFarlane, Robert. *Original Copy: Plagiarism and Originality in Nineteenth-Century Literature.* Oxford University Press, 2007.

Magendie, Francois. *An Elementary Compendium of Physiology.* Translated by E. Milligan, 4th ed., Edinburgh: John Carfrae & Son, 1831.

Martin, Meredith. *The Rise and Fall of Meter: Poetry and English National Culture, 1860–1930.* Princeton University Press, 2012.

Maudsley, Henry. *Body and Mind.* London: Macmillan and Co., 1870.

Mays, Kelly J. "The Disease of Reading and Victorian Periodicals." *Literature in the Marketplace: Nineteenth-Century British Publishing and Reading Practices.* Edited by John O. Jordan and Robert L. Patten, Cambridge University Press, 1995, pp. 165–194.

Mazzeo, Tilar J. *Plagiarism and Literary Property in the Romantic Period.* University of Pennsylvania Press, 2007.

McGann, Jerome J. "The Meaning of the Ancient Mariner." *Critical Inquiry*, vol. 8, no. 1, 1981, pp. 35–67.

The Poetics of Sensibility: A Revolution in Literary Style. Clarendon Press, 1996.

McGivering, John H. "'Wireless': Some Reflections on a Story by Kipling, a Poem by Keats, and the Early Days of Wireless Telegraphy." *Kipling Journal*, vol. 68, Sept. 1994, p. 33.

McLane, Maureen. "Ballads and Bards: British Romantic Orality." *Modern Philology*, vol. 98, no. 3, 2001, pp. 423–443.

McLuhan, Marshall. *Understanding Media: The Extensions of Man.* Reprint. MIT Press, 1994.

Menke, Richard. *Telegraphic Realism: Victorian Fiction and Other Information Systems.* Stanford University Press, 2008.

[Merivale, John Herman.] Unsigned obituary for Samuel Taylor Coleridge in *The Edinburgh Review.* Reprinted in J. R. de J. Jackson, editor, *Coleridge: The Critical Heritage*, vol. II: 1834–1900, Routledge, 1991, p. 47.

Meynell, Alice. "A Letter from a Girl to Her Own Old Age." *Broadview*, pp. 1087–1088.

Moore, Dafydd. "Tennyson, Malory and the Ossianic Mode: *The Poems of Ossian* and 'The Death of Arthur'." *Review of English Studies*, vol. 57, no. 230, 2006, pp. 374–391.

Moretti, Franco. "Conjectures on World Literature." *New Left Review*, vol. 1, 2000, pp. 54–68.

Morgan, Benjamin. *The Outward Mind: Materialist Aesthetics in Victorian Science and Literature.* University of Chicago Press, 2017.

Müller, Johannes. *The Physiology of the Senses, Voice, and Muscular Motion, with the Mental Faculties.* Translated by William Baly, London: Taylor, Walton, and Maberly, 1848.

Muri, Allison. *The Enlightenment Cyborg: A History of Communications and Control in the Human Machine, 1660–1830.* University of Toronto Press, 2006.

Myers, Frederic W. H. "Automatic Writing II." *Proceedings of the Society for Psychical Research*, vol. 3, 1885, pp. 1–64.

"Automatic Writing III." *Proceedings of the Society for Psychical Research*, vol. 4, 1886–1887, pp. 209–261.

Human Personality and Its Survival of Bodily Death. 1903. Longmans, Green, and Co., 1904. 2 vols.

"On a Telepathic Explanation of Some So-called Spiritualistic Phenomena." *Proceedings of the Society for Psychical Research*, vol. 2, 1884, pp. 217–237.

"Tennyson as Prophet." 1889. *Science and a Future Life, with Other Essays.* London: Macmillan and Co., 1893.

"On the Trance-Phenomena of Mrs. Thompson." *Proceedings of the Society for Psychical Research*, vol. 17, June 1902, pp. 67–74.

Myers, Frederic W. H., Edward Gurney, and Frank Podmore. *Phantasms of the Living.* 1886. Edited by Eleanor Mildred Sigwick, University Books, 1962.

Nicolai. "A Memoir on the Appearance of Spectres or Phantoms occasioned by Disease, with Psychological Remarks. Read by NICOLAI to the Royal Society of Berlin, on the 28th of February, 1799." *Journal of Natural Philosophy, Chemistry, and the Arts,* vol. 6, Sept./Dec. 1803, pp. 161–179.

Nussbaum, Martha. *Poetic Justice: The Literary Imagination and Public Life.* Beacon, 1995.

Ong, Walter J. *Orality and Literacy: The Technologizing of the Word.* Edited by Terence Hawkes, Methuen, 1988.

Oppenheim, Janet. *The Other World: Spiritualism and Psychical Research in England, 1850–1914.* Cambridge University Press, 1985.

Parry, Caleb Hillier. *Elements of Pathology and Therapeutics.* Vol. 1: General Pathology. 2nd ed., Edinburgh: Crutwell, 1825.

Paterson, Robert. "On Spectral Illusions." *Edinburgh Medical and Surgical Journal,* vol. 59, 1843, pp. 77–102.

Peters, John Durham. *Speaking into the Air: A History of the Idea of Communication.* University of Chicago Press, 1999.

Pfordresher, John. *A Variorum Edition of Tennyson's Idylls of the King.* Columbia University Press, 1973.

Picker, John. *Victorian Soundscapes.* Oxford University Press, 2003.

Piddington, J. D. "Supplementary Notes on 'A Series of Concordant Automatisms'." *Proceedings of the Society for Psychical Research,* vol. 24, Mar. 1910, pp. 11–30.

Pinch, Adela. *Strange Fits of Passion: Epistemologies of Emotion, Hume to Austen.* Stanford University Press, 1996.

Price, Leah. *The Anthology and the Rise of the Novel from Richardson to George Eliot.* Cambridge University Press, 2000.

Prins, Yopie. "Historical Poetics, Dysprosody, and *The Science of English Verse.*" *PMLA,* vol. 123, no. 1, 2008, pp. 229–234.

"Voice Inverse." *Victorian Poetry,* vol. 42, no. 1, 2004, pp. 43–59.

Psomiades, Kathy Alexis. "She Has a Lovely Face: The Feminine and the Aesthetic." *Beauty's Body: Femininity and Representation in British Aestheticism.* Stanford University Press, 1997, pp. 23–57.

Rainey, Lawrence. "Taking Dictation: Collage Poetics, Pathology, and Politics." *Modernism/Modernity,* vol. 5, no. 2, 1998, pp. 123–153.

Rauber, D. F. "The Fragment as Romantic Form." *Modern Language Quarterly,* vol. 30, 1969, pp. 212–221.

Reade, Charles. *Trade Malice: A Personal Narrative.* London: Samuel French, 1875.

"Reading Aloud." *Chambers's Edinburgh Journal,* vol. 42, Oct. 19, 1844, pp. 248–249.

Rée, Jonathan. *I See a Voice: A Philosophical History of Language, Deafness and the Senses.* HarperCollins, 1999.

Reed, Edward S. *From Soul to Mind: The Emergence of Psychology from Erasmus Darwin to William James.* Yale University Press, 1997.

Reiman, Donald R., ed. *The Romantics Reviewed: Contemporary Reviews of British Romantic Writers. Part A: The Lake Poets.* Garland, 1972. 2 vols.

Review of "Christabel," by Samuel Taylor Coleridge. *Academic*, Sept. 15, 1821, pp. 339–341. Reprinted in Reiman, vol. I, pp. 1–2.

Review of "Christabel," by Samuel Taylor Coleridge. *Augustan Review* III, July 1816, pp. 14–24. Reprinted in Reiman, vol. I, pp. 33–38.

Review of "Christabel," by Samuel Taylor Coleridge. *The Times* 20 May 1816, n.p. Reprinted in Reiman, vol. II, pp. 890–891.

Review of *Poems* (3rd ed.), by Samuel Taylor Coleridge. *Annual Review* 2, 1804, p. 556. Reprinted in Reiman, vol. I, p. 12.

Richards, I. A. *Practical Criticism: A Study of Literary Judgment.* Harcourt, 1929.

Principles of Literary Criticism. New Harcourt, Brace, and Co., 1947.

Richardson, Alan. *British Romanticism and the Science of the Mind.* Cambridge University Press, 2001.

Roberts, William. Review of "Christabel," by Samuel Taylor Coleridge. *British Review*, vol. VIII, Aug. 1816, pp. 64–81. Reprinted in Reiman, vol. I, pp. 238–247.

Robson, Catherine. *Heart Beats: Everyday Life and the Memorized Poem.* Princeton University Press, 2012.

"Standing on the Burning Deck: Poetry, Performance, History." *PMLA*, vol. 120, no. 1, 2005, pp. 148–162.

Rossetti, Christina. "Song: When I Am Dead." *Broadview*, pp. 857–858.

Rossetti, Dante Gabriel. "The Blessed Damozel." *Broadview*, pp. 806–808.

"My Sister's Sleep." *Broadview*, pp. 808–809.

"The Portrait." *Broadview*, pp. 815–817.

Rudy, Jason R. *Electric Meters: Victorian Physiological Poetics.* Ohio University Press, 2009.

Russett, Margaret. *Fictions and Fakes: Forging Romantic Authenticity, 1760–1845.* Cambridge University Press, 2006.

Saint-Amour, Paul. *The Copywrights: Intellectual Property and the Literary Imagination.* Cornell University Press, 2003.

Schwenger, Peter. "The Obbligato Effect." *New Literary History*, vol. 42, no. 1, 2011, pp. 115–128.

Sconce, Jeffrey. *Haunted Media: Electronic Presence from Telegraphy to Television.* Duke University Press, 2000.

Scott, Walter. *Letters on Demonology and Witchcraft.* 2nd ed., John Murray, 1831.

Shakespeare, William. "Sonnet 111." *The Riverside Shakespeare.* 2nd ed., Houghton Mifflin, 1997, p. 1863.

The Tragedy of Romeo and Juliet. The Riverside Shakespeare. 2nd ed., Houghton Mifflin, 1997, pp. 1101–1145.

Shelley, Percy Bysshe. *A Defence of Poetry. Essays on Poetry: Peacock, Shelley, Browning.* Edited by H. F. B. Brett-Smith, Houghton Mifflin, 1921, pp. 21–60.

"Remembrance." *The Complete Poems of Percy Bysshe Shelley.* Modern Library, 1994, pp. 681–682.

"The Sensitive-Plant." *The Complete Poems of Percy Bysshe Shelley*. Modern Library, 1994, pp. 627–633.

Siskin, Clifford, and William Warner. "This Is Enlightenment: An Invitation in the Form of an Argument." *This Is Enlightenment*. Edited by Siskin and Warner, University of Chicago Press, 2010, pp. 1–36.

Small, Helen. "A Pulse of 124: Charles Dickens and a Pathology of the Mid-Victorian Reading Public." *The Practice and Representation of Reading in England*. Edited by James Raven, Helen Small, and Naomi Tadmor, Cambridge University Press, 1996, pp. 263–290.

Smith, Adam. *The Theory of Moral Sentiments*. Vol. 1, London: J. Richardson and Co., 1822.

Stainton, Moses [M. A. ("Oxon")]. *Spirit-Identity*. London: W. H. Harrison, 1879.

Stead, W. T. "The Mystery of Automatic Handwriting." *Review of Reviews*, vol. 6, no. 31, 1892, p. 44.

Stewart, Dugald. *Elements of the Philosophy of the Human Mind*. London: A. Strahan, 1792.

Stewart, Garrett. *Dear Reader: The Conscripted Audience in Nineteenth-Century British Fiction*. Johns Hopkins University Press, 1996.

Reading Voices: Literature and the Phonotext. University of California Press, 1990.

Stewart, Susan. "Notes on Distressed Genres." *Journal of American Folklore*, vol. 104, no. 411, 1991, pp. 5–31.

Sword, Helen. *Ghostwriting Modernism*. Cornell University Press, 2002.

Tate, Gregory. *The Poet's Mind: The Psychology of Victorian Poetry 1830–1870*. Oxford University Press, 2012.

Taylor, Jenny. "The Gay Science: The 'Hidden Soul' of Victorian Criticism." *Literature and History*, vol. 10, no. 2, 1984, pp. 189–202.

Tennyson, Alfred. "The Coming of Arthur." *Idylls of the King*. 1873. Edited by J. M. Gray, Penguin, 1996, pp. 21–35.

"Edward Gray." *The Poems of Tennyson*. Vol. II. Edited by Christopher Ricks, University of California Press, 1987, pp. 165–166.

"The Epic" and "Morte d'Arthur." *Broadview* pp. 189–194.

"The Higher Pantheism." *Broadview*, p. 279.

In Memoriam A. H. H. Broadview, pp. 204–252.

"The Last Tournament." *Idylls of the King*. 1873. Edited by J. M. Gray, Penguin, 1996, pp. 248–268.

"Ode on the Death of the Duke of Wellington." *The Poems of Tennyson*. Vol. II. Edited by Christopher Ricks. University of California Press, 1987, pp. 480–492.

"The Passing of Arthur" [1869]. *The Holy Grail and Other Poems*. London: Strahan and Co., 1870.

"The Passing of Arthur" [1873]. *Idylls of the King*. 1873. Edited by J. M. Gray. Penguin, 1996, pp. 288–300.

Tennyson, Hallam. *Alfred Lord Tennyson: A Memoir*. Greenwood Press, 1969.

Terada, Rei. "Phenomenality and Dissatisfaction in Coleridge's Notebooks." *Studies in Romanticism*, vol. 43, no. 2, 2004, pp. 257–282.

Thurschwell, Pamela. *Literature, Technology and Magical Thinking, 1880–1920.* Cambridge University Press, 2001.

Tod, David. *The Anatomy and Physiology of the Organ of Hearing.* London: Longman, Rees, Orme, Brown, Green, and Longman, 1832.

Travers Smith, Hester. *Psychic Messages from Oscar Wilde [excerpts]. Gender and Modernism: New Geographies, Complex Intersections.* Edited by Bonnie Kime Scott, University of Illinois Press, 2007, pp. 633–647.

Voices from the Void: Six Years' Experience in Automatic Communications. E. P. Dutton & Company, 1919.

Trumpener, Katie. *Bardic Nationalism: The Romantic Novel and the British Empire.* Princeton University Press, 1997.

Tucker, Herbert F. "Dramatic Monologue and the Overhearing of Lyric." *Lyric Poetry: Beyond New Criticism.* Edited by Chaviva Hosek and Patricia Parker, Cornell University Press, 1985, pp. 226–243.

Tennyson and the Doom of Romanticism. Harvard University Press, 1988.

Verrall, Mrs. A. W. "Notes on Mrs. Willett's Scripts on February, 1910." *Proceedings of the Society for Psychical Research*, vol. 25, 1911, pp. 176–217.

Vincent, David. *Literacy and Popular Culture: England 1750–1914.* Cambridge University Press, 1989.

Warren, Samuel. *Passages from the Diary of a Late Physician.* Paris: Baudry's European Library, 1838.

Wilde, Oscar. "The Burden of Itys." *The Complete Works of Oscar Wilde*, Vol. I. Edited by Bobby Fong and Karl Beckson, Oxford University Press, 2000, pp. 57–67.

Wilson, John [Christopher North]. *Essays Critical and Imaginative: Christopher at the Lakes.* Vol. II. London: Blackwood, 1856, pp. 109–152.

Wilson, Leigh. "The Cross-Correspondences, the Nature of Evidence and the Matter of Writing." *The Ashgate Research Companion to Nineteenth-Century Spiritualism and the Occult.* Edited by Tatiana Kontou and Sarah Willburn, Ashgate, 2012, pp. 97–119.

Wolfson, Susan. *Formal Charges: The Shaping of Poetry in British Romanticism.* Stanford University Press, 1997.

Wordsworth, Dorothy, and William Wordsworth. *The Letters of William and Dorothy Wordsworth.* Vol. I: *The Early Years, 1787–1805.* Edited by Ernest de Selincourt, Clarendon Press, 1967.

Wordsworth, William. "Essay, Supplementary to the Preface." *Poems.* London: Longman, Hurst, Rees, Orme and Brown, 1815. 2 vols.

"Lines Composed a Few Miles Above Tintern Abbey." *Romanticism: An Anthology.* 2nd ed., Edited by Duncan Wu, Blackwell, 2004, pp. 265–270.

"Note to 'The Ancient Mariner'." 1800. *Lyrical Ballads and Related Writings.* Edited by William Richey and Daniel Robinson, Houghton Mifflin, 2002, pp. 389–390.

The Poetical Works of William Wordsworth. Edited by Ernest de Selincourt and Helen Darbishire, Clarendon Press, pp. 1940–1949. 5 vols.

"Preface [to *Lyrical Ballads*]." 1802. *Lyrical Ballads and Related Writings*. Edited by William Richey and Daniel Robinson, Houghton Mifflin, 2002, pp. 390–411.

"A slumber did my spirit seal." *Romanticism: An Anthology*. 2nd ed., Edited by Duncan Wu, Blackwell, 2004, p. 327.

Wright, Edward. "The Art of Plagiarism." *Contemporary Review*, vol. 85, January 1904, pp. 514–518.

Index

CAMBRIDGE STUDIES IN NINETEENTH-CENTURY
LITERATURE AND CULTURE

GENERAL EDITOR: Gillian Beer, *University of Cambridge*

Titles published

1. *The Sickroom in Victorian Fiction: The Art of Being Ill*
   MIRIAM BAILIN, *Washington University*
2. *Muscular Christianity: Embodying the Victorian Age*
   edited by DONALD E. HALL, *California State University, Northridge*
3. *Victorian Masculinities: Manhood and Masculine Poetics in Early Victorian Literature and Art*
   HERBERT SUSSMAN, *Northeastern University, Boston*
4. *Byron and the Victorians*
   ANDREW ELFENBEIN, *University of Minnesota*
5. *Literature in the Marketplace: Nineteenth-Century British Publishing and the Circulation of Books*
   edited by JOHN O. JORDAN, *University of California, Santa Cruz* and
   ROBERT L. PATTEN, *Rice University, Houston*
6. *Victorian Photography, Painting and Poetry*
   LINDSAY SMITH, *University of Sussex*
7. *Charlotte Brontë and Victorian Psychology*
   SALLY SHUTTLEWORTH, *University of Sheffield*
8. *The Gothic Body: Sexuality, Materialism and Degeneration at the Fin de Siècle*
   KELLY HURLEY, *University of Colorado at Boulder*
9. *Rereading Walter Pater*
   WILLIAM F. SHUTER, *Eastern Michigan University*
10. *Remaking Queen Victoria*
    edited by MARGARET HOMANS, *Yale University* and ADRIENNE MUNICH, *State University of New York, Stony Brook*
11. *Disease, Desire, and the Body in Victorian Women's Popular Novels*
    PAMELA K. GILBERT, *University of Florida*
12. *Realism, Representation, and the Arts in Nineteenth-Century Literature*
    ALISON BYERLY, *Middlebury College, Vermont*
13. *Literary Culture and the Pacific*
    VANESSA SMITH, *University of Sydney*
14. *Professional Domesticity in the Victorian Novel Women, Work and Home*
    MONICA F. COHEN
15. *Victorian Renovations of the Novel: Narrative Annexes and the Boundaries of Representation*
    SUZANNE KEEN, *Washington and Lee University, Virginia*
16. *Actresses on the Victorian Stage: Feminine Performance and the Galatea Myth*
    GAIL MARSHALL, *University of Leeds*

For EU product safety concerns, contact us at Calle de José Abascal, 56–1°,
28003 Madrid, Spain or eugpsr@cambridge.org.

www.ingramcontent.com/pod-product-compliance
Ingram Content Group UK Ltd.
Pitfield, Milton Keynes, MK11 3LW, UK
UKHW020326140625
459647UK00018B/2041